On Clear and Confused Ideas

An Essay about Substance Concepts

RUTH GARRETT MILLIKAN

University of Connecticut

CAMBRIDGE
UNIVERSITY PRESS

PUBLISHED BY THE PRESS SYNDICATE OF THE UNIVERSITY OF CAMBRIDGE
The Pitt Building, Trumpington Street, Cambridge, United Kingdom

CAMBRIDGE UNIVERSITY PRESS
The Edinburgh Building, Cambridge CB2 2RU, UK   http://www.cup.cam.ac.uk
40 West 20th Street, New York, NY 10011-4211, USA   http://www.cup.org
10 Stamford Road, Oakleigh, Melbourne 3166, Australia
Ruiz de Alarcón 13, 28014 Madrid, Spain

© Ruth Garrett Millikan   2000

First published 2000

Printed in the United States of America

Typeface Bembo 10.5/13 pt.   *System* QuarkXPress [BV]

A catalog record for this book is available from the British Library.

Library of Congress Cataloging in Publication Data
Millikan, Ruth Garrett.
On clear and confused ideas : an essay about substance concepts / Ruth Garrett
Millikan.
p.   cm.
Includes bibliographical references.
ISBN 0-521-62386-3 (hardcover) – ISBN 0-521-62553-X (pbk.)
1. Substance (Philosophy)   I. Title.
BD331 .M47   2000
121'.4–dc21
99-058059

ISBN   0 521 62386 3   hardback
ISBN   0 521 62553 X   paperback

Contents

Preface

When my mother was three, her father came home one evening without his beard and she insisted he was Uncle Albert, my grandfather's younger and beardless brother. She thought he was, as usual, being a terrible tease, and she cried when he didn't admit his real identity. Only when he pulled out her daddy's silver pocket watch with its distinctive and beloved pop-up cover was she willing to be corrected. But just who was it that she had been thinking was being so mean, this man (her daddy) or Uncle Albert? This is what I mean by a confused idea.

I have an old letter from Yale's alumni association inquiring whether I, Mrs. Donald P. Shankweiler, knew of the whereabouts of their "alumnus" Ruth Garrett Millikan. This seemed a sensible question, I suppose, as according to their records we lived at the same address. Since I lived with myself, perhaps I knew where I was? By not owning up I evaded solicitations from Yale's alumni fund for a good many years.

More often, confusions about the identities of things are disruptive rather than amusing. It is fortunate that we generally manage recognition tasks so well, and our ability to do so deserves careful study. I will argue in this book that the most central job of cognition is the exceedingly difficult task of reidentifying individuals, properties, kinds, and so forth, through diverse media and under diverse conditions.

Traditionally, failure to manage this task well has been assimilated to making false judgments or having false beliefs – in the Fregean tradition, judgments or beliefs employing different modes of presentation: judging that this man is Uncle Albert; assuming that Mrs. Donald P. Shankweiler is not Ruth Garrett Millikan. On the contrary, I will argue, this sort of failure causes confusion in concepts, which is something quite different, and at the limit causes inability to think at all. It results in corruption of the inner representational system, which comes to represent equivocally, or redundantly, or to represent nothing at all.

The very first duty of any cognitive system is to see to the integrity of its own mental semantics. This involves correctly recognizing sameness of content in various natural signs encountered by the sensory systems, these sources of incoming information being what determines conceptual content for basic empirical concepts. For animals with any sophistication, it also involves the continuing development of new empirical concepts, and the enrichment and sharpening, by training and tuning, of those already possessed, to attain greater variety and accuracy in methods of reidentification.

This book concerns only one kind of empirical concepts, but these are the most fundamental. Echoing Aristotle, I call them concepts of "substances." The book is about what substance concepts are, what their function is, how they perform it, what ontological structures support them, how they are acquired, how their extensions are determined, how they are connected with words for substances, what epistemological considerations confirm their adequacy, and how they have been misunderstood in the philosophical and psychological traditions. Having a substance concept is having a certain kind of ability – in part, an ability to reidentify a substance correctly – and the nature of abilities themselves is a fundamental but neglected subject requiring attention. If it's not an act of judgment, what it is to reidentify a thing also needs to be addressed. Reidentifying is *not* analogous to uttering a mental identity sentence containing two descriptions or terms referring to the same. Indeed, careful examination of this act undermines the notion that there even exist modes of presentation in thought. So an understanding must be reconstructed of the phenomena that have made it seem that there were.

The whole discussion will be placed in an evolutionary frame, where human cognition is assumed to be an outgrowth of more primitive forms of mentality, and assumed to have "functions." That is, the mechanisms responsible for our capacities for cognition are assumed to be biological adaptations, evolved through a process of natural selection.[1] Very many of the claims and arguments of this book can stand apart from this assumption, but not all.

This naturalist perspective has a methodological implication that should be kept constantly in mind. If we are dealing with biological

---

1 This framework for the study of human cognition is defended in Millikan (1984, 1993a Chapter 2 and in press b) as well as in Chapter 15 and Appendix B.

phenomena, then we are working in an area where the natural divisions are divisions only de facto and are often irremediably vague. These divisions do not apply across possible worlds; they are not determined by necessary and/or sufficient conditions. If you were to propose to pair a set of dog chromosomes with a set of coyote chromosomes and then swap every other gene, you would not find any biologist prepared to debate what species concept to apply to the (in this case, really possible) resulting pups. Biological theories begin with normal cases, or paradigm cases of central phenomena, and work out from there only when needed to systematize further existing phenomena. Similarly, I will be concerned to describe substance concepts as they normally function, how their extensions are normally determined, the sorts of ontological structures to which they paradigmatically correspond, and so forth. But I will show no interest, for example, in what a person might be "credited with" referring to, or thinking of, or having a concept of, and so forth, in possible-worlds cases, or even in queer actual cases. Such questions rest, I believe, on false assumptions about the kind of phenomena that reference and conception are and tend to be philosophically destructive. The thesis and argument of this book itself are, of course, calculated to support this opinion.

Help from friends with the contents of individual chapters is acknowledged in footnotes. Some parts of Chapters 1 through 6 and Chapter 12 are revised from "A common structure for concepts of individuals, stuffs, and basic kinds: More mama, more milk and more mouse" (Millikan 1998a) and "With enemies like this I don't need friends: Author's response" (Millikan 1998b), in *Behavioral and Brain Sciences*, reprinted with the kind permission of Cambridge University Press. Some portions of other chapters have also been taken from earlier papers – in a few cases, also the chapter titles. These sources are acknowledged in footnotes. My main debt of gratitude, however, is for the warmhearted personal support I have consistently received from my colleagues at the University of Connecticut, recently also from the higher administration at Connecticut, always from my department chairman, and from graduate students both at home and abroad. To tell it truthfully, I have been quite thoroughly coddled and spoiled. At best, this book may match some small portion of that debt.

1

Introducing Substance Concepts

§1.1 ONE SPECIAL KIND OF CONCEPT

One use of the word "concept" equates a concept with whatever it is one has to learn in order to use a certain word correctly. So we can talk of the concept *or* and the concept *of* and the concepts *hurrah, the, because, necessarily, ouch, good, true, two, exists, is* – and so forth. We can talk that way, but then we should remember Wittgenstein's warning: "Think of the tools in a toolbox: there is a hammer, pliers, a saw, a screwdriver, a glue pot, nails and screws – The functions of words are as diverse as the functions of these objects" (1953, Section §11). Given this broad usage of "concept," there will be little or nothing in common about any two of these various concepts. We mustn't expect a theory of how the tape measure works to double as a theory of how the glue works.

In this book, I propose a thesis about the nature of one and only one kind of concept, namely, concepts of what (with a respectful nod to Aristotle) I call "substances." Paradigmatic substances, in my sense, are individuals (Mama, The Empire State Building), stuffs (gold, milk), and natural kinds (mouse, geode). The core of the theory is not, however, about grasp of the use of *words* for substances (although I will get to that). Rather, the core belongs to the general theory of cognition, in exactly the same way that theories of perception do. Substance concepts are primarily things we use to think with rather than to talk with. A reasonable comparison might be between the proposal I will make here and David Marr's first level of analysis in his theory of vision. I attempt something like a "task analysis" for substance concepts, a description of what their job or function is, why we need to have them. Marr claimed

1

(rightly or wrongly) that the task of vision is to construct representations of three dimensional objects starting from retinal images. I will claim that the task of substance concepts is to enable us to reidentify substances through diverse media and under diverse conditions, and to enable us over time to accumulate practical skills and theoretical knowledge about these substances and to use what we have learned.

There is another tradition that treats a theory of concepts as part of a theory of cognition by taking a concept to be a mental word. If one takes it that what makes a mental feature, or a brain feature, into a mental word is its function, then this usage of "concept" is not incompatible with my usage here. Indeed, during the first part of this book I will rely rather heavily on the image of a substance concept as corresponding to something like a mental word (while plotting subsequently to demolish much that has usually accompanied this vision). But if a substance concept is thought of as a mental word, it must constantly be borne in mind that the category "mental word for a substance," like the category "tool for scraping paint," is a function category. My claims will concern the function that defines this category. If a mental word for a substance is to serve a certain function, the cognitive systems that use it must have certain abilities. It is onto these abilities that I will turn the spotlight, often speaking of a substance concept simply as *being* an ability.

In this chapter I will roughly sketch the general sort of ability I take a substance concept to be. In later chapters I will fill in details, but some rough understanding of the whole project is needed first.

§1.2 WHAT ARE "SUBSTANCES"?

From the standpoint of an organism that wishes to learn, the most immediately useful and accessible subjects of knowledge are things that retain their properties, hence potentials for use, over numerous encounters with them. This makes it possible for the organism to store away knowledge or know-how concerning the thing as observed or experienced on earlier occasions for use on later occasions, the knowledge retaining its validity over time. These accessible subjects for knowledge are the things I am calling "substances." Substances are, by definition, what can afford this sort of opportunity to a learner, and where this affordance is no accident, but is supported by an ontological ground of real connection. The category of substances is widely extensive, there being many kinds of items about which it is possible to learn from one encounter something about what to expect on other encounters. I will discuss the ontology of substances in Chapter 2.[1] Here I illustrate with just a few paradigmatic examples.

I can discover on one temporal or spatial encounter with cats that cats eat fish and the knowledge will remain good on other encounters with cats. That is, I can discover from the cat over here eating fish that the cat over there will probably also eat fish, or from a cat now eating fish that a cat encountered later will eat fish. I also can discover numerous other anatomical, physiological, and behavioral facts about cats that will carry over. There is the entire subject of cat physiology and behavior studied by those attending veterinary schools. I can learn how to hold a frightened cat on one or a few occasions, and this may hold good for a lifetime of cat ownership.

Similarly, I can discover that Xavier knows Greek on one encounter and this will remain good on other encounters with Xavier. Or I can discover that he has blue eyes, that he is tall, that he likes lobster, and that he can easily be persuaded to have a drink, and these will, or are likely to, carry over as well. I can discover that ice is slippery and this will remain good when I encounter ice again, either over there with the next step I take, or next winter. I can learn how to avoid slipping on ice, and this will carry over from one encounter with ice to the next. And for any determinate kind or stuff, there is a vast array of questions, such as "what is its chemistry?," "what is its melting point?," "what is its specific gravity?," or "what is its tensile strength?" that can sensibly be asked about it and answered, once and for all, on the basis, often, of one careful observation. For these reasons, catkind, Xavier, and ice are each "substances." Besides stuffs, real kinds, and individuals, the category *substances* may include certain event types (here's breakfast again), cultural artifacts, musical compositions, and many other things such as McDonald's and the Elm Street bus, but I will ignore these others in this introductory chapter.

§1.3 KNOWLEDGE OF SUBSTANCES

It is is not a matter of logic, of course, but rather of the makeup of the world, that I can learn from one observation what color Xavier's eyes are or, say, how the water spider propels itself. It is not a matter of logic that these things will not vary from meeting to meeting. And indeed,

---

1 The ontology is discussed with a different emphasis in Millikan (1984), Chapters 16 and 17.

the discovery on one meeting that cat is black does not carry over; next time I meet cat it may be striped or white. Nor does the discovery that Xavier is talking or asleep carry over; next time he may be quiet or awake. Nor does discovering that ice is cubical or thin carry over, and so forth. Although substances are, as such, items about which enduring knowledge can be acquired from one or a few encounters, only certain types of knowledge are available for each substance or broad category of substances.

Furthermore, most of the knowledge that carries over about ordinary substances is not certain knowledge, but merely probable knowledge. Some cats don't like fish, perhaps, and a stroke could erase Xavier's Greek. But compare: No knowledge whatever carries over about non-substance kinds, such as *the red square* or *the two-inch malleable object*, or *the opaque liquid*. There is nothing to be learned about any of these kinds except what applies to one or another of the parts of these complexes taken separately, that is, except what can be learned separately about red, about square, about malleability, liquidity, and so forth.

Classically, simple induction is described as a movement from knowledge about certain instances of a kind to conclusions about other instances of the same kind. Forced into this ill-fitting mold, learning what the properties of a substance are would be viewed as running inductions over instances of the second order kind *meetings with substance S*: meetings with Xavier, meetings with ice, meetings with cat, and so forth. If we then made the usual assumption that running inductions over members of a kind involves having concepts of the various instances of the kind on the basis of which an inference is made, we would get the strange result that learning that Xavier has blue eyes involves beginning with concepts of meetings with (or instances of, or time slices of . . . ?) Xavier. But to have a concept of a meeting with Xavier, presumably you must first have a concept of Xavier. If having a concept of Xavier requires knowing how to generalize productively from one meeting with Xavier to another, as I will argue it does, then a regress results if you must begin with a *prior* concept of Xavier in order to do this. I will discuss the psychological structure of substance concepts in Chapter 5. At the moment, let me just note that when I speak of "running inductions" over occasions of meeting with various substances, I do not imply that this kind of "induction" can be unpacked in the usual way. Possibly "generalization" would be a less misleading word. Its usage in "stimulus generalization," for example, does not imply that inferences are involved that start with premises containing concepts of stimula-

4

tions. On the other hand, the central thesis to be argued in this book implies that a great many logical/psychological moves that have traditionally been treated as examples of simple induction, in particular, inductions over the members of real kinds, need not begin with such concepts either, so it is best, in general, not automatically to shackle the notion "induction" with its classical analysis.

§1.4 WHY WE NEED SUBSTANCE CONCEPTS

The next step in articulating the notion of a substance concept is to ask ourselves *why* a person, or animal, needs to carry knowledge of the properties of a substance from one encounter with it to another. Why is it helpful to learn about a substance and remember what has been learned? Notice that if all of a substance's properties were immediately manifest to one upon every encounter with it, there would be no need to learn and remember what these properties were. If every cat I encountered was in the process of eating a fish, I would not need to remember that cats eat fish, and if Xavier was always speaking Greek when I encountered him, I would not need to remember that he speaks Greek. Carrying knowledge of substances about is useful only because most of a substance's properties are not manifest but hidden from us most of the time. This is not, in general, because these properties are "deep" or "theoretical" properties, but because observing a property always requires that one have a particular perspective on it. To observe that butter is yellow you must be in the light, to observe that it is greasy you must touch it, to observe that the sugar is sweet it must be in your mouth, to observe that the milk is drinkable and filling you must tip the cup and drink. You do not find out that the cat scratches until you disturb it, or that the fire burns unless you near it. The bright colored design on the front of the quilt is not seen from the back, and although Xavier knows Greek he is seldom come upon speaking it. Different properties and utilities of a substance show themselves on different encounters. Were it not for that, there would be no point in collecting knowledge of a substance over time and remembering it.

§1.5 THE ABILITY TO REIDENTIFY SUBSTANCES

Yet a sort of paradox lurks here that, I believe, takes us straight to the most central problem there is for cognition. The difficulty is that it won't help to carry knowledge of a substance about with you unless

5

you can recognize that substance when you encounter it again *as* the one you have knowledge about. Without that you will be unable to apply whatever knowledge you have. But if different properties of a substance show themselves on different encounters with it, how is one to know when one is encountering the same substance again? The very reason you needed to carry knowledge about in the first place shows up as a barrier to applying it. Indeed, not only substances but also their properties reveal themselves quite differently on different occasions of meeting. The enduring properties of substances are distal not proximal, and they affect the external senses quite differently under different conditions and when bearing different relations to the perceiver.

This is a problem, moreover, not merely for the application of knowledge of substances one already has, but for the project of collecting knowledge of substances. How can you collect knowledge of a substance over time, over a series of encounters, if you cannot recognize that it is the *same* substance about which you have learned one thing on one encounter, another thing on another encounter? Clearly it is essential to grasp that it is the *same* thing about which you have these various bits of knowledge. Suppose, for example, that you are hungry and that you know that yogurt is good to eat and that there is yogurt in the refrigerator. This is of no use unless you also grasp that these two bits of knowledge are about the same stuff, yogurt. *To caricature*, if you represent yogurt to yourself in one way, say, with a mental diamond, as you store away the knowledge that yogurt is good to eat, but represent it another way, say, with a mental heart, as you store away the knowledge that it is in the refrigerator, these bits of information will not help you when you are hungry.[2] Indeed, the idea that you might be collecting information about a thing without grasping that it was the same thing that any of these various pieces of information was about is not obviously coherent. Russell's claim that "it is scarcely conceivable that we can make a judgment or entertain a supposition without knowing what it is we are judging or supposing about" (Russell 1912, p. 58) has an intuitive appeal and a plausible application (Chapters 13 and 14).

From this we should conclude, I believe, that a most complex but crucial skill involved for any organism that has knowledge of substances must be the ability to reidentify these substances efficiently and with

---

2 To model the act of reidentifying a substance in thought as using the same mental term again, as I have playfully done here, is a crude and misleading expedient, to be criticized at length in Chapter 10.

fair reliability under a variety of conditions. The other side of this coin is that a fundamental ability involved in all theoretical knowledge of substances must be the capacity to store away information gathered about each substance in such a way that it is understood which substance it concerns. Information about the same must be represented by what one grasps *as* a representation of the same.

This capacity is central to the capacity to maintain a coherent, non-equivocal, nonredundant, inner representational system, which means, I will try to persuade you, that it is essential for representing something in thought (i.e., conceptually) at all. That these capacities are specifically conceptual capacities, not to be confused with judgmental capacities, will be argued culminating in Chapter 12.

§1.6 FALLIBILITY OF SUBSTANCE REIDENTIFICATION

The ideal capacity to identify a substance would allow correct reidentification under every physically possible condition, regardless of intervening media and the relation of the substance to the perceiver. The ideal capacity also would be infallible. Obviously, there are no such capacities. If the cost of never making an error in identifying Xavier or ice or cats is almost never managing to identify any of them at all, then it will pay to be less cautious. But if one is to recognize a substance a reasonable proportion of the time when one encounters it, one will need to become sensitive to a variety of relatively reliable indicators of the substance, indeed, to as many as possible, so as to recognize the substance under as many conditions as possible.

Reasonably reliable indicators of substances may come in a variety of epistemic types. One kind of indicator may be various appearances of the substance to each of the various senses, under varying conditions, at varying distances, given varying intervening media, or resulting from various kinds of probing and testing, with or without the use of special instruments of observation. That is, one kind of indicator may allow recognition of the substance directly, without inference. Another kind of indicator may be possession of various pieces of information about the presented substance – that it has these or those objective properties that indicate it reliably enough. In Chapter 6, I will argue that words also can be indicators of substances, but that requires a special story.

In the case of familiar substances, typically we collect over time very numerous means of identification, but all of these are fallible, at least in principle. There is no such thing as a way of identifying a substance that works with necessity and that one also can be sure one is actually using on a given occasion. All methods of identification rest at some point on the presence of conditions external to the organism, and attempting to identify the presence of these conditions poses the same problem over again. Nor is any particular method or methods of identification set apart as "definitional" of the substance, as an ultimate criterion determining its extension or determining what its concept is of. The purpose of a substance concept is not to sustain what Wettstein (1988) aptly calls "a cognitive fix" on the substance, but the practical one of facilitating information gathering and use for an organism navigating in a changing and cluttered environment.

Consider, for example, how many ways you can recognize each of the various members of your immediate family – by looks of various body parts from each of dozens of angles, by characteristic postures, by voice, by footsteps, by handwriting, by various characteristic activities, by clothes and other possessions. None of these ways nor any subset *defines* for you any family member, and probably all are fallible. There are, for example, conditions under which you would fail to recognize even your spouse, conditions under which you would misidentify him, or her and conditions under which you might mistake another for him or her. The same is true of your ability to identify squirrels or wood. To be skilled in identifying a substance no more implies that one never misidentifies it than skill in walking implies that one never trips. Nor does it imply that one has in reserve some infallible defining method of identification, some ultimate method of verification, that determines the extension of each of one's thoughts of a substance, any more than the ability to walk implies knowing some special way to walk that could never let one trip.

§1.7 FIXING THE EXTENSIONS OF SUBSTANCE CONCEPTS:
ABILITIES

If this is so, it follows that it cannot be merely one's disposition to apply a substance term that determines its referent or extension. The question emerges with urgency, then: What *does* determine the extension? When my mother stoutly insisted her father was "Uncle Albert," it seems clear that the name "Uncle Albert," for her, did not in fact refer to her father. She applied "Uncle Albert" incorrectly according to her own standards, not just the standards of adults. By contrast, in a passage characteristic of the psychological literature, Lakoff remarks, "It is known, for example, that two-year-olds have different categories than adults. Lions and tigers as well as cats are commonly called "kitty" by two-year-olds . . ." (1987, p. 50). How does Lakoff know that two-year-olds don't think that lions and tigers *are* housecats, for example, housecats grown big or giant kitties, just as my mother thought her father was Uncle Albert? Perhaps with more experience the child will change her mind, not on the question what "cat" means, but on reliable ways to recognize kitties. A child who has got only partway toward knowing how to ride a bicycle has not learned something different from bicycle riding, but *partially* learned how to ride a bicycle. Won't it be the same for a child who has got only partway toward recognizing Uncle Albert, or housecats?

The issues here turn, I will claim, on the question what "an ability to reidentify X" is, other than a disposition to identify X. If having a concept of cats requires having an ability to reidentify cats, and if an ability were just a disposition, then whatever the child has a disposition to identify as a cat would have to be part of the extension of her concept. It is crucial, I will argue, that an ability is *not* a disposition – of any kind. The question what a given ability is an ability to do, even though it may not accomplish this end under all conditions, is the same as the question what substance a given substance concept is of (Chapters 4, 13, and 14).

§1.8 SUBSTANCE TEMPLATES

The practical ability to reidentify a substance when encountered, so as to collect information about it over time and to know when to apply it, needs to be complemented with another and equally important ability. Having a concept of a substance requires a grasp of what kinds of things can be learned about that substance. It requires understanding from which kinds of experienced practical successes to generalize to new encounters with the substance, or if the concept is used for gathering information, it requires understanding what sorts of predicates will remain stable over encounters with the substance, that is, what some of the meaningful *questions* are that can be asked about the substance.[3] You can ask how tall Mama is, but not how tall gold is. You can ask at what temperature gold melts, but not at what temperature chairs (as such) do – the latter is a question that can be answered only for certain individual chairs. There is much that you can find out about the internal organs of each species of animal but not about the gross internal

---

3   See Millikan (1984), Chapter 15, p. 252 ff, and Chapters 16 and 17.

parts of gold or mud. Having a concept of a substance does not involve knowing an essence. Rather, it involves understanding something of what recognition of the substance might be good for, in the context either of developing practical skills or theoretical knowledge.

To have the concept of any individual person, you must know what kinds of questions can be asked and answered about individual people; to have the concept of any individual species, you must know some of the questions that can be asked and answered about species; to have the concept of any chemical element, you must know some of the questions that can be asked and answered about chemical elements, and so forth. The primary interest of groupings like *persons, species,* and *chemical elements* is not that they themselves correspond to substances, but that they bring with them "substance templates." Many of the same sorts of questions can be asked and answered though not, of course, answered the same way, for all members of each of these groups. They are natural groups, the members of which display a common set of determinables rather than, or in addition to, a common set of determinates.[4] All chemical elements have, for example, some atomic number or another, some specific chemical combining properties or others, some electrical conductivity or other.

Physical object seems to be a pure substance template. To be a physical object in the broadest sense, a thing need have no particular determinate properties at all, but it has to have some mass, some charge, some position and velocity at each time, some extension, be composed of some particular material, and so forth. With rare exceptions, however, categories that bring with them substance templates also bring at least a bit more. They correspond to substances displaying at least a few common properties as well as bringing substance templates with them.

§1.9 CONCEPTIONS OF SUBSTANCES

The practical ability to reidentify a substance is typically composed of a variety of different ways of identifying it. These multiple means are used conjointly and alternatively for identifying the substance, each being employed whenever possible under the given circumstances, and given the thinker's particular current relation to the substance. None of these

4 Determinables are not specific properties like *red* or *square,* but rather disjunctions of contrary properties like *colored* (equals red or blue or green or . . .), and *shaped* (equals square or triangular or circular or . . .).

ways defines the extension of the concept, nor are the means of identifying that one person employs likely to be exactly the same as another person's. What should we understand, then, by the notion "same concept?" What will it mean to say that two persons share a concept?

Concepts are abilities, and there is an ambiguity in the notion "same ability" from which an ambiguity in the notion "same concept" results. Let us suppose, for example, that you tie your shoes by looping one lace into a bow, encircling it with the other, and pulling through, while I tie my shoes by looping each lace separately, then tying them together. The results that we get will be exactly the same, but do we exercise the same ability? Sometimes what counts as "the same ability" is what accomplishes the same: We share the ability to tie our shoes. Other times what counts as "the same ability" is what accomplishes the same by the same means: We do not exercise exactly the same abilities in tying our shoes. Similarly, consider a child and an organic chemist. Each has an ability to identify sugar and collect knowledge about it. Does it follow that there is a concept that they both have, hence that they have "the same concept?" In one sense they do, for each has the ability, one more fallibly, the other less fallibly, to identify sugar, and each knows some kinds of information that might be collected about sugar. But in another sense they do not have "the same concept." The chemist has much more sophisticated and reliable means at her disposal for identifying sugar and knows to ask much more sophisticated questions about sugar than the child. Similarly, we could ask, did Helen Keller have many of the same concepts as you and I, or did she have largely different ones? She had a perfectly normal and very large English vocabulary, which she employed in a perfectly normal way so far as reference and extension are concerned, but her means of identifying the substances she was receiving information about was largely different from yours and mine. She received most of her information through touch and vibration alone.[5]

Having understood what the problem is, we can solve it by introducing a technical distinction. I will say that the child has "the same concept" as the chemist, namely, "the concept of sugar," but that she has a very different "conception" of sugar than does the chemist. Similarly, Helen Keller had very many of the same concepts as you and I, but quite different conceptions of their objects. This fits with the ordinary way of speaking according to which people having very different information or beliefs about a thing have "different conceptions" of it, given

5   I will discuss using language to identify substances in Chapter 6.

11

that having information about a substance presupposes a grasp of its associated property invariances, moreover, that information one has about a substance is often used to help identify it. The "conception" one has of a substance, then, will be the ways one has of identifying that substance plus the disposition to project certain kinds of invariances rather than others over one's experiences with it.[6]

Having introduced this technical distinction, we should notice not merely the points in which it agrees with common or traditional usages of the terms "concept" and "conception," but also where there are points of friction. Suppose you were to assume, as it was traditional to assume for kinds and stuffs, that a person's conception of a substance determines the extension of their thought, which in turn determines the extension of their term for the substance. Assume also that different conceptions, for kinds and stuffs, determine different extensions across possible worlds, and that extension across possible worlds is what the thought of such a substance is fundamentally about, hence what one's term for it "means." That is, assume, putting things in Kripke's (1972) terms, that terms for substances are *non*rigid designators. Then the distinction between concept and conception would disappear. For each substance kind or stuff that might be thought of or meant, there would correspond but one possible conception. There would no longer be an equivocation in speaking of "the same concept." For example, if two people each had "a concept of cats," they would necessarily have both "the same concept" and also "the same conception" in our defined senses. For each extension across possible worlds that might be conceived of or meant, there would correspond but *one* possible conception. Similarly, for each univocal word in a language for a substance kind or stuff there would correspond just one conception.

I am opposing this tradition. There is no such thing as either as "the" conception of a substance nor as "the" conception that corresponds to a public language term for a substance. Different people competently speaking the same language may have quite different – indeed, *nonoverlapping* – conceptions corresponding to the same substance term, and a single person may have quite different conceptions corresponding to the same substance at different times. This divergence from a more traditional position results in some necessary friction over terminology, however. What I am calling a "conception" is in many ways much like what tradition has called a "concept." But then tradition speaks of

6   In Millikan (1984), I rather confusingly called these conceptions "intensions."

12

"THE concept cat," not of "A concept cat" and I claim there is no such thing as "THE concept cat" if what is meant is a conception. I reserve the term "concept" then for what we do have only one of per person per substance, and only one of per word for a substance, namely, for abilities to recognize substances and to know something of their potential for inductive use. Or, since these abilities are what lend thoughts of substances their referential content, their representational values, as mentioned earlier, we also can think of substance concepts as corresponding to mental representations of substances, say, to mental words for substances *but qua meaningful.*

But this is not quite right either. Indeed, it does not take into account a phenomenon to which I am most anxious to draw attention in this book, namely conceptual confusions and, more generally, the possibility of redundancy, equivocation and emptiness in substance concepts. Substance concepts do not always correspond one-to-one to substances. This complication is closely connected with the question what happens to Fregean senses and their kin given this view of substance concepts. The answer will be that they have to be pretty much trashed (Chapters 11 and 12).

§1.10 IDENTIFYING THROUGH LANGUAGE

The claim that having a substance concept involves an ability to recognize that substance contrasts sharply with the more classical view that substance concepts correspond to descriptions or sets of properties understood by the thinker uniquely to distinguish the substance. According to the classical view, to distinguish a substance in the way needed to conceive of it, you must merely have its distinguishing properties in mind – you must think of them and intend them to distinguish the substance and that is the end of it. According to the view I am defending, you need instead to distinguish when natural information[7] about that substance is what is arriving *at your sensory surfaces.* This is an entirely different matter. It certainly is not obvious, for example, how knowing that Benjamin Franklin was uniquely the inventor of bifocals could help

---

7   I use the term "natural information" to mean natural informationC as defined in Appendix B. There Dretske's, Fodor's and Gibson's notions of natural information are discussed and compared to informationC. As a first approximation, the reader can interpret the natural information referred to in the body of this book as something that is, anyway, akin to Dretske's or Gibson's natural information, even though that reading will take one only halfway in the end.

you to distinguish when natural information about Benjamin Franklin is arriving at your sensory surfaces, or how knowing that molybdenum is the element with atomic number 42 will help the nonchemist to do so. For each of us, a very large percent of the substances we can think about are substances that we do not have any capacity to identify, as it were, in the flesh.

I will argue that human language is merely another medium, such as light, through which natural information is conveyed. It is just one more form of structured information-carrying ambient energy that one's senses may intercept. Thus the capacity to identify when the language one hears concerns a certain substance constitutes an ability to identify the substance. The substance is encountered "in the flesh" through language just as surely as by seeing or hearing it (Chapter 6).

§1.11 EPISTEMOLOGY, AND THE ACT OF REIDENTIFYING

Clearly what I am proposing is a form of "meaning externalism." In Chapter 7 I will discuss the epistemology of substance concepts. I will answer the question that has been urgently raised for meaning externalists concerning how it is possible for us to know whether our would-be substance concepts are of real substances, and how we know they are not redundant or equivocal.

The second part of this book (Chapters 8–14) mainly concerns the nature of the *act* of identifying a substance, asking what an ability to re-identify really is. Results are compared with the language of thought tradition and the neo-Fregean tradition. The question of what determines reference is then explored more carefully. Chapter 15 places the whole project in the context of Darwinian evolution. But I think it will not help to introduce the themes of these later chapters here. Why a study of the act of identifying should be of such crucial importance in explaining conception must unfold in its own time. Enough of the general picture has been sketched, I believe, to begin filling in.

2

Substances: The Ontology[1]

§2.1 REAL KINDS

Substances are those things about which you can learn from one encounter something of what to expect on other encounters, where this is no accident but the result of a real connection. There is a reason why the same or similar properties characterize what is encountered. We can begin with examples of substances that are kinds. I will call these substances "real kinds," contrasting this, as is traditional, with "nominal kinds."

Most of the various definitions currently offered of "natural kinds" capture real kinds of one sort or another. Sometimes, however, the term "natural kind" is used to refer merely to a class determined by a "projectable" property, that is, one that might figure in natural laws. Then "is green" and "is at 32° Fahrenheit" denote "natural kinds," predicates projectable over certain classes of subjects. What I am calling real kinds, on the other hand, must figure as subjects over which a variety of predicates are projectable. They are things that *have* properties, rather than merely *being* properties.[2] That is why Aristotle called them "secondary substances," putting them in the same broad ontological class as individuals, which he called "primary substances." True, unlike the Aristotelian

1 Portions of Section 2.2 were revised from "On swampkinds" in *Mind and Language* (Millikan 1996), with the kind permission of Blackwell Publishers, and from "Historical Kinds and the Special Sciences" (Millikan 1999), with kind permission from Kluwer Academic Publishers.

2 A discussion of the ontological distinction between substances and properties is in Millikan (1984, Chapters 15–17).

tradition, in modern times concepts of stuffs and real kinds have traditionally been treated as predicate concepts. That is, to call a thing "gold" or "mouse" has been taken to involve saying or thinking that it bears a certain *description*. One understands something as being gold or a mouse or a chair or a planet by representing it as having a certain set, or a certain appropriate sampling, of properties. Or one represents it as having certain relations to other things, or having a certain kind of inner nature or structure, or a certain origin or cause. But I am going to argue, on the contrary, that the earliest and most basic concepts that we have of *gold* and *mouse* and so forth are subject concepts. Their abstract structure is exactly the same as for concepts of individuals like Mama and Bill Clinton. This is possible because Aristotle's various "substances" have an identical *ontological* structure when considered at a suitably abstract level. That is, surprisingly to us moderns, the Aristotelian term "substance," though very abstract is univocal.

Real kinds are not classes defined by one property, nor are they defined by a set of properties. Compare them with natural kinds. "Natural kinds" are sometimes taken as defined by sets of properties set apart because they are "correlated" in nature (e.g., Markman 1989). Similarly, while agreeing with Russell on the term "natural kind," Hacking explains that Russell "made a rather charming comparison between natural kinds and topological neighborhoods, saying that the former may be thought of as intensional neighborhoods, in which every member is close to a great many other members according to some notion of closeness to be explained" (Hacking 1991a, p. 112, referring to Russell 1948). These descriptions don't capture the sort of real kinds I intend. Just as, for a realist, a natural law is not merely a perfect correlation between properties but must correspond to a real ground in nature that is responsible for the correlation, a real kind is not determined merely by a correlation of properties but requires a real ground to determine it.

Thus, J. S. Mill said about his "Kinds" (the capitalization is in Mill) that "a hundred generations have not exhausted the common properties of animals or plants . . . nor do we suppose them to be exhaustible, but proceed to new observations and experiments, in the full confidence of discovering new properties which were by no means implied in those we previously knew" (from Hacking 1991a, p. 118). Surely we are not to understand this confidence as grounded in accidental historical convergence. Mill clearly had in mind that it is grounded in nature by a supporting natural ground of induction. Mill's "Kinds" are supposed to be genuinely projectable kinds, not the result of accidental correlations, accidental heaps of piled up properties. Mill's "Kinds" are real kinds.

In recent years, a number of psychologists have been interested in the structure of concepts of "natural kinds" and in the development of children's understanding of these kinds (e.g., Carey 1985; Gelman and Coley 1991; Keil 1989; Markman 1989). Natural kinds are said to be distinguished in part by the fact that many true generalizations can be made about them, and that, as such, they provide an indispensable key to the acquisition of inductive knowledge. For example, according to Gelman and Coley (1991), people develop natural kind concepts

> . . . with the implicit . . . goal of learning as much as possible about the objects being classified. . . . For example, if we learn that X is a "cat," we infer that it has many important properties in common with other cats, including diet, body temperature, genetic structure, and internal organs. We can even induce previously unknown properties. For example, if we discover that one cat has a substance called "cytosine" inside, we may then decide that other cats also contain this substance. . . . (p. 151)

Gelman and Coley (1991) call this feature "rich inductive potential." Clearly a concept having this sort of potential does not emerge by ontological accident. If a term is to have genuine "rich inductive potential," it had better attach not just to an accidental pattern of correlated properties, but to properties correlated for a good reason.

Kinds are not real if they yield inductive knowledge by accident. Consider, for example, the kind that is jade. As Putnam (1975) informs us, jade is either of two minerals, nephrite or jadeite, which have many properties in common but not for any univocal reason. Rather, each has these properties for its own reasons. Similarly, Putnam's earth water (H_2O) and twinearth water (XYZ) were conceived as having numerous observable properties in common, but not in common for any univocal reason. Inductive inferences from samples of nephrite to samples of jadeite, when the conclusions happen to come out true, are not true for a reason grounded in a common nature. There is no ontological *ground* of induction underlying such inferences. For this reason, jade is not a real kind. Nor, if Putnam's twinearth story were true, would generic water, conceived to be multiply realized either as H_2O or XYZ, be a real kind.

Real kinds are kinds that allow successful inductions to be made from one or a few members to other members of the kind not by accident, but because supported by a ground in nature. What we need to clarify is what various sorts of natural grounds there might be that would hold the members of a kind together so that one member would be like another by natural necessity. There are, I believe, a number of different types of reasons for the occurrence in nature of real kinds, these accounting in different ways for success in generalizing over encounters.

§2.2 KINDS OF REAL KINDS

Perhaps the best-known real kinds are the sort Putnam called "natural kinds" in "The Meaning of 'Meaning' " (Putnam 1975). These are real kinds by virtue of possessing a common inner nature of some sort, such as an inner molecular structure, from which the more superficial or easily observable properties of the kind's instances flow. The inner structure results by natural necessity in a certain selection of surface properties, or results in given selections under given conditions. Popular examples of this sort of kind are the various chemical elements and compounds. Putnam gave water and aluminum as his examples. Strictly speaking, these are not kinds but stuffs, but we could treat samples of these as members of kinds. Certainly water molecules, electrons, protons, and so forth, form real kinds of this sort. Portions of water have an inner structure in common that produces different surface properties given different temperature conditions. Stars, planets, comets, asteroids, and geodes form real kinds, not because their properties flow always from exactly the same inner nature, but because they were formed by the same natural forces in the same sort of circumstances out of materials similar in relevant ways. Real kinds of these various sorts can be said to have "essences" in a very traditional sense, essences that are not nominal but real, discovered through empirical investigation. The ontological ground of induction for such kinds, the reason that the members have many properties in common, is that they have a few fundamental properties and/or causes in common that account with natural necessity for the others.

I will call real kinds of this sort "ahistorical" or "eternal" kinds. They are ahistorical because the location of the members of the kind relative to one another in historical time and space plays no role in explaining the likenesses among them. Less well known are historical kinds, kinds for which historical location does play a role in explaining likeness.

Aristotle thought that the various animal and plant species were ahistorical kinds. He thought that the members of each species were alike because of a common inner nature or form from which various more superficial properties flowed or would flow if this form was supplied with the right matter. Modern biologists disagree. The kind *Homo sapiens*, for example, displays no identity of inner structure, or none that has relevance, specifically, to being human. Your genes and my genes are not the same gene types, but are merely taken from the same gene pool. Indeed, there are almost no genes in the human pool that have no alleles left at all. Nor should it be thought that the genes that most of us happen to have in common are what really make us be human, the rest causing inessential differences. On the contrary, alternate alleles frequently perform essential developmental functions. According to contemporary biology, what species an individual organism belongs to depends not on its timeless properties, either superficial or deep, but on its historical relations to other individuals — relations essentially embedded in real space and time. Dogs must be born of other dogs, not merely like other dogs; sibling species count as two or more for the same reason that identical twins count as two, not one, and so forth. In the case of sexually reproducing species, species membership is usually determined in part by reference to interbreeding, and there is some reference to lineage in all but the most radical cladists' attempts at defining both species and higher taxa. What these references to interbreeding and lineage do is effectively to confine each species and higher taxon to a historical location in this world. Indeed, M. T. Ghiselin (1974, 1981) and David Hull (e.g., 1978) claim that by biologists' usage, species are not similarity classes but big, scattered, historical *individuals* enduring through time.

From this Hull concludes, "there is no such thing as human nature" (p. 211), and it does follow, at least, that there is no such thing as a single set of founding properties, an inner human essence, from which all other properties characteristic of humans flow. On the other hand, given any species, there are innumerable traits that most of its members have in common with one another *not by accident but for a very good reason*. Hull himself emphasized that species as well as individuals (here he quotes Eldredge and Gould 1972) "are homeostatic systems. . . . amazingly well-buffered to resist change and maintain stability in the face of disturbing influences" (Hull 1978, p. 199, Eldredge and Gould 1972, p. 114). Stability results from continuity of selection pressures in a niche, which continually weed out the deleterious mutations that arise, thus preserving the well adapted status quo. And it results from the necessity for the various genes in a gene pool to be compatible with one another, so that throwing chromosomes together randomly from among the available alleles almost always results in a viable reproductive individual. This is what Eldredge, Gould, and Hull refer to as "homeostasis" in the gene pool.

Underlying these stabilizing forces, however, is an even more fundamental force. New gene tokens are copied from old ones. A massive replicating process is at work in the continuation of a species. The role of the forces producing homeostasis is secondary, keeping the reproducing or copying relatively faithful over periods of time. The role of homeostatic forces is to see that the kind does not do as Achilles' horse did and "run off in all directions," but remains relatively stable in its properties over time.

In sum, the members of biological taxa are like one another, not because they have inner or outer causes of the same ahistorical type, but because they bear certain historical relations *to one another*. It is not just that each exhibits the properties of the kind for the same ahistorical or eternal reason. Rather, each exhibits the properties of the kind because other members of the kind exhibit them. Inductions made from one member of the kind to another are grounded because there is a causal/historical link between the members of the kind that causes the members to be like one another. Biological taxa are historical kinds.

I have mentioned that the ontological ground of induction for many stuffs is ahistorical, for example, the ground of induction for the various chemical elements and compounds is ahistorical. But there also are stuffs whose ground of induction is historical, for example, peanut butter retains its basic properties over encounters because it is what is made by grinding up peanuts, which constitute a historical kind, and cowhide does because it is the hide of the historical kind cow.

The two most obvious sorts of historical reasons why members of a kind might be caused to be like one another are, first, that something akin to reproduction or copying has been going on, all the various members having been produced from one another or from the same models and/or, second, that the various members have been produced by, in, or in response to, the very same ongoing historical environment, for example, in response to the presence of members of other ongoing historical kinds. A third and ubiquitous causal factor often supporting the first is that some "function" is served by members of the kind, where "function" is understood roughly in the biological sense as an effect raising the probability that its cause will be reproduced, that it will be "selected for reproduction." It is typical for these various reasons to be combined. For example, many artifact kinds combine these features. Thus Frank Keil remarks,

Chairs have a number of properties, features, and functions that are normally used to identify them, and although there may not be internal causal homeostatic mechanisms of chairs that lead them to have these properties, there may well be external mechanisms having to do with the form and functions of the human body and with typical social and cultural activities of humans. For example, certain dimensions of chairs are determined by the normal length of human limbs and torsos. . . . (Keil 1989, pp. 46–7)

Chairs have been designed to fit the physical dimensions and practical and aesthetic preferences of humans, who are much alike in relevant respects for historical reasons. Moreover, the majority of chairs have not been designed from scratch, but copied from previous chairs that have satisfied these requirements. They thus form a rough historical kind owing to all three of the above reasons. Clearly there are reasons that go well beyond (mysteriously agreed on) points of definition why one knows roughly what to expect when someone offers to bring a chair. Similarly, one knows what to expect when someone offers to lend a Phillips screwdriver (designed to fit screws that were designed to fit prior Phillips screwdrivers), or to take one to see a Romanesque church – or, of course, to replace your back doorknob.[3]

The members of some historical artifact kinds are similar in nearly the same detail as members of animal species. In Millikan (1984), I spelled out why the 1969 Plymouth Valiant 100 was a "secondary substance":

. . . in 1969 every '69 Valiant shared with every other each of the properties described in the '69 Valiant's handbook and many other properties as well. And there was a good though complicated explanation for the fact that they *shared* these properties. They all originated with the selfsame plan – not just with identical plans but with the same plan *token*. They were made of the same materials gathered from the same places, and they were turned out by the same machines and the same workers . . . or machines similar and workers similarly trained [on purpose] . . . [Hence all the Valiants] had such and such strengths, dispositions and weaknesses . . . placement of distributor . . . size of piston rings . . . shape of door handles. . . . Valiants, like most other physical objects, are

---

3   The reference is to Fodor (1998).

things that tend to persist, maintaining the same properties over time in accordance with natural conservation laws. . . . Also, there are roughly stable prevailing economic and social conditions . . . in accordance with which working parts of automobiles tend to be restored and replaced with similar parts. . . .

[The Valiant also] has an identity relative to certain kinds of conditional properties. . . . For example, the fenders of the '69 Valiant that has not been garaged tend to rust out whereas the body stands up much better; the ball joints are liable to need replacing after relatively few thousands of miles whereas the engine . . . is not likely to burn oil until 100,000 miles. . . . (Millikan 1984, pp. 279–80)

Historical kinds of a somewhat less concrete nature are, for example, retail chains (McDonald's, Wal-Mart) and buses on a certain bus line (bus #13, the Elm Street bus).[4] Many kinds of interest to social scientists, such as ethnic, social, economic, and vocational groups, are historical kinds. For example, school teachers, doctors, and fathers form historical kinds when these groups are studied as limited to particular historical cultural contexts. Members of these groups are likely to act similarly in certain ways and to have attitudes in common as a result of similar training handed down from person to person (reproduction or copying), as a result of custom (more copying), as a result either of natural human dispositions or social pressures to conform to role models (copying again) and/or as a result of legal practices. More generally, they are molded by what is relevantly numerically the same historical niche, a certain homeostatic ongoing historical social context that bears upon them in ways peculiar to their social status. Boyd (1991) claims that members of some social groups may exhibit properties characteristic of the group as a result of being classified into these groups rather than conversely, but he argues that this does not compromise these social kinds as possible scientific objects. Members may come to form a cohesive social kind "only because" other members of the society class them together (stereotyping, prejudice, taboos), but the "because" here is causal, not logical, resulting in certain derived uniformities among members of the group. The kind that results is then real, not merely nominal. If social groups were not real, there could be no gain in empirical studies concerning them, for example, studies of the attitudes of American doctors toward herbal medicines, and so forth. Doctors are an actual-world group, not a set of possible properties in a set of possible worlds. That is why their attitudes and practices can be studied empiri-

4   The latter example is Richard Grandy's (from conversation).

22

cally. On the othe hand, insofar as social scientists sometimes generalize across radically different cultures, not just, say, across Western cultures, the common historical thread across social groups is mainly just human psychology, the common psychological dispositions of the historical species *Homo sapiens*.

Historical kinds do not have "essences" in the traditional sense. On the other hand, a kind is real only if there is some univocal principle, the very same principle throughout, that explains for each pair of members why they are alike in a number of respects. That is, the principle explains the *likeness* between members, not, in the first instance, the properties themselves. (To explain why a photocopy is *like* the original is not to explain why either has the properties it has. I can know why the photocopy is like the original without knowing what specific properties either of them has.) Only in some cases does the best explanation of this likeness concern likeness in inner constitution. In the case of historical kinds, although a statistically significant likeness among inner constitutions may *result* from the principles that group the members into the kind (most of your and my genes are the same[5]), this probabilistic result is not what defines the species' unity. Most real kinds do not have traditional essences, but to be real they must have ontological grounds, and these could, I suppose, be called "essences" in an extended sense. One or another kind of glue must hold them together, making it be the case that properties exhibited by one member of the kind are always or often exhibited also by other members, so that induction is supported. We could extend the term "essence" so that it applies to whatever natural principle accounts for the instances of a kind being alike. But it is probably safer to stay with the term "ontological ground of induction" to avoid any possibility of misunderstanding.

§2.3 INDIVIDUALS AS SUBSTANCES

Not only real kinds but all substances must be held together by some kind of ground of induction. That is what makes them substances. A substance is something that one can learn things about from one encounter that will apply on other occasions and where this possibility is not coincidental but grounded. There is an explanation or cause of the samenesses.

---

5 About 90 percent are likely to be the same. It does not follow that there are many (even any) genes common to everybody. (To conclude so would commit the fallacy of composition.)

Ghiselin and David Hull said that species are "individuals" because they are held together not by a traditional essence but through historical causal connections. The other side of this coin is that individuals are rather like species: Their ontological ground of induction is similar. If Xavier is blue-eyed, tall, good at mathematics, and intolerant of gays today, it is likely he will be so tomorrow and even next year. This is because he too is a "homeostatic system . . . amazingly well-buffered to resist change and maintain stability in the face of disturbing influences," and because Xavier tomorrow will be a sort of copy of Xavier today. Xavier today is much like Xavier yesterday because Xavier today directly resulted from Xavier yesterday, in accordance with certain kinds of conservation laws, and certain patterns of homeostasis, and because of replications of his somatic cells. Ghiselin and Hull say that species are individuals; conversely, some philosophers have thought of Xavier as a class consisting of Xavier timeslices, each of which causes the next. Either way, there is a deep similarity between individuals and many historical kinds.

Because of the rich ontological ground of induction on which biological species rest, one can run numerous inductions over the members of any species, learning about most members from observing one or a few. The elementary student learns about sulphur from experiments with one sample. Similarly, she learns about frogkind by dissecting one frog, and about the human's susceptibility to operant conditioning by conditioning one friend to blink for smiles. One can learn from sample members of a species about the whole species for much the same reason one can learn about one temporal stage of a person from other temporal stages of the same person, and vice versa.

§2.4 KINDS OF BETTERNESS AND WORSENESS IN
SUBSTANCES

Unlike eternal kinds, historical kinds are not likely to ground many, if any, exceptionless generalizations. The copying processes that generate them are not perfect, nor are the historical environments that sustain them steady in all relevant respects. This is true of individuals as well. Depending on the category of individual and what it is made of, some properties will be less likely to change than others, but usually there are very few that could not change under any conditions. The idea that either a historical individual or a historical kind is somehow defined for all possible worlds, not just this one, such that there are definite properties that *must* endure for the individual to remain in existence, or that *must* be present for the kind member really to exemplify the kind, is mistaken. Who is really and truly a member of the working class? Here the principle or principles that cause or tend to hold the kind together catch up some members more squarely than others. Was Theseus's ship still the same ship after its last plank was replaced? There is nothing in nature to draw such distinctions. Historical kinds typically have naturally and irreducibly vague boundaries. So do historical individuals. If their boundaries happen to be sharp, as they sometimes are in practice, this is a matter of historical fact, not some deeper necessity.

Real kinds are domains over which predicates are nonaccidentally projectable. There are good reasons in nature why one member of a real kind is like another. So, although real kinds can have vague boundaries, still, the question whether an item belongs to a certain real kind or not, or whether it is on its border, is written in nature, not just in English or !Kung. Whether a seemingly marginal item is or is not a member of a certain real kind often is a straightforward substantive question about how the world is, not a question of how we humans or we English speakers like to classify. If it is not like other members of the kind for the very same reason they are like one another, then no matter how many properties it has in common with them, it is not a member of the same real kind. Similarly, we take it quite rightly that whether a correct identification of an individual has been made is a matter of how the world is, not of how we humans or we English speakers like to identify. This has not, of course, stopped philosophers interested in such questions from thinking up numerous bizarre possible-world examples where it would not be clear whether this individual thing would be numerically the same as that one. Similarly, they might raise the question whether a dog with, say, ¼ or ⅕ or ⅒ coyote genes spliced in would be a dog. But the home of *historical* substances is in *this* world. Questions concerning their identities in other worlds are, in fact, subtly incoherent.

Historical substances are not likely to ground exceptionless generalizations. But many substances interest us not because they afford such reliable inductions, but because they afford so many inductions. They bring a great wealth of probable knowledge with them.[6] This gives rise,

---

6 Andrew Milne suggests that historical kinds may be likely to have more projectible properties than ahistorical ones because "with historical kinds, often things that are nomically quite separate are still projectible. . . . Properties that are only contingently correlated, in the sense that it is perfectly lawful for one to occur without the other, may nonetheless be

25

presumably, to the typicality effects explored by contemporary psychologists studying categories. It seems natural that people should work with a stereotype taken from knowledge of the most stable properties of substances when asked to describe the substance, in making guesses about category membership, when asked to make inferences about unobserved members, and so forth.

Because the occurrence of causative factors accounting for similarities can be more or less regular or irregular, and because the number of grounded similarities characterizing a substance can be larger or smaller, there are two different continua from richer to poorer along which historical substances can range. These reflect (1) the reliability of the inferences supported, and (2) their multiplicity. Substances vary widely in both of these dimensions. If the substance is sufficiently impoverished in both of these dimensions, whether there exists a real kind at all can be a vague matter. There is no sharp line between what is and is not a substance. Rather, some things are, as it were, better substances than others, some are worth understanding as substances, others are too marginal or uninteresting. One might argue that even Californians form a very rough or vague historical kind. They are of the same species, many have copied behavioral patterns from one another, they have been subject to certain social and physical environmental influences from the same sources; hence, certain very rough and uncertain generalizations can be made over them for good reason. There is a long, graded continuum between historical kinds suitable, say, to project sciences over and a great variety of poorer and less exact historical kinds that are nonetheless not nominal but real.

§2.5 ONTOLOGICAL RELATIVITY (OF A NONQUINEAN SORT)

The category of substances, as I have defined it, is at root an epistemological category. As such, it cuts straight across many more familiar distinctions in ontology. What makes a substance a substance is that it can be appropriated by cognition for the grounded, not accidental, running of inductions, or projecting of invariants. This will be possible in differ-

projectible, because if one is copied the other may be too. So, for instance, while there is no law (so far as I know) connecting having a chitinous exoskeleton and having more than four legs, it is reasonable to assume that something with a chitinous exoskeleton has more than four legs because something with the exoskeleton is a copy of something else with an exoskeleton that had more than four legs" [private correspondence].

ent cases for very different reasons, due to very different sorts of causes, which is, of course, exactly what interests me about substances. It is their variety, considered from other ontological perspectives, that makes it easy to overlook their similarity relative to the projects of cognition. I have illustrated the category of substance by reference to individuals, stuffs and certain kinds whose members are ordinary physical individuals. But other ontological types can be substances too. Beethoven's Fifth Symphony has many properties that are unlikely to vary from performance to performance. You can recognize it and know what is coming next. This is also true of tellings of *The Three Bears*. Places have properties many of which remain the same over time. Dinner time and siesta time have pretty definite properties, in many cultures. War among humans has certain properties that seem to remain pretty much the same over the ages. Western industrial economies can be studied as a real kind.

There is not one set of ontological "elements," one unique way of carving the ontology of the world, but a variety of crisscrossing overlapping equally basic patterns to be discovered there. Cubes are things one can learn to recognize and learn a number of stable things about such as how they fit together, how they balance, that their sides, angles and diagonals are equal, and so forth. In their commentary on Millikan (1998a), Cangelosi and Parisi (1998) remark (correcting me) that *white thing* is something one can learn about. White things, they said, get dirty easily and, I now add, show up easily in dim light, stay cool in sunlight, but also tend to blind us, and so forth. Understood as substances, however, I think that these entities are most naturally and also most correctly named with simple nouns: "Cubes don't stand on edge easily," "White stays cool in sunlight," "squares have equal diagonals" and so forth. This reflects the fact that qua naming substances, the terms "cube," "white," and "square" express subject-term thoughts. As substances, white and square are not predicates, not properties; they *have* properties. The same thing can be a property relative to certain substances and also a substance relative to certain properties.[7] Which way a thinker is understanding such an entity is generally expressed in the grammar.

---

7 For more on this theme, see Millikan (1984), Chapters 15–17. There I claim, for example, that unlike substances, properties are, as such, members of contrary spaces. These are groups whose members oppose one another, by natural necessity, on the ground of certain kinds of substances.

Just as properties do not have to have natural demarcation lines between them in order to be real, there are substances that have no natural boundaries along certain dimensions. Water shades into mud on one side and into lemonade and then lemon juice on another. Substances of this sort are organized around paradigms, or around peak points, or gradient shifts, at which causally intertwined properties are either historically or ahistorically determined to be collected together. Other cases often diverge from the paradigms along several dimensions. Closer approximation to the paradigm essences or paradigm historical causes linking these cases together yields closer approximation to the other of typical properties of the substance as well.

§2.6 SUBSTANCE TEMPLATES AND HIERARCHY AMONG SUBSTANCES

I can observe today that Xavier has blue eyes and knows Greek, and unless Xavier is very unlucky, this will hold true when I meet him tomorrow. But if Xavier is sitting or angry or playing tennis when I meet him, this probably will not be true tomorrow. Similarly, if I observe the approximate adult size, preferred diet, variety and placement of internal and external organs (two eyes, two kidneys, one heart on the left) and general physiology of one member of the species *Felis domesticus*, all of these observations will probably yield correct predictions about the next member of *Felis domesticus*. But if my observations concern color, certain kinds of behavior patterns, and the pattern of torn ears, they will be unlikely to carry over to the next cat I meet. If they do, it will be a matter of accident. Again, if I have determined the color, boiling point, specific gravity, volatility, and chemical combining properties of diethyl ether on one pure sample, then I have determined the color, boiling point, specific gravity, volatility, and chemical combining properties of diethyl ether, period. If the experiments need replication, this is not because other samples of diethyl ether might have a different color, boiling point, and so forth, but because I may have made a mistake in measurement or analysis. But I cannot in this way determine the shape, volume, or purity of diethyl ether. These are not properties that generalize from one meeting to the next.

Now about diethyl ether you probably take me to be right, *not* because you know that the above is true of diethyl ether specifically. Rather, you know it is true of chemical compounds generally. You know that chemical compounds do not vary with respect to color, boiling point, combining properties, and so forth, but that they do vary, when encountered, with respect to size, weight, shape, ownership, monetary value, place they were mined (for mined minerals), and so forth. You know that there are properties that the chemical kinds have *qua* being those very chemicals again, and that there are other properties that only samples of them have. This is because you understand the category *chemical compound* to correspond not merely (if at all) to a substance (what, if any, are the *determinate* properties that every chemical compound has?) but to a substance *template* (Section 1.8). Similarly, you probably take me to be right about Xavier, not because you know him personally, but because you understand him to fall under the substance template *human being*, and you have a good idea what determinables are likely to be constant for substances falling in this category.

But if you also agreed with me about *Felis domesticus*, why was that? Was it because you know that every species of animal is uniform, for example, with respect to adult size? But snakes and alligators keep right on growing. Or because you know that every species of animal is liable to vary in color from individual to individual? But this is not true of most species. Nor is it true of most species – perhaps only of mammals and some birds – that their behavior patterns may vary significantly from individual to individual. *Animal* is not as well focused a template as either *chemical compound* or *human being*. Knowing just that something is an animal, you will have lots of ideas about the kinds of questions that can be asked about it, but for a significant proportion of these, you may not know in advance whether they can be answered univocally for the species as a whole. If you are given that the animal is a mammal, of course, this may help quite a lot. Categories like *animal* and *mammal* correspond, of course, to substances – each has some univocal properties of its own – but, more important, for the project of gathering knowledge, they bring with them substance templates. The categories *animal species, mammal species, person, crab, pebble, bridge, road, musical composition, chemical element*, and *book*, for example, are all substance templates as well as corresponding to substances in their own right. As templates, they take predicates like "have shapes," "have colors," "have metabolism rates," "have specific gravities," "have spatial lengths," "have temporal lengths," "have designers," "are written in languages (French, German)," and so forth.

I have mentioned that substances vary both in the number of inductions they support and in the reliability of the inductions they support. Here we have a third kind of variability in substance quality. Substances vary in the availability and sharpness of focus of recognizable substance templates covering them. Where good substance templates are available and known, concepts of the substances falling under them are extremely easy to develop, for it is known in advance what kinds of determinables will be determinate for these substances, hence what kinds of inductions they can support. The discovery of substance templates requires something like meta-inductions, although there is some evidence that certain meta-inductions may be bypassed by human infants. Some grasp of certain templates, some grasp of the structure of certain substance domains, may be wired in (compare Atran 1989; Boyer 1998; Carey 1985; Gallistel et al. 1993; Gelman and Coley 1991; Keil 1979, 1989; Markman 1989; Marler 1993, Spelke 1989, 1993). For those disciplines systematic enough to be clearly labeled as well-developed empirical sciences, the substances studied typically fall under well-focused substance templates, or under a hierarchy of such templates. Especially, well-founded second-order inductions of this sort would seem to underlie all of what Kuhn labeled "normal science." The basic principles of good scientific induction are never found in logic alone; all inductive reasoning rests on a posteriori projectability judgments (compare, for example, Boyd 1991).

Many substances do not fall under well-focused substance templates, however. Consider, for example, the substance *chair*. I have argued that this is a historical substance, but what substance template do chairs fit under? It is clear that one would not want to project a science of furniture, for example, for although there may be one or two questions pretty certain to have answers for each kind of furniture (what was it designed to be used for?), there are not nearly enough to delimit in advance all or most of the determinables that are relatively reliably determined for most chairs.

Aristotle thought there was a hierarchial ordering among all substances. According to the doctrine of "real definition" or of natural ordering by genus and differentia, substances were supposed to form a logical tree. I think this doctrine was seriously wrong. The structure of the domain of substances is frankly a logical mess, a mare's nest of overlappings and crisscrossings. There are multitudes of entwined substances, very very many more, surely, than we have ideas of. The ones that are picked up by thought and by language are only those that have properties of interest to us. But that they are interesting does nothing, of course, to make their status as substances less than fully objective. Tree structure is good for a general classification system to have (Section

30

3.2), but it is not the structure of the logical space of substances nor of most of its subspaces.

Consider butter on the one hand and human beings on the other. Clearly there is no way to hang these on the same logical tree. They are neither beside one another (horizontal) under some higher substance, nor is one included in the other (vertical), nor is there some more inclusive substance covering them both. (Aristotle might have said they are both subsumed under *substance* and under *Being*, but *substance* is not a substance and neither is *Being*.) When we look within domains rather than across them, matters are no tidier. Susan is a 1990s American mother and a professor and a diabetic. Each of these is a rough substance category, but there is no logical tree on which they all hang. Heated modern debates among biologists about principles of classification (phenetics, cladistics, evolutionary classification) reflect exactly this: There is no natural way to organize the substances that are of interest to the zoologist or botanist into a single hierarchy. The demand that biological taxonomy should settle on a single hierarchy is of course quite rational. A good classification system is needed for information storage and retrieval among the various biologists. The actual systems of classification used by biologists are compromises between good classification and respect for natural substance boundaries (compare Mayr 1981). In the natural domain of substances there is a confusing crisscrossing, every which way. On the other hand, wherever there exist substances that are also substance templates, a degree of hierarchy and order is naturally imposed on the domain of substances.

For every substance, one can ask how many inductions, if I knew to venture them, would yield reliable results. We also can ask how many of these inductions I could know to venture in advance through grasp of a good template for the substance. The latter question is the more interesting to the epistemologist. The interesting question of inductive potential concerns how many determinables you *know* you can find stable values for, not how many stable properties the substance actually has. The best substances are the ones for which there are rich, known, substance templates, for example, the chemical elements and compounds, the various living species, and also individual members of these species, and most more ordinary individual physical objects. These are things we know how to learn many things about without wasting time on dozens of observations verifying the stability of each trait.

A question that has sometimes been asked by psychologists interested in categorization concerns which level of substance categories are inductively the most "fertile" to have a grasp of (see Komatsu 1998). The question assumes, of course, some degree of hierarchial structure within the domain to be considered. Now if one were to recognize only the lowest level substances, say, only the individual animals or only the species, although it is true that these have the greatest number of properties, learning about these properties would be a hopelessly inefficient process. One would have to start all over with each individual object or species, exploring its individual features, with no contribution from prior knowledge of higher substances carrying substance templates, either about its properties or its relevant determinables. It seems that there is no particular level at which greatest "fertility" lies. It results, rather, from an interaction between levels.

3

Classifying, Identifying, and the Function of Substance Concepts

Substances, as I have described them, are whatever one can learn from given only one or a few encounters, various skills or information that will apply on other encounters. Further, this possibility must be grounded in some kind of natural necessity. The function of a substance concept is to make possible this sort of learning and use of knowledge for a specific substance. For this, the cognizing organism must be able to recognize the specific substance under a variety of different conditions, as many as possible. It needs to do this, first, to grasp that the substance it is learning about over various encounters is one and the same so that knowledge of it can accumulate and, second, so that the accumulated knowledge can be applied. For substance concepts to be employed in the service of theoretical knowing – employed for knowing *that* rather than knowing *how* – the substance must be represented in thought in a univocal way, the same substance always represented *as* being the same. This makes possible a stable, unequivocal, and nonredundant inner representational system.

The ability to recognize what is objectively the same substance again *as* the same despite wide variations in the faces it shows to the senses is necessarily fallible. Although you surely have many ways of identifying each member of your immediate family – similarly for water and for cats – there will always be possible conditions under which you would misidentify them, mistaking them for someone or something else. If a concept is genuinely a substance concept, if its extension is really a substance, this extension is not determined by one's fallible dispositions to recognize it. These dispositions, given any of numerous adverse conditions, would break up the extension of the substance or mix it with other things. The extension of a substance concept is determined not by one's dispositions (rightly or wrongly) to recognize it but, first, by the real extent of the substance in nature.

The purpose of this chapter is to clear the ground of certain rubble left by classical and contemporary theories according to which dispositions to identify do determine the extensions of substance concepts.[1] Chapter 4 will then begin the foundation for another explanation of how a substance concept hooks onto its extension – onto a substance, whole – and how it is determined onto which substance it is hooked.[2] It will begin to establish a version of what is sometimes called "direct reference" theory.

To understand how the extension of a substance concept is determined, first we must understand more exactly what the functions of substance concepts are, hence to what sort of things in nature they need to be hitched in order to serve these functions. The standard view has been that terms for kinds and stuffs correspond to capacities to classify instances falling under these terms. I claim instead that most such terms correspond in the first instance to abilities to identify substances, and that they are only secondarily used as classifiers. The result of the standard view has been a thorough confusion between two quite different kinds of functions, the functions of identifying and the functions of classifying.

§3.2 THE FUNCTIONS OF CLASSIFYING

Sharpening the distinction between the terms "identify" and "classify" somewhat for expository purposes, the difference between identifying and classifying lies both in purpose and in the psychological structure of these acts. The purposes of classification and identification are hopelessly entangled, for example, in the following contemporary descriptions by psychologists of the functions of what the authors call "categorization" and "concepts":

---

1 Appendix B also concerns this matter. It concerns information theories of mental content according to which to have a concept of Xes, one must be able to "discriminate" between Xes and all other things.

2 The explanation will not be completely finished, however, until the full implications of the theory of abilities to be introduced in Chapter 4 have been drawn out in Chapters 13 and 14.

34

Categorization . . . is a means of simplifying the environment, of reducing the load on memory, and of helping us to store and retrieve information efficiently. (Markman 1989, p. 11)

Without concepts, mental life would be chaotic. If we perceived each entity as unique, we would be overwhelmed by the sheer diversity of what we experience and unable to remember more than a minute fraction of what we encounter. And if each individual entity needed a distinct name, our language would be staggeringly complex and communication virtually impossible." (Smith and Medin 1981, p. 1)

. . . concepts are used to classify . . . if you know nothing about a novel object but are told it is an instance of X, you can *infer* that the object has all or many of X's properties. . . . (Smith and Medin 1981, p. 8)

A good classification system aids efficient information storage, retrieval, and transfer of information, or efficient storage and retrieval of the objects classified, or, in a different but related way, efficient communication. It aids the efficient storage and retrieval of what we already know when we use dictionaries, encyclopedias, telephone books, guide books, filing systems, classification systems in libraries, and so forth. It aids in putting objects away where they can be found again in grocery stores, hardware stores, museums, home workshops, and again, libraries. It aids in communication in the following way. Shared classification systems allow one person efficiently to convey enough information about a thing for another to retrieve it, either literally or from memory. For example, saying it is "the red book on my table in my study" that I want you to bring will get me what I want only if we share a way of classifying things into those that are studies and those that are not, those that are mine and those that are not, and into books and nonbooks, red things and nonred things, tables and nontables. Then I can swiftly convey enough for you to retrieve the object I intend.

These being its principle uses, an ideal *general* classification system, designed to cover a general domain, will draw sharp lines around the classes it contains, so that each member in its domain falls determinately either in or out of each class. General domain classification systems are used, for example, by libraries and grocery stores. These lines need not cut between items in all possible worlds, however, but only in the actual domain where the classification system is to be used. Classification for purposes of communication, on the other hand, does not correspond to a single general domain. The domains that are involved in ordinary informal communication typically are severely restricted by context, varying radically from one speaker-hearer pair and from one occasion to another. For this reason, words whose natural extensions have very vague boundaries can still be used in specific communicative contexts to classify objects precisely. I refer to what I want simply as "red," but given the books on my table it is clear enough what object I want, even though the entire domain of red things shades off gradually into pink things, purple things, orange things, and so forth. If both my hearer and I know my intended local domain and I choose my words well with reference to it, I can often use very vague words to effect accurate hearer classifications in context. It remains true, however, that clear boundaries between classes relative to the actual members in the domain of its use is helpful for all of the functions of classification.

An ideal general classification system also has a tree or a grid structure, so that each item can be located within it by answering a determinate set of questions in order. This assures that each member of the relevant domain has one and only one location within the classification system, hence that it can be efficiently put away and retrieved. This is true also for classification used for communication. In asking for "the red book on the table in my study," each of my descriptive words, used here as classifiers, partitions my intended domain into two classes in such a way that, taken together, they separate off just the intended (unit) class.

The initial data for a classification task must include a specification of each property of each object to be classified that is relevant to its classification. It must be possible to answer each of the questions determining its classification. A librarian would not try to classify a book, for example, without carefully examining its contents, and to classify an object as a red book on the table in my study you must know it is red, a book, on a table, in a study, and that the study is mine – every one of these. On the other hand, most of the myriad properties of any object will not be relevant to a given classification task. Librarians don't need to note the colors, numbers of pages, numbers of illustrations, publishers, type fonts or, usually, the shapes and sizes of the books they classify. But the properties that define the classes in the classification system being used obviously do need to be determined, whether by observation or by inference, as either present or absent for each instance of a domain *prior* to classifying it. Consonant with this, in classical "categorization" experiments in psychology, since these are usually taken to be studies of classification, all properties of each "stimulus" and each "test item" considered to be relevant to the classification to be learned are clearly exhibited to the learner.

Now consider Smith and Medin's claim quoted above that ". . . concepts are used to classify . . . if you know nothing about a novel object but are told it is an instance of X, you can *infer* that the object has all or many of X's properties. . . ." Suppose that the extension of "X" is, as suggested, *merely* a class and not also a substance. In that case, you will not have to do any *inferring* in order to know that the object "has all or most of X's properties." For in that case, the properties of the object must include all of those properties used to determine that it falls in class X, and no other properties will be inferable in a grounded way. This is because grounded inferences from properties of some members of a class to other members are possible only if the extension of the class is a substance. Being a substance is the same thing as being something that grounds inferences of this kind; if no substance, then no grounded inference. Concepts that merely classify, and do not also identify substances, contain exactly as much information as is analytically put into them, no more and no less. If without concepts of this kind we would be "unable to remember more than a minute fraction of what we encounter," we would be just as unable with them. Use of words that are shorthand for strings of memorized properties may make classification and communication more efficient, but it cannot make memory or thought more efficient.

Similarly, when a classification system is used for storing away information in encyclopedias or libraries, it is not the classification *system* that contains the information. The information is in the encyclopedia entries and in the books, not in the classification system. In order to retrieve the information, one must first find the right entries or retrieve the right books. And it is exactly the same when I use words to classify what I am talking about. By classifying my subject matter as a "red book on the table in my study," I hand you tools with which to circumscribe that object, but if you are to retrieve any more information about it than is already contained in my classification, you will either have to go and find the extension itself and inspect it, or find it in your memory so as to retrieve things you already happen to know about it. (On the other hand, exactly because the word "book" is not merely a classifier but corresponds to a rough substance, you also may retrieve from memory what you know about books generally and apply it to this case.)

Contrast now the functions of reidentifying. Reidentifying is required not primarily for information storage, retrieval, and transfer, but for information *acquisition* and information *use*. Rather than knowing its relevant properties in advance, as when one classifies something, one identifies a substance in order to *come* to know its properties. Identifying is necessary in order to collect together over time knowledge of a thing's properties, hence in order to know its properties on particular occasions, since many of these properties are manifest on encounter only some of the time. Identifying is also necessary in order to apply one's knowledge of things. One applies one's knowledge by managing to recognize a substance on the basis of whatever properties *do* happen to be currently manifest, and then applying one's prior knowledge of *others* of its properties, properties not currently observed.

Notice first that these functions do not require the substance recognized to have sharp boundaries. Grasp of substances very often affords knowledge that is not invariant over the substance's entire extension. If the edges of the substance are vague, the variance is more marked toward these edges. Well-fashioned substance concepts, well-fashioned abilities to exploit substances as objects of knowledge, will include the ability to recognize a difference between more central and less central areas in the extent of the substance, and to portion out degrees of reliance on accumulated knowledge of the substance accordingly. When, as is often the case, the boundaries of substances really *are* vague, obviously there is nothing, other than taking this into account, that the organism can do about it. Artificially imposing precision will not help. By contrast, ideal general classification systems, I have said, are more efficient if precise relative to the entities actually in their domains. Where substance boundaries are vague in nature, the purposes of *classification* are sometimes served by drawing artificial boundaries around the extensions of these substances. For certain classificatory purposes, for example, what counts as war and who counts as a member of the working class or as a full-time student may be quite sharply but artificially defined.

Notice, second, that substances are not generally organized into tree or grid structures. This was argued in Section 2.6.

Notice, third, that unlike a task of classifying, the task of identifying a substance doesn't require that any one particular set of the substance's properties be known or manifest to one, or that different people should use the same properties of the substance in order to identify it. Any of very numerous means of recognizing the substance may be applied. Each of these methods will be fallible in principle. Identifying a substance and exploiting its possibilities is as fallible as any other practical activity one engages in. One may always stumble and fall.

§3.4 UNDERSTANDING EXTENSIONS AS CLASSES VERSUS AS SUBSTANCES

Although substance concepts, hence words for substances, can be used for the purpose of classifying, the reverse does not hold in general. There is a big difference between understanding something merely as a class and understanding it as a substance. Conceptions used to classify need only carve out some clear unequivocal extension within the domain to be classified. Conceptions that govern substance concepts must locate genuine ontological grounds of induction. A substance concept is distinguished by the role it is ready to play, accumulating additional means of identification, and anticipating certain kinds of inductions as likely to hold. A substance concept will be successful only if there really is some substance out there it is hooked into. One reason it is an error to place great value on operational definitions in science, for example, is that operational definitions, as such, are merely *classifiers*, hence do not necessarily correlate with substances. But it is substances rather than classes that are of interest to science.

Because *conceptions* filling out substance concepts can sometimes be used also as conceptions of classes, words for substances can vacillate between being understood as standing for substances and as standing only for classes. When confidence is lost in the reality of a substance or in the univocity of a substance term, it may begin to be used in a strictly classificatory way. For example, terms for many mental disorders have vacillated over the years between being understood as capturing substances, naming single diseases for which single etiologies and therapies might eventually be discovered, and as being merely classificatory, defining useful groupings of symptoms for efficient transfer of information.

Nominals that are used only to express concepts of classes typically are complexes built out of prior terms. They wear their analytical natures on their sleeves. Their extensions are functions of unions and disjuncts of the extensions of the prior terms that compose them. Typically, this sort of construction will be built up in the same way by all who understand the syntactic forms of the language. Thus, although prior conceptions attaching to the element terms in the complex may differ from one speaker of the language to another, the mode of construction of complex conceptions out of prior conceptions will be common. These terms express analytical concepts, concepts only of classes. Substance concepts, on the other hand, are synthetical. A person's conception of a substance may employ prior concepts used in the process of identifying, but the substance concept is not equivalent to any mere function of prior concepts.

But there are, of course, many exceptions to the rule that synthetical concepts are expressed with simple nouns, analytical concepts with compounds. Consider the term "red sulfur." Red sulfur is not just sulfur that is red, but an allotrope of sulfur, a substance in its own right with its own suite of properties different from other forms of sulfur. On the other hand, red sulfur also happens to be the only substance that is both red and (pure) sulfur. Does the nominal "red sulfur" correspond, then, to a synthetical or an analytical concept?

Whether a word express an analytical or a synthetical concept may sometimes depend on the user. For some people the concept for "red sulfur" may be synthetical and for others analytical. A person who did not understand that sulfur that is red happens to be a substance in its own right would only have an analytical concept corresponding to the term "red sulfur." Accordingly, they would never recognize any part of the extension of "red sulfur" in any way other than by noting that it was sulfur and also noting that it was red. And they would not attempt inductions from samples of red sulfur to other samples of red sulfur that they would not have attempted either from samples of red to other samples of red or from samples of sulfur to other samples of sulfur. On the other hand, a person might instead have a synthetical concept of "red sulfur." That is the kind chemists have, for example. More interesting, it would be possible to have a concept of this stuff, this substance, without knowing either that it is red or that it is sulfur. One might recognize it as the sticky so-smelling substance typically found in such-and-such context, and be surprised to learn that it is always red, and that it is a kind of sulfur.

Similarly, should "Californian" correspond to a vague sort of substance, as suggested in Section 2.4, then although the "-ian" suffix suggests an analytical concept, there will be at least two ways to have a concept for "Californian," one analytical and the other synthetical. It is less plausible, of course, that one might have a reliable way of *identifying* Californians that did not depend on first determining that they came from California. Not every legitimate substance is reliably identifiable in multiple ways, if one counts as "identifying in the same way," using descriptions employing concepts of the same *things* in the same way. (These prior concepts might each be governed by variable conceptions, however.) Especially, as is true in this particular case, ways of identifying that relate directly to the real ontological ground of a substance may be uniquely reliable. Whether a substance concept is legitimately a one criterion concept or not does not rest on something ephemeral called "the rules of our language" (wherever they live) but lies in nature. If it is necessary that a vixen be a female fox, the deep reason is that it is sets of fox chromosomes that include two X chromosomes, copied from prior sets of this sort (close enough), that are responsible for causing the characteristic likenesses among vixens. Being a female fox is the *real* essence of vixenhood, nor is this a purely a priori matter.

One last difference between identifying and classifying. Classifying requires recognizing that a predicate applies to some definite *subject*. Suppose, for example, that we tried to model the act of classifying individual objects into the red ones and the green ones as, just, responding in one way to the red individuals, in another to the green individuals. What would determine that these responses constituted the classifying of *individuals*, rather than of time slices of individuals, or facing surfaces of individuals, or dye stuffs found on the surfaces of individuals, or pattens of ambient light impinging on retinas? You can't classify without some grasp of *what* you are classifying. You have to be able independently to think of the object you want to classify before you can classify it. Identifying an object, on the other hand, does not always require something conceptually prior. Identifying a substance as animals do, merely for practical purposes, requires only that behavioral responses the animal is disposed to learn by employing the concept should be appropriate to that substance, that is, they should be responses that are effective because of the properties or dispositions of that substance. True, identifying a substance for theoretical use does require that you have some appropriate *predicate* concepts, ones that you understand as applicable to, whether or not they are true of, the substance. I am not claiming that the only things we reidentify are substances.[3] But whatever it is that one *classifies*, it is clear that the capacity to think of members within the domain to be classified is more fundamental than the ability to classify. Identifying is a skill prior to classifying.

3 In Millikan (1984) Chapter 16, I talked quite a lot about reidentifying properties, and the analysis of the act of reidentifying to be offered below in Chapters 9 through 12 applies equally to concepts of substances and concepts of properties.

The traditional view among philosophers and psychologists has been that the ability to apply a term for a kind or a stuff is an ability to classify. This view has often taken the form of assuming that kind terms and stuff terms are descriptive, each corresponding to some sort of configuration of properties. If the concepts corresponding to these terms are concepts of configurations of properties, their extensions are naturally determined analytically as a direct function of the extensions of those properties. Both among contemporary psychologists and also in some philosophical circles, this view is still much the most common form of a more general position I will call "conceptionism." Conceptionism is the view that the extension of a concept or term is determined by some aspect of the thinker's *conception* of its extension, that is, by some *method* that the thinker has of identifying it. I am fully in charge of the extensions of my concepts; whatever I am, after due consideration, disposed to apply them to is what they are concepts of.

One way of identifying a substance, of course, is by means of the knowledge that it has certain properties or falls under a certain description peculiar to that substance. The classic form of conceptionism holds that the conception that determines the extension of a substance term is such a set of properties or such a description. We can call this classic view "descriptionism." Another form of conceptionism holds that the extension of certain concepts or terms is determined by means of identification procedures not employing prior concepts of properties. Concepts whose extensions are thought to be determined in this direct manner are sometimes called "recognitional concepts." Thus Fodor remarks "if a concept is recognitional, then having certain kinds of experience would, in principle, show with the force of conceptual necessity that the concept applies" (Fodor 1999). "Conceptionism" in either form contrasts, of course, with "direct reference" theories of conceptual content.[4]

§3.5 DESCRIPTIONISM IN THE PSYCHOLOGICAL LITERATURE

Conceptionist views – the view that substance concepts are basically classifiers, their extensions being determined by dispositions to apply

---

4 In Millikan (1998a and 1998b), I referred to both kinds of conceptionism as "descriptionism." This resulted in understandable confusion on the part of several commentators. Here I am shifting to what I hope is a more perspicuous terminology.

them – underlie a surprising proportion of the masses of recent work on "concepts" and "categories" in the psychological literature. It will be worth spelling this out in some detail. I will try to show, indeed, that throughout the changing variety of competing theories of concepts and categorization developed by psychologists in the last half century, the theoretical assumption of conceptionism, generally in the form of descriptionism, has managed to go completely unchallenged. This is true, despite the fact that Putnam's and Kripke's famous arguments (or at least their conclusions) against descriptionism (Kripke 1972; Putnam 1975) have been rehearsed numerous times in the psychological literature, and despite a number of brave attempts to integrate these insights into the psychological tradition (Gelman & Coley 1991; Keil 1989; Komatsu 1992; Lakoff 1987; Markman 1989; Neisser 1987 Ch. 2). The difficulty, I believe, results from the fact that Putnam's and Kripke's insights were almost entirely negative. They told us how the extensions of certain substance concepts are *not* determined, but they supplied no adequate theories of how they *are* determined. Moreover, the tentative positive views that they offered focused more on the extensions of *words* in a public language than on the nature of concepts, leaving obscure the nature of the psychological states or processes that would constitute an *understanding* of the meanings of the words discussed. Thus, they offered little aid to psychologists. One aim of this book is to help remedy that.

The descriptionist holds that the referent or extent of a substance term is determined by its falling under a description associated with the term by the term user. Certain properties, relations, facts about origins, facts about causes, similarities to prototypes, similarities to given exemplars, and so forth – certain "information" about each portion of the extent – determines it to be a portion of the extent, and the thinker or the thinker's "mental representation" determines which information is to play this role. In the psychological literature, this view is sometimes found in caricature in the statement that concepts *are* features or properties, for example, "many properties are concepts themselves" (Barsalou 1987, p. 129).

Using the concept *chair* as his example, Komatsu (1992) expresses what he claims is the most general question that psychological theories of concepts have attempted to answer, thus: ". . . *what information, very generally, is represented by the concept chair*, so that people are able to reason about chairs, recognize instances of chairs, and understand complex concepts . . ." (1992, p. 500, italics mine). Building on Medin and Smith (1981, 1984), he applies this descriptionist formula to each of five accounts of concepts:

... the classical view (e.g., Katz 1972, Katz & Fodor 1963) ... the family resemblance view (e.g., Rosch & Mervis 1975) ... the exemplar view (e.g.,
Medin & Schaffer 1978) ... the schema view [Komatsu later cites Bartlett
(1932), Minsky (1975), Piaget (1926), Rumelhardt (1980), Schank & Abelson
(1977), Winograd (1975), and Neisser (1975)] ... the explanation-based view
(e.g., Johnson-Laird 1983, Lakoff 1987, Murphy & Medin 1985) [later he men-
tions the work of Gelman and Keil].

Descriptionism is most obviously compatible with nominalism, the
view that the members of the kinds that words name are grouped together either conventionally, according to the dictates of culture, or
according to patterns natural to human perception and thought. For
example, heavily sprinkled throughout the literature we find references to "learning about people's categorization decisions." On this
view, the descriptions that govern concepts have their source either in
the conventions of society, or in peculiarities of the human perceptual
and cognitive systems, that is, in ways it is natural to us to generalize.
For example, in classical studies of concept learning, subjects were
typically set the task of learning imaginary categories defined by ar-
bitrarily chosen sets of properties, and many studies exploring family
resemblance or prototype or exemplar views of categorization have
also set arbitrary tasks. The view that the human mind has its own
ways of imposing various groupings of things into kinds, ways that
languages must respect in order to be learnable, has been evident especially since Rosch's work on color categories (e.g., Rosch 1973,
1975). In this tradition, the psychological problem concerning categorization is understood to be that of ferreting out exactly what these
psychologically imposed principles are – those principles in accordance with which children or adults "prefer to sort" (Markman
1989). Thus, for example, Lakoff subtitles his 1987 book, "What Categories Reveal about the Mind."

But descriptionism need not be allied with nominalism or conven-
tionalism. It also has been combined with realism about human categories. The realist holds that many of our categories correspond to kinds
that are grouped together by nature independently of mind. As we acquire categories, we learn not merely, say, how to communicate with
others, but how to grasp structures that were already there in nature.
The view of substances that I am advocating is, of course, a variety of
realist view. It might seem that there is an incompatibility between realism and descriptionism. If the extent of a category is determined by
nature, then it cannot be determined by fitting a certain description as-

44

sociated with a word. But in fact there are a number of ways in which realism and descriptionism have been combined.

The simplest way is to take the extent of a substance term to be fixed by one, or a set, of definite descriptions of the substance. Whether it is supposed that the description is used rigidly or nonrigidly makes no difference in this context. In either case, the thinker entertains a prior description that determines the extent of his word or category. Thus the classical twentieth-century view was that Aristotle himself was a natural unit in nature, and that to have a concept of Aristotle was to capture him in thought under a description such as "the teacher of Alexander," or under a suitable disjunct of descriptions. Similarly, there has been a tendency in the psychological literature to interpret Kripke's (1972) and Putnam's (1975) apparently antidescriptionist views on the meaning of proper names and natural kind terms as invoking definite descriptions on a metalevel. Kripke is thought to have claimed that the referent of a proper name N is fixed in the user's mind by the description "whoever was originally baptized as N," and Putnam is thought to have claimed that the extent of a natural kind term is fixed for laymen by the description "whatever natural kind the experts have in mind when they use term T." This is what Fumerton calls "Russelling," a theory of direct reference (Fumerton 1989). It transforms it, of course, into a descriptionist theory instead.

Theories that language categories are organized "probablistically" (Medin 1989) by family resemblance or by reference to prototypes often combine realism with descriptionism. Families and prototypes are usually taken to center over highly correlated properties, and these correlations are taken to be empirically discovered. Thus, prototype theory is naturally compatible with the view that many concepts end up paired with real kinds. But probablistic theories are regularly interpreted as explaining only how the learner's experience *generates* the category. Then the actual extension of the category is taken to be determined, not by the real extent of a kind, but by how the learner is inclined to classify new examples. The same is true of exemplar theories and for variations on these two views. Thus, Billman suggests that we should compare and test psychological models of structure and processing of concepts by examining the function from "learning instances plus the target items to categorize" to "the set of possible *category judgments*" (Billman 1992, p. 415, emphasis mine) and Ward and Becker state that "category structure" can mean "the set of items that the learner considers to be members of the category in question (i.e., the category extension)" (1992,

p. 454). Made explicit, the idea here seems to be that experience with a natural kind may inspire the category, but the category extent is determined by the thinker's potential decisions on exemplars. When all goes well, our psychologically determined kinds may contain the same members as the natural ones, that is all. Similarly, the realists Gelman and Byrnes tell us, explicitly making reference to Chomsky's theory of innate grammar, that "[w]e can determine how languages and conceptual systems are constrained by examining the forms and meanings that children construct, and which errors they *fail* to make" (1991, p. 3). That is, it is the child's inclinations that constrain the concepts.

Most explicitly realist in their approach to concepts are contemporary researchers holding what Komatsu calls an "explanation-based view" of concept structure. Komatsu (1992) characterizes this view by quoting Keil:

No individual concept can be understood without some understanding of how it relates to other concepts. Concepts are not probablistic distributions of features or properties, or passive reflections of feature frequencies and correlations in the world; nor are they simple lists of necessary and sufficient features. They are mostly about things in the world, however, and bear nonarbitrary relations to feature frequencies and correlations, as well as providing explanations of those features and correlations. If it is the nature of concepts to provide such explanations, they can be considered to embody systematic sets of beliefs – beliefs that may be largely causal in nature. (Keil 1989, p. 7)

Note that the view is not just that concepts designate kinds for which there exist explanations of property correlations, but that the concept actually *consists* in essential part of an understanding or, looking beyond Page 1 of Keil's text, a partial understanding of these explanations. Interpreting this in the terms of the last chapter, the concept consists in part of a partial understanding of the ontological ground of induction that underlies the concept. Of particular interest to the explanation theorists, for example, has been Medin's work showing that people behave as though believing that beneath their categories there are hidden essences making the things in the categories what they are (e.g., Medin and Ortony 1989). Keil, Carey, Gelman, and Markman are among those who have done very interesting work tracing the development of children's natural kind concepts and artifact concepts, for example, documenting the transition from reliance on superficial characteristic properties for identification of these kinds to use of rudimentary and then more sophisticated "theories" about the underlying causes of the unity of the kind.

These advocates of explanation-based views have remained strongly influenced by the characteristic mid-twentieth-century doctrine that a "theory" is a set of inference connections among concepts, that the net of theory in which a concept is caught up determines its "meaning," and that the meaning of a concept determines its reference. Thus, to introduce or change theories threatens to change meanings hence reference:

How can one be sure that one is even talking about the same concept at all if all concepts are relative to theories? . . . We do not want every change in theoretical beliefs to make the concepts embedded in them completely different from those that were embedded before the change; yet no precise method is offered [by Smith, Carey, & Wiser 1985] for making a decision. . . . These are difficult issues, and it is hardly surprising that they are not yet resolved. (Keil 1989, pp. 21–2)

Following Smith, Carey, and Wiser, Keil speaks of " 'tracking' concepts across theory change" and agrees with them that probably "[d]escent can be traced . . . because of several properties of theories that stay fixed through change" (Smith, Carey, & Wiser 1985, p. 182). And he agrees with Fodor that it is not obvious how the classical view could be true that "children and adults could have different kinds of concepts for the same terms," for that makes it seem as though [quoting Fodor 1972] "they must misunderstand each other essentially" (Fodor, 1972 p. 88; Keil 1989, pp. 15–16). Again, the view here is conceptionist. There is no suggestion that the extent of the concept, its "meaning" in the most fundamental sense, might be directly fixed by the extent of a natural unit in nature, reference remaining the same while conceptions change. (For an exception to this, see Gopnik & Meltzoff 1996.)

My claim is that all this traditional work, supposedly on the nature of concepts, has actually concerned merely conceptions. For example, changes in theories about the underlying grounds of induction for specific kinds of substances are changes in conceptions, not in what the corresponding substance concepts are of. You cannot have a theory about something, say, about what makes dogs to be dogs (remember that Aristotle had a false theory about this), unless you can first think of the thing you would theorize about. Changes in your theory are not, then, changes in your concept or in its extension. It does not follow that these psychological studies, when they have concerned substance concepts, have not had, and will not continue to have, great value. Nor does it follow that they simply have not concerned meanings. Conception is definitely one of the things that "meaning" can mean. But these studies need to be reinterpreted *as* studies of conceptions if their value is to be secured. For example, their relevance to understanding word meanings will be problematic should it be common for different speakers of the same language to have quite different conceptions of the same substance yet use the same word for it. And indeed, beginning in Chapter 6, I will argue that radical divergence in speaker conceptions of exactly this sort are the rule rather than the exception.

§3.6 HOW THEN ARE THE EXTENSIONS OF SUBSTANCE CONCEPTS DETERMINED?

If substance concepts are not just classifiers, so that conceptions of substances are not what determines the extensions of their corresponding concepts, how then *are* the extensions of these concepts determined? To argue that the extensions of substance *words* are not determined by conceptions and to explain how these words do hook onto their extensions instead was, of course, supposed to be part of Kripke's project in *Naming and Necessity* (1972) and Putnam's project in "The Meaning of 'Meaning' " (Putnam 1975). If Kripke was right, "Bill Clinton" does not attach to Bill Clinton by means of speakers associating with "Bill Clinton" any particular properties or relations, ipso facto not by means of associating with it any inner or outer causes, any essence, any particular kind of ontological ground. A proper name is not, as I have been putting it, a classifier but an identifier. Similarly, Putnam argued that to call a thing "water" or "elm" is not to describe it. Natural kind terms do not work by being associated with properties. Rather, the extensions of "water" and "elm," like the extent of "Bill Clinton," are natural units in nature, units to which the concepts *water* and *elm* do something like pointing, and to which they can continue to point despite large changes in the properties the thinker represents these units as having. Taking Lakoff's example discussed in Section 1.7, large changes can occur in the manner in which a child identifies cats, hence in the things the child is willing to call "kitty," without affecting the extension of the child's word "kitty." The difficulty, of course, is to cash out the metaphor of "pointing." Speaking literally, what determines *which* substance is the extension of a given substance term or concept on the present view?

Putnam spoke of "indexicality" rather than "pointing," and Kripke suggested (without actually endorsing it) a causal theory of the reference of proper names. As mentioned earlier, a difficulty with both of these suggestions was that they tended to collapse into more complicated descriptionist views (see Fumerton 1989). The situation was exacerbated by the fact that Kripke and Putnam both used a form of argument that seems to assume the very thing it is trying to disprove. Their arguments proceeded by offering examples, taken either from this world (Kripke) or from other possible worlds (Putnam), in which our intuitions cry out that wrong results follow from some particular classical view of the kind of description that determines reference. But if our intuitions are really the final judges here, that would certainly suggest that we have *in mind* what determines reference, and this brings us back either to a descriptionist view, or at least to a conceptionist view. Compare Russell's early view of demonstratives, where "This is a book" unpacks into something like "the thing at which I am pointing is a book." And compare Ned Block's view (1986), according to which the way we would make decisions about its extension in possible cases determines what sort of Kaplan-style character, what sort of function from possible worlds to extensions, a concept expresses, for example, whether its referent is indexically determined as its cause, or as bearing some other relation to the concept.

Still, what else could possibly determine the extensions of our concepts if not our own intentions or dispositions? And if something else does determine the extension, what determines that *this is* what determines it, if not our prior intentions or dispositions? After all, what is an extension anyway? What is it for something to have an "extension"? Isn't an extension made into an extension by the fact that we apply the word "extension" in this way and not that? Aren't extensions determined by how we intend or are disposed to apply the term "extension"?

Is there a way to stop pulling at our bootstraps?

Consider: No one supposes that the function of vision is determined by the intentions of the individuals who happen to have eyes. Similarly, why should functions of the developmental processes responsible for concept formation and the functions of the concepts these processes shape be determined by the intentions of the individuals in which these processes happen to occur? It is not the purposes of individuals, but the biological functions – the unconscious purposes – of their inborn concept-tuning mechanisms that connect substance concepts with certain extensions.

I have proposed a theory telling what the most general function of substance concepts is. It is their job to make it possible to utilize substances as these are objectively defined in nature for purposes of gathering and applying information. In order to do this, they must include skills in reidentifying substances. Only in so far as they succeed in this task can they help us to proceed with successful inductions. My claim will then be that the extension of a substance concept is whatever substance in the world it is the job of that particular concept, given its particular phylogenetic and ontogenetic history of development, to be reidentifying or conceptually "tracking." Many mechanisms are involved in the development of a substance concept, and different kinds of mechanisms effect the development of concepts of different kinds of substances. Some speculations about these mechanisms, and about their particular phylogenetic and/or ontogenetic origins, will be offered in Chapter 5. But the rough idea is that the specific functions of the mechanisms or abilities responsible for originating a particular substance concept, whether these functions or abilities originated through evolution of the species or through individual learning, determine whether the concept is of anything definite and if so of what. This claim will need to be filled out a great deal before it will be plausible (or clearly understandable). The core of the project will be an analysis of what an ability, hence an ability to identify, is that does not equate abilities with dispositions (Chapter 4), and that explains how it is determined what a particular ability is an ability to do, even though the ability may be currently operating under conditions that fail to express it properly (Chapters 4 and 14).

You can call whatever the conception filling out a certain person's concept happens to corral, that is, whatever the person *takes* to be part of the concept's extension, by the name "the concept's extension" if you like. Humpty Dumpty was right about that. But then "extension" becomes a notion with very little interest, and we will need to coin another term for the thing it was the real purpose of that particular conception to capture. A parallel would be to label whatever a frog happens to snap up with its tongue reflex – for example, beebees – as its "prey," and then have to coin another term to designate the things its reflex snap was *designed* to capture.

4

The Nature of Abilities: How Is Extension Determined?

§4.1 ABILITIES ARE NOT DISPOSITIONS OF THE MOST COMMON SORT

The conception you have of a substance does not determine the extension of your concept. The extension is the extent of a certain substance in nature, not whatever you would identify as part of the extension. But the extent of *which* substance? That question is crucial. What determines, in the particular case, what particular substance one's perhaps stumbling, sketchy, and inadequate conception is aiming at? This chapter will make some progress toward answering that question. Further pieces of the puzzle will be added in Chapter 5, and the last pieces will finally settle into place at the end of Chapter 14.

Substance concepts are abilities of a certain kind. They are, in part, abilities to reidentify their assigned substances. How are these substances assigned? It is not a function of the cognitive systems as handed down by natural selection to identify any particular substance. Natural selection did not endow me with the ability to identify either 1969 Plymouth Valiants, or gasoline, or my husband. What I was endowed with was the capacity to acquire these abilities. Thus the general form of the question what determines the reference of a certain substance concept is: What determines what a learned ability is an ability to do? It will help to tackle the matter in this entirely general form.

The question of what abilities are deserves a lot of attention that it hasn't gotten. The modern philosophical tradition has unreflectively assimilated abilities to capacities and capacities to dispositions. This affords a slippery slope. A "capacity" can be either a living thing's abilities (the capacity of a camel to go without water for weeks) or a nonliving thing's dispositions (the capacity of gold to resist corrosion) but abilities and dispositions, in these contexts, are not the same. An ability is very much more than a disposition in one way, I will argue, and less in another.

In the usual philosophical sense, for something to have a "disposition" to behave in a certain way, say to do A, is for there to be circumstances under which it will do A in accordance with natural law. But to say merely that there are circumstances under which a thing will do A is nearly vacuous. If put in the right circumstances – for example, if hooked up to the right gadgets and so forth – any kind of thing can probably be made to supply a contributing cause to any kind of outcome you please. So usually one has in mind a disposition to do A in some definite circumstances C. To speak without restriction of a disposition to perform in a certain way must be either (1) to imply that the actual conditions, or the most likely conditions, are such as to realize the disposition, or such that it is often realized or (2) to assume or implicitly to refer to some specific sort of circumstances in which it will be realized. It is in the first way that people are said, for example, to have bad dispositions or sunny dispositions, or to be well disposed toward one another, and so forth. It is in the second way that salt is said to have a disposition to dissolve.

Sense (1) certainly is not the same as the notion of having an ability. Sunny dispositions are not, as such, abilities. Moreover, we all have dispositions, in sense (1), to depress the carpet on which we walk, to attract nearby mosquitoes and frighten nearby mice, and also to slip on ice. None of these are abilities. Moreover, we have many abilities that we have no dispositions at all, in sense (1), to realize. I have, for example, the ability to kill cats, to stand on my head on the commuter train, and to play bebop on the violin, but I have no sense (1) disposition to do any of these things. At the very least, something else must be added to a sense (1) disposition to make it into an ability. And it has to be subtracted that one is or is likely to be in conditions that realize it.

Perhaps abilities are dispositions in sense (2) if we fill in the conditions in the implicit antecedent of the conditionals correctly. An ability to do A is a disposition to do A if – what? The obvious suggestion is, "if one tries."

The first thing to notice about this answer is that it will require us to unpack the notion *trying*, and that this is not easy. We cannot do it, for example, by making reference to an *intention* to do A, if intending to do x requires having a concept of A. That would probably leave many animals with no abilities at all, and it would certainly leave us without most of our cognitive abilities. Especially, it would leave us without the ability to identify substances. We cannot suppose that in order to have a substance concept one must first have a prior concept of the substance one is trying to identify so that one can intend to identify it. We would have to unpack "trying" by reference instead to some kind of purpose more primitive than that involved in explicitly intending, in terms, for example, of biological purpose. I will come back to this later.

But no matter how we unpack *trying,* an ability is not the same as a disposition to succeed when one tries. My abilities often fail me. I have the ability to walk, but also, under certain circumstances, the disposition to slip or trip, and I do this exactly when trying to walk. I know how to cook, but I may still burn the dinner tonight. Many people with the ability to swim have drowned, presumably when they were trying to swim. We got into the question what abilities are by noting that the ability to reidentify a substance is fallible. Sometimes I misidentify things, but I would not do that if it were not, in some sense, my purpose to identify them. It seems that something else has to go into the antecedent besides "if I try," if abilities are to be understood as dispositions. If I try under what conditions?

There is a standard reflex answer to this sort of question: "under normal conditions." This combines disposition in sense (1) with disposition in sense (2). We saw that abilities can't just be what one has a disposition to do under the circumstances one is in or is likely to be in. Nor are they just what one has a disposition to do when one tries. Are they, then, what one has a disposition to do if one tries under the circumstances one is in or is likely to be in — under circumstances that are "normal"? That is, are abilities dispositions for the most part to succeed if one tries? The reference to likelihood would explain why, for example, although lots of people try and succeed in catching fish on hook and line, we do not say that a person knows how to catch fish, but only that they know how to fish. Reasonably, this is because they do not regularly succeed when they try to catch fish. It might also help to explain how different people can have abilities to do the same thing, but some can be better at it than others. Some are more likely to succeed when they try than others. So let us explore this answer.

I have an ability to swim granted I am likely to succeed if I try. I am now sitting at my desk in a dry sunny room. I now have the ability to swim, indeed I have had that ability ever since I was six. But if I try to swim sitting at my desk in a dry sunny room will I be likely to succeed?

Not likely. I know how to swim, but I am not in a position at the moment to swim. Indeed, most of the time I am not in a position to swim. I go down to the lake only once in a while. So it can't be that knowing how to swim is the same as being likely to succeed if I try – what has gone wrong?

§4.2 HAVING AN ABILITY TO VERSUS BEING ABLE TO

Focus on the antecedent, "if I try." Is the idea that if I just tried, I could do it? – that all that is needed for me to accomplish swimming is to add in a trying? That, we have just seen, cannot be the right idea. Certainly I could not immediately swim just by trying. It might be, of course, that if I tried I could bring about a situation in which I would *then* be in a position to swim. But this is not true for all abilities either. There is a difference, a surprisingly wide one, between being able to and having the ability to. I may know exactly how to invest a thousand to make a million, except that I haven't got any money at all. I have the required ability, but I am not able to exercise it, nor am I necessarily in a position to get myself into a position to invest a thousand to make a million. I may know how to make a marvelous gourmet dish for which the ingredients are completely unavailable. If there was a time when people knew how to make tasty dodo stew, they didn't suddenly stop knowing how on the expiration date of the last dodo. They still had the ability, but they were no longer able to apply it. True, in ordinary speech the word "ability" may be a little fuzzy around this edge. But let us settle on using it in this unwavering manner. Abilities don't disappear just because the world is uncooperative in supplying the necessary conditions for their exercise.

You may have noticed that I have been slipping back and forth between "knowing how to" and "having the ability to," whereas there are some differences in how these terms are typically used. One difference is exactly that "having the ability to" tends to slide a bit toward actually being able, whereas "knowing how to" does not. Whether I am in a position to do a thing virtually never bears on whether I "know how" to do it. Also, "knowing how" is more likely to be used for learned skills, "having the ability" for innate skills. I know how to do sums and ride a bicycle. I don't know how to see. Instead, I have the ability to see. I will continue to ignore this distinction. It won't be pertinent for our purposes.

Here is another way to interpret "if I tried." Usually I will not try something unless I believe I have a fair chance of succeeding. For example, you could not possibly induce me to try to swim while sitting at my desk in a dry sunlit room. You might induce me to pretend to try, but not really to try. Perhaps what we need then is this. One's abilities are what one has a disposition to do if one tries under the circumstances one would likely be in were one to try. Let us see how far this definition will take us.

Abilities can be more or less well developed. You can know very well how to read or swim or ride a bicycle, or you can know these things but not very well. I know a small child who replied when asked "Are you learning how to play the violin?" with a denial: "No, I already know how to play the violin; I'm learning how to play it better." What does learning how to do something better consist in? In the case of violin playing, of course, it consists in learning how to turn out a more polished product. But there are two other dimensions in which abilities can improve.

You can learn to do the same thing under more circumstances. For example, you might learn to drive a car safely even on ice, or how to ride a bike without slipping even over muddy paths, or how to row a straight line even in a crosswind, or how to peel potatoes neatly with only an ordinary knife available rather than a potato peeler. If abilities are dispositions to do something when you try in circumstances you are then likely to be in, then it would be wrong to think of learning these various things as acquiring *new* abilities. It is the same thing you are aiming at, whether the wind blows crosswise or from the stern, whether the bike path turns out muddy or dry. You are trying for the same thing; it is just that the circumstances are different. You are not aiming at the circumstances. They were just the ones that happened to come along. (Of course it also is possible to aim, specifically, at rowing-straight-in-a-crosswind. You purposefully go out in a wind, and then purposefully row across it while trying to keep a straight course. That is a different thing to do. For example, in that case you don't succeed if you don't find a crosswind.)

Notice that learning to do the same thing under a wider variety of conditions need not produce a more reliable disposition to do that thing when you try. So long as throughout your learning you are pretty good at distinguishing conditions, given your current ability level, under which you would succeed from conditions under which you would fail, and so long as you don't try unless reasonably sure you will succeed, no change in the frequency of your failures necessarily occurs. So this might seem to be a way to get better at something, to improve an ability, without becoming more likely to succeed when you try. On the other hand, the harder it is to see the ground ahead with a project, the more difficult it is to see at the start whether conditions necessary for success lie ahead, hence whether to begin trying. Then learning how under more conditions will increase the probability of succeeding when you try. So far so good for our proposed definition.

This brings us to the second way in which you can improve an ability. You can learn to recognize better the circumstances in which you will succeed if you try. Adults fall down less often than children, and have to be rescued from drowning less often. This is not just because they are better coordinated. They are better at recognizing risky situations, better at knowing when not to try, or not to try this way but rather to try some other way. It is not just that adults are more cautious. They know better when to be cautious. This way of improving an ability necessarily makes it more reliable. It improves the chances of succeeding when you try, because it improves the chances of trying only at times when you will succeed.

Granted these ways that an ability can improve, notice that we can't interpret "normal conditions" for exercise of an ability as conditions people generally are in when they try that activity. Different people may know how to do the same thing in quite different ways, under quite different conditions, so that the conditions under which they would try are quite different. Perhaps neither would be able to do it under the conditions the other finds most suitable. This sort of effect is especially evident and especially important in the area we are most interested in. Different people can have entirely different conceptions of the same substance, entirely different ways of recognizing it, so that neither would recognize it under the conditions the other would. People also can have skills that no one else has, skills developed under conditions, perhaps, in which no other human has been. Consider, for example, skills developed by space walkers engaged in specialized tasks. Similarly, a person can have a concept of a substance of which no other person has a concept. Any reference to "normal conditions," if it were to help in defining abilities would have to be made not just relative to the particular ability but also to the particular person who is able.

56

Is it true that my ability to do A is a disposition that I have to do A un- der conditions I would probably be in if I tried? How is a probability concerning only one person to be defined? In fact it is a very tough question how to interpret a probability of this kind, and merely waving one's hands toward something called "individual propensities," as some now do in the philosophy of biology, is certainly a step in the wrong di- rection. But I will let these issues lie. Whatever sense might be made of the notion of an individual's own personalized probability of being in certain conditions when they try, still an ability can't be defined in terms of an individual's probability of succeeding should they try. Here's why.

At the start of this discussion, I argued that an ability can't be merely a disposition one has under conditions one is likely to be in, citing as counterinstances those dispositions that make up one's temperament, one's disposition to depress the carpet on which one stands, and to slip on ice. A reason to reject these dispositions as abilities is that so far as I, the organism, am concerned, these dispositions are entirely accidental, having nothing to do with purposes, either of nature's design or of mine. I then added a reference to tryings, thus importing a dimension of purpose – of what happens not by accident but by design – and this helped us quite a lot. But defining an ability as an individual's likeliness to succeed should they try in conditions they would likely be in if they tried snags on exactly the same problem one level up. The conditions I am in may not be conditions I was designed by nature to be in, or that my abilities were designed through learning processes to operate in. If (1) I have a disposition to succeed if I try, or if (2) I fail to have such a disposition, these could be purely coincidental matters, hence might not indicate an ability.

Consider the second case first, the case where I have an ability but fail to have any such disposition. Suppose, for example, that the last dodo is dead but the dodo stew chef doesn't know it. And suppose there are people about still posing as dodo pedlars, and that it is quite likely the dodo stewmaker will be taken in by them. Then it will not be true that if the dodo stewmaker tries to make dodo stew he will most likely succeed. If he tries to make dodo stew it will be because he is mistaken in thinking he has bought dodo meat. Recalling the distinc- tion noted earlier between knowing how to do A and being in a posi- tion to do A, it is clear that something has gone wrong. The dodo stew chef surely does have the ability to make dodo stew, though he is in no position to exercise it. But he lacks a disposition to make dodo stew when under conditions he would probably be in if induced to try.

Now consider a case in which a disposition to succeed if one tries is present but does not correspond to an ability. Macaffee the cat has learned how to get himself let in the door by stretching up tall and scratching by its side window, thus making himself both heard and seen from inside. (Our cat does this.) Now the house changes owners, but Macaffee won't stay in his new home and returns to the old. The new owners dislike cats and have no disposition at all to let him in. However, soon after his return they have an automatic door installed for a wheelchair occupant with a wide push button outside at exactly the place Macaffee is disposed to scratch. Now the first day after the installation it is true that Macaffee has a disposition to get the door open for himself if he tries under the circumstances he is in or is likely to be in when he tries. But he no more knows how, at this point, to let himself in than you know how to win the state lottery if, happily, you happen to do so. What one does successfully only by pure chance is not something one knows how to do.

Now, in the preface to this book I promised not to play Counter Examples in Queer Possible Worlds, and I do not mean to be doing so here. My point is not that we wouldn't *say* Macaffee knows how to let himself in, that this is not how "our concept of an ability" is fashioned. Rather, my point is that the same *principle* is involved here as in cruder cases where dispositions very obviously do not equal abilities. Abilities are distinct from dispositions in having a necessary involvement in the purposive and nonaccidental order. A consistent theoretical definition of abilities will consistently take this into account. What is interesting and central about abilities will not be captured if we let in cases where results are achieved coincidentally, or if we exclude cases where failures to achieve results are coincidental.

Notice also that the attempt to turn abilities into dispositions with the antecedent "if one tried," as we came to interpret that phrase, was a cheat all along. It is not just that *trying* requires an analysis and is unlikely itself to unpack into dispositions. Rather, the conditionals corresponding to dispositions are supposed to refer to causes in their antecedents and effects in their consequents, and we did not use "if one tries" in that way. *If the match lit, then it was struck* may be a true conditional, but it does not correspond to a disposition for the match to be struck if it lights. Similarly, our "if one tries" was not used merely as a reference to a cause. The idea was that if one tries that must be because one believes one can succeed, and that in turn will likely be because one recognizes one is in conditions that will make success possible. The only true disposition here is the disposition to succeed if one tries under certain conditions, namely, the ones one attempts to recognize. Moreover one attempts to recognize these conditions *under that very description*, namely, *as* certain conditions *under which one can succeed*. The description of this disposition thus appears to be empty. One has a disposition to succeed if one is right that conditions under which one will succeed are present.

§4.5 DISTINGUISHING ABILITIES BY MEANS OR ENDS

We are still seeking the relation of an ability to the conditions of its successful exercise. Let me start fresh with an example that may bring out this relation more clearly. Suppose that you once learned how to use WordPrefab 2.2, but for the last fifteen years you have had a stenographer and haven't looked at any more recent word processing programs. WordPrefab 2.2 is now completely extinct and nobody anywhere has kept it either on their computers or on disk. It is clear then that you will no longer succeed in word processing if (without retraining) you try, no matter how we interpret the antecedent of the conditional. But do you still know how to do word processing?

A temptation is to reply that you don't know how to do word processing period; you only know how to do word processing in or by means of WordPrefab 2.2. But consider: No one knows how to do word processing without employing some program or other, some means or other. So from that sort of reasoning it would follow that nobody knows how to do word processing period. Similarly, since everyone employs some stroke or other in order to swim, and since if we cut strokes finely enough, surely no one knows how to employ every possible swimming stroke there is, it would follow that nobody knows how to swim period. Indeed, since everything accomplished in, or in relation to, the world outside one is accomplished by some means or another, requiring some definite conditions or other to be in place in that outside world, it will turn out that no one has any abilities to affect the world outside period. Rather, all abilities are hedged with specific means and conditions.

In Section 1.9, I pointed out that we have two ways of distinguishing or designating abilities: by ends, or by ends plus means. Where abilities to identify substances are concerned, this is the distinction between what I called "concepts" and what I called "conceptions." What has happened just above is that we have distinguished abilities by means rather than merely by ends. If we distinguish abilities by means, then of course no one ever knows how to do something full stop. The various means they know must always be described in saying what they know how to do. It is also true that if we cut designations by means finely enough, it may well be that two people seldom if ever have exactly "the same ability."

Now, there is nothing wrong with distinguishing abilities in this manner for some purposes. But that should not blind us to the legitimacy of distinguishing them by ends alone for other purposes. For many purposes, it is quite legitimate to say that some people know how to swim whereas others don't, and that all those people who know how to swim have the same ability. Similarly, it is quite legitimate to say of the person who knows how to do word processing using WordPrefab 2.2 that they know how to do word processing. They can have an ability to do word processing, even though, unfortunately, the conditions required for the means they employ (presence of a WordPrefab 2.2 program on an accessible computer) are unavailable, so they are not in a position to exercise that ability. Having an ability is not the same thing as being able.

To see the distinction between counting abilities by their ends and counting them by their ends-plus-their-means clearly, it is important to keep another distinction made earlier in mind (Section 4.2). This is the distinction between aiming at an end while also knowing to use certain means to that end in certain circumstances, and aiming at getting to the end in those very circumstances or by the use of those very means. Aiming at word processing and aiming at word-processing-with-WordPrefab 2.2 are two different things to aim at; knowing how to do these two things corresponds to two different abilities when abilities are counted by ends only. This is very easy to confuse with the fact that there are two different ways to count abilities, either by reference to ends only or by reference also to means. Similarly, abilities as counted by ends often have, for a given individual, many alternative means, employed under different conditions. This is not the same as the person having many alternative ends. It is not the same as the person's having many alternative abilities as counted by ends. For it may be that the person never aims at any of the specific means, or at being in conditions in which these means specifically can be used. Thus, you walk on a mountain trail constantly adjusting your means to the conditions coming up underfoot, but you aim at none of these means nor at being in any of the conditions requiring these means.

§4.6 ABILITIES ARE NOT DISPOSITIONS BUT DO IMPLY DISPOSITIONS

We have settled then that the person who learned how to use WordPrefab2.2 learned and still knows how to do word processing period, whether or not WordPrefab2.2 still exists in any form. But there is no possibility at all in their current situation that their ability to do word processing will manifest itself, whether or not they try. Thus it appears that knowing how to do word processing has nothing at all to do with this person's dispositions in their current situation. At the same time, it is clear under what possible conditions this ability *could* be manifested – namely, under the condition that this person would have WordPrefab2.2 on the computer they used. What then IS the relation between this person's ability and the circumstances under which it would necessarily be manifested?

The relation, it seems, is historical. The conditions in which this ability would be manifested are the conditions in which it was historically designed as an ability. In general, the conditions under which *any* ability will manifest itself are the conditions under which it was historically designed as an ability. These are conditions in which it was learned, or conditions in which it was naturally selected for. They are conditions necessary to completing the mechanisms by which past successes were reached by the systems or programs responsible for the abilities. Past presence of these conditions helped account for the selection or maintenance of the systems or programs constituting the abilities. What I know how to do I must once have learned how to do. Otherwise it would not be knowledge but mere luck. Or what I have an ability to do is what my systems were maintained or selected for doing. That is my suggestion. I know of no other way to understand what abilities are that is consonant with the case advanced above against their merely being current dispositions of some kind. (This can also be taken as a challenge, of course, to come up with alternative suggestions.)

To an ability there always corresponds a disposition, but it does not follow that an ability IS a disposition. If an ability to do A were a disposition to do A under specified conditions, then we should be able to specify the conditions under which anyone must be disposed to do A if and only if they have an ability to do A. But these conditions cannot be specified for the general case. Because different people who have learned to do the same thing may have learned to do it in different ways, relying on different conditions, the conditions under which a given ability (defined by its end) might manifest itself may be entirely different for different people. There is no such thing as *the* set of conditions under which it is necessary that any person be able to manifest their ability to do word processing or to swim. For each person, there is an independent reference here to personal history. Each person's ability to do A rests on a disposition defined through their particular past. Each has a disposition to do A if they try to do A under the conditions that accounted for their own past successes in doing A. If they have no such disposition, of course, then they have lost the ability to do A. It does not follow that their ability IS a disposition. Rather, which disposition(s) it is that can manifest the ability to do A is determined by which conditions helped account for the acquisition of this particular person's ability. To attempt to define the ability by reference to its historically enabling conditions would move one in a circle.[1]

Another question that has been running in the background is now easily answered as well. How should we understand the notion "trying" such that an ability is manifested when one succeeds in what one tries under historically enabling conditions, yet such that there can be mental abilities the goals of which we do not represent to ourselves or even understand, hence do not "try" to reach in the most oridnary sense of "try"? "Trying" to do A, *in the needed sense*, is simply the initiation and running to the point of success or failure of a mechanism or program that is designed to do A.

§4.7 WHAT DETERMINES THE CONTENT OF AN ABILITY?

What then determines what a learned ability is an ability to do? The difficulty, recall, was that the kinds of parts, systems, and programs that embody abilities have innumerable dispositions that are not abilities, and

---

1 The conditions under which a person with the ability to do A necessarily has a disposition to do A if they try can be thought of as a peculiar sort of normal conditions, namely, conditions that were normally present and active on the occasions of their past successes. These are conditions of the sort that I labeled with the capitalized term "Normal" in Millikan (1984). "Normal" conditions for proper functioning of any mechanism are conditions that obtained and were active on occasions of successful past performance leading to selection of the mechanism.

also that real and even strong abilities can fail, the outer conditions necessary to support them being absent and the absence remaining undetected. So a look only at the mechanism that has or embodies abilities – at what its various dispositions are – will not reveal what its abilities are. What then does determine what its abilities are? I had originally raised this question as a more general form of the question: What determines, in the particular case, what particular substance one's perhaps stumbling, sketchy and inadequate conception is aiming at?

In the case of innate abilities, no matter what dispositions a mechanism happens to have, what determines its abilities is what it was selected for doing.[2] In the case of learned abilities, what natural selection selected for was the ability to learn in a certain way. It selected for mechanisms that became tuned through interaction with the environment to do things of useful kinds. For an organism to know how to do A as a result of learning is for it to possess an intact mechanism that is biologically designed to be tuned to do things like A and that has been tuned to do A as designed. That is, it became tuned in the same manner, following the same principles, as its successful ancestors when they were learning to do similar kinds of things.[3] We humans possess at least a number, possibly very numerous, different kinds of learning mechanisms, including various mechanisms for trial-and-error learning, learning by association, by imitation, by figuring something out, and so forth. Each of these mechanisms works in accordance with its own principles, tailoring learned abilities in its own manner. To know how to do something as a result of learning, one must have a disposition to succeed in doing it under the conditions one learned under that afforded previous successes or under the conditions that helped to tune one to do it by affording successes, and this learning or tuning must have been of the kind the learning mechanisms involved were selected for doing. Otherwise one does not know how, but does what one does only by accident.

Some learning mechanisms are extremely general in their possible applications and some are extremely quick. Of very general application, for example, are our abilities to learn something by figuring it out or

---

2 Things that a mechanism was selected for doing are its "proper functions," as defined in Millikan (1984, Chapters 1 and 2). Those concerned about the heavy but informal use of the notions of "function" and "design" throughout this book are referred to these chapters, where a tight definition is offered.

3 Abilities that have been learned correspond to mechanisms that have "adapted and derived" proper functions. For details on adapted and derived proper functions, see Millikan (1984, Chapter 2) and Millikan (in press b).

thinking it through, using materials gained from previous experience, including knowledge of our prior abilities. So we often claim correctly that we know how to do something that we have never tried to do, for example, that we know how to get to Plainfield, or that we know how to make a certain kind of repair. If conservative, we may say only that we think we know how, but we are often right that we know. Similarly, observing only once that you have a certain capacity can immediately turn it into an ability. Anything that you find out you can effect immediately becomes an ability. Having observed that stirring the red strawberries into the vanilla ice cream turns it pink, the child knows how to make pink ice cream.

We need not think of abilities, then, as characteristically derived from elaborate *specialized* training or tuning histories. They are, however, often derived from very numerous prior abilities that have been strung or blended together. The idea that one might count the number of a person's abilities, or count the abilities that go into a certain activity, often is not really coherent. Like patterns, however, or like patches of ground, abilities can be clearly distinguished and designated even when they have no clear criteria of individuation.

§4.8 THE EXTENSIONS OF SUBSTANCE CONCEPTS

In the last chapter (Section 3.6), I claimed that it is not the purposes of individuals but the subpersonal biological functions of their inborn concept-tuning mechanisms that connect their substance concepts with certain extensions. Similarly, the function of my eyes or my liver is not determined by *my* intentions for their use. We must suppose that natural selection has endowed us, specifically, with the ability to learn to identify substances, or, more likely, with a variety of abilities, each specific to learning to identify members of a different domain of substances (see Chapter 5) or, at the very least, the ability to acquire abilities of the latter kind through learning. Considering the centrality of the ability to reidentify substances for any animal that acquires and applies either practical or theoretical knowledge (Section 1.4), the likelihood that natural selection has tailored capacities very specifically to this purpose in such animals is about as high as the likelihood that it has tailored their capacities specifically for obtaining nourishment and mates.

Granted this, we can begin to answer the question how specific substances become assigned to specific substance conceptions — how the extensions of substance concepts are fixed. Chapter 5 will fill the picture out more with some speculations about *how* one's abilities to re-identify specific substances are learned or develop, and Chapter 14 will complete the discussion of how conceptual abilities are focused on corresponding substances.

We encounter substances, better, we encounter natural signs of substances (see Appendix B) in perception (or in the speech of others – see Chapter 6). We bring to bear certain innate abilities, or we bring to bear general skills acquired earlier in life (grasp of substance templates, grasp of general methods applicable to specific substance domains), or we proceed by trial-and-error learning in attempting inductions over encounters. In these ways we often manage to keep track, and we learn better how to keep track, of when we are encountering the same substances again. Thus the information gathered about each substance is brought together and brought to bear on future encounters with it. The important point is that the way this all happens is no accident. That is what it means to say that it is done using "abilities" and "skills" and by "learning." It is all done according to principles by which feats of the same abstract sort were accomplished by our ancestors, thus accounting for selection of the innate abilities and learning mechanisms responsible.

Now there will be times when a substance is misidentified, and for every substance, of course, innumerable unrealized *dispositions* to misidentify it under adverse conditions. There also may accumulate considerable misinformation about certain substances. These mistakes occur because conditions on which past successes in keeping track or learning to keep track depended – historically enabling conditions for the cognitive mechanisms' development and use – are not currently present. Unless the cognitive mechanisms are malformed or damaged,[4] mistakes are always caused by the presence of *abnormal* conditions, not necessarily in the sense of *unusual* conditions, but merely of conditions other than those under which the utilized mechanisms were operating on those specific occasions that historically afforded successes, hence accounted for their selection or for their tuning through learning. If current conditions were exactly the same as the historically enabling conditions for these mechanisms, they would obviously succeed. This is what distinguishes one's dispositions to identify from one's abilities to identify. It separates acts of misidentification from correct identifications and dispositions to misidentify from dispositions to identify correctly.

---

4   A definition of normal structure for devices with proper functions, including the functions corresponding to abilities, is offered in Millikan (1984, Chapter 1).

In clear cases, then (I will soon discuss some that are less clear), a substance concept has as its referent or extension a substance encountered at the very start of such a process of keeping track nonaccidentally and that fits the general abilities to keep track that have been brought to bear. It causally originates from encounters with the substance to which it refers, and the general abilities that are brought to bear in attempting reidentification determine the substance's ontological category. They determine, for example, whether it is the function of the concept to reidentify a stuff or an individual or a kind of individual, and if the latter, what sort of substance template is involved (see Section 14.1). The concept is a concept of A, rather than B, not because the thinker will always succeed in reidentifying A, never confusing it with B, but because A is what the thinker has been roughly keeping track of and picking up information about not accidentally but in accordance with abilities, skills, and know-hows.

Here is another way to approach the same matter, but that leaves it more open whether to buy into the historical theory of the nature of cognitive abilities I have proposed. Traditionally, it is supposed that what a substance concept is of is whatever fits certain features or properties it represents its extension as having. Its extension is what fits these properties, even though one may not always be able to recognize exactly when something does. In this way the concept can have a definite extension, even though you sometimes make mistakes in recognizing that extension. But then the prior question can be raised, what determines which *features* or *properties* are the ones you are representing and trying to recognize? This cannot be determined by your representing prior properties that the represented properties must themselves have, without regress. Nor can it be determined merely by your dispositions to recognize these properties, since no one is infallible at recognizing properties any more than substances.

A standard reply is that we do recognize certain properties infallibly when we are in "normal conditions," and that this is what defines what properties our property concepts represent. For example, red is whatever appears red to me under normal conditions for seeing colors. But how then do we define "normal conditions," such that they are, for example, appropriately different for seeing the shapes of big things like mountains and the shapes of small things like fleas, appropriately different for hearing loud sounds and soft ones, and different for hearing sounds, for seeing colors and for identifying tastes, and so forth (consider how tea tasters must prepare themselves)? We must take care that "normal conditions" do not turn out to be, just, the conditions under which one perceives each of these various properties correctly, for that would be marching in place. On the other hand, if there is any noncircular way of defining "normal conditions" for the perception of various properties, we should be able to use exactly the same technique to define "normal conditions" for keeping track of various kinds of substances. The two problems are exactly parallel. How then should we understand these "normal conditions"?

Biologists are usually concerned, first, to understand normal function. They may be interested in diseases or other abnormal functions, too, but these are defined relative to normal function. I have proposed that normal function, in this context, is best defined relative to a history of natural selection,[5] but you may supply your own favorite theory of normal function, should you have one, and it will serve the argument as well. My claim here is only that whatever normal function is, philosophers and cognitive psychologists, too, are, or should be, interested in it as well as biologists. I add that for the most part biological items require to be in rather definite conditions in order to perform normally. My own preference is then to define "normal conditions" relative to selectionist history also – as conditions under which that function was performed historically such as to be selected for Millikan (1984,1993a). But if you can supply a better definition, there is no objection. The point is that if we can give a definition of normal biological function and normal conditions for performance of this or that function, we can apply it also to performance of psychological functions, such as the development of substance concepts and their application. We can say what normal conditions for keeping track of substances are.

Grant then that there is a normal way or normal ways for development of substance concepts to occur, perhaps different for different substance domains. Or what is the same thing, grant that normal developmental cognitive psychology is a viable field. There will be a normal way or ways that the child or adult first recognizes the manifestations of a new substance impinging on their perceptual organs and a normal way or ways that they attempt to keep track of that substance, or learn to keep track of it better, and so forth. And there will be normal conditions for success in keeping track, in building conceptions adequate to the substance. When everything goes exactly normally, then, there will

---

5   1984, Chapters 1 and 2; 1993a, Chapter 1 and 2.

be no question what the concept is of, even if there is a disposition to apply it incorrectly under conditions that are not normal for expression of these abilities.

But problems can arise when things do not go exactly, when they deviate from the ideal. It can happen that each of two substances is kept track of in a normal way over a variety of encounters, but that there are also mistakes made so that information gathered from both gets collected under the same concept. For example, one might have two people "mixed up" or "confused" in one's mind. Similarly, mass and weight were not distinguished throughout most of the history of science. More than two substances might also be entwined under one concept. If it is not definite which among various similar, closely related, overlapping or nested substances was the one primarily responsible for the information that has been gathered and/or for the tuning of the (would-be) tracking dispositions, then the concept is equivocal or vague. Two or more are being thought of as one. It is likely that normal development of many kinds of concepts involves a process of differentiating between substances originally confused together. Perner calls this a process of "focusing reference" (Perner 1998). It is tempting to interpret much of the history of science as an attempt to focus reference, for example, distinguishing weight from mass and oxygen from other oxidizers.

We also can imagine much more serious confusions than simple equivocation where it is not clear what if any substance or substances have been kept track of at all. Biological items are, in general, defined relative to an ideal. A diseased or damaged or malformed heart is a heart none the less because of historical relations it has to hearts that performed normally. But having described how normal hearts are structured and how they function, it is of no interest to biologists how far away from that ideal a thing has to be before one stops calling it a "heart." There are no exact borders of the substance *heart* in nature, and the biologist is concerned with nature. Similarly, I suggest, to press the question, in sufficiently abnormal cases, "But please, really, what is the extension of this person's substance concept?" is pointless. What, if anything, for example, was the referent of "phlogiston"?[6, 7]

6   I take these matters up again at the end of Chapter 14.
7   I am grateful to Andrew Milne for some very helpful suggestions on this chapter.

5

More Mama, More Milk
and More Mouse:
The Structure and Development
of Substance Concepts

§5.1 EARLY WORDS FOR SUBSTANCES

The bulk of a child's earliest words are concrete nouns, including names of individuals, names of concrete kinds, and some names for stuffs ("milk," "juice"). These are acquired in a rush by the dozens between about one and one half and two years old: "this vocabulary spurt is often called the *naming* explosion to reflect the large preponderance of nouns that are learned" (Markman 1991, p. 81).[1] Adjectives come later and more slowly, and abstract nouns later still. This suggests that the ability to distinguish concrete individuals in thought and the ability to distinguish concrete kinds and stuffs may have something in common, and that concepts of properties and of other abstract objects may not be required for these tasks. There is much independent evidence that children come to appreciate separable dimensions, such as color, shape, and size, only after a considerable period in which "holistic similarities" dominate their attention (see Keil 1989, for discussion). Thus, concepts of properties again appear as less fundamental than those expressed with simple concrete nouns.

We can interpret this data as suggesting that concepts of substances are the easiest for a child to obtain, and more surprising, that the ontological distinction among individuals, real kinds, and stuffs does not produce a difference in ease of early learning. I have proposed that, despite their obvious ontological differences, individuals, real kinds, and

---

1 See Gentner 1982 and Ingram 1989 for reviews, Dromi 1987 for some reservations. There is evidence that Korean children may usually have a "verb spurt" a month or two before their "noun spurt" begins. Still the number of nouns soon overtakes the number of verbs (Choi and Gopnik 1993).

stuffs have something important in common that bears directly on what it is to have concepts of them. I will now propose that this similarity makes them all knowable in a very similar way, and prior to properties. Though concepts of individuals, real kinds, and stuffs are traditionally considered to be quite different in structure, I believe that their *root* structure is in fact identical. Only as they become more fully developed do defining differences appear among them. This is because their corresponding substances have an identical ontological structure when considered at a suitably abstract level, and because it is possible to have unsophisticated substance concepts that rest only on this abstract structure.

§5.2 INITIAL IRRELEVANCE OF SOME FUNDAMENTAL ONTOLOGICAL DIFFERENCES

I have argued that different domains of substances are differentiated according to the kinds of ontological grounds that hold them together, supporting successful inductions over encounters with them. One can learn on one encounter with Xavier what to expect on other encounters with Xavier for a different reason than one can learn from one encounter with the element silver or with the species dog what to expect on other encounters. And I have argued that we do not always have a correct understanding of the grounds of induction that underlie our successful substance concepts. For example, it is only recently that we have come to the understanding we now have, as opposed to the understanding Aristotle had (Section 2.2), of what holds the various biological species together, and we still don't have many details in the case, for example, of asexual animals and easily hybridized plants. Although, ontologically speaking, individuals are space-time worms while real kinds are, instead, collections of similar space-time worms, to have the capacity to understand this ontological distinction would require a grasp of space-time structure and temporal relations of a sort not acquired by children until years after they are proficient in the use of both proper and common names (Nelson 1991). It seems it cannot be *necessary* to having the concept of a substance that one understand its ontological ground. This suggests that it may be possible in general, even though it may not be ideal, for the concept of a substance to rest merely on its most abstract structure *as* a substance, hence for primitive concepts of substances within the various domains to have a common structure. Small children might have concepts of individuals, real kinds, and stuffs

70

prior to any understanding at all of the differences among the ontological grounds that in fact organize these domains, and these various concepts might all be formed in much the same way.

What would seem to be primary in the early experience of a child is merely that milk and mouse retain many of their properties and potentials for use or interaction over various encounters with them exactly as Mama does. Given this, we might expect the child, indeed we might expect any animal, in the first instance, to learn how to relate to, and what to expect from, each of these various items in much the same way. Putting it Quine's way, the child's first recognitions (and those of the dog) are merely of *more Mama, more milk*, and *more mouse* (Quine 1960, p. 92). To grasp this possibility, however, it is crucial to keep in mind the differences between classifying and identifying explored in Chapter 3. If a child's primary concepts of, for example, milk and mouse were classifying concepts, then of course they could not have the same structure as her concept of Mama.

The child observes things about Mama when she encounters her, not things about samples or instances of Mama. The child identifies Mama; she does not classify Mama. The psychological structure of classification is the structure of subject-predicate judgment. To classify an item requires differentiating the item to be classified in thought and applying a predicate to it. To do the latter, the child would need to have prior concepts of instances of Mama — concepts of timeslices of Mama, I suppose. But concepts of timeslices of Mama clearly are analytical concepts, resting on prior concepts of Mama and of times, and thus we go around in a circle (Section 3.4).

In a similar way, to learn things about milk, the child need not think of or keep track of instances or portions of milk. And the very point of having the concept *mouse* would seem to be that under it, one does not *distinguish* Amos from Amos's brother, but thinks of them as the same. Classifying animals as mice versus cats versus dogs would involve thoughts of Fidos and Spots, Felixes and Macaffees, Amoses and brothers of Amoses, each individual to be judged a member of its proper kind. But there is no more reason to suppose that this is the way the child first conceives of mouse than that this is how she conceives of Mama. She need not have concepts of individual mice in order to recognize mouse again. Early substance concepts, even when what they are of, ontologically, is kinds, need not be predicate concepts applied to prior subject concepts. They need not be understood as *descriptions* of anything.

In Chapter 4, I discussed how abilities typically rest on alternative means. My ability to get from home to school rests on many alternative means, as do my abilities to swim and to tie my shoes. Similarly, the capacity to identify a substance typically rests on a variety of alternative conceptual means. The number of ways I can identify each of my daughters is nearly innumerable – through appearance of body or body parts from a hundred angles, by voice through many mediating conditions, by posture, clothing, sounds of feet, handwriting, characteristic habits and activities, various nicknames, and hundreds of identifying descriptions. On the other hand, as with my other abilities, none of these ways is infallible. Having an ability does not require one unfailingly to recognize when the required conditions for its means obtain, or even that one understand what these conditions are. Surely none of these methods of recognizing my daughters, either taken collectively or taken singly, constitutes a *definition* or *criterion* of any of my daughters. Concepts of one's friends are not analytical concepts but synthetical, nor are they "recognitional" concepts (Section 3.4). Exactly the same is undoubtedly true for the infant's concept of milk and of mouse. Indeed, the same is true of any adult's concepts of these things in so far as they operate *as* substance concepts. There are lots of ways to recognize milk quite reliably: by look, by taste, by context, by the sorts of stains it makes, by chemical analysis, and so forth. Similarly, there are lots of ways of recognizing mice. None of these ways plays any role in *defining* milk or mice. (These are defined in nature.) And none, of course, is infallible. (Failure to understand these points is called "verificationism.")

Concepts of Aristotle's secondary substances, such as *mouse* and *dog*, show themselves in English grammar as simple subjects of judgment by vacillating among singular, plural, definite, and indefinite forms to express the same secondary-substance thoughts. Thus "The lion is tawny," "Lions are tawny," and "A lion is tawny" have, in most contexts, exactly the same meaning. The apparent determiners and the indication of number are doing no semantic work in these sentences. The grammar of English mandates use of some determiner with every count noun, but the name of a secondary substance does not, as such, express a counting thought. Nor is there a quantifier implicit in these sentences. They are not equivalent to "All lions are tawny," "Some lions are tawny," or "Most lions are tawny," despite the efforts of elementary logic texts to force them into one or another of these molds. Many languages, for example Bengali, Finnish, and Japanese, are more semantically transparent in this respect, using secondary substance names bare to express this kind of thought.

§5.3 THE STRUCTURE COMMON TO ALL SUBSTANCE CONCEPTS

What the infant identifies is more Mama, more milk and more mouse. Better, since the idea is not that the infant mistakes Mama and mouse for stuffs (that would require grasping the ontology of stuffs), what the infant understands is "here's Mama again," "here's milk again," and "here's mouse again."[2] But various substances and various domains of substances differ, of course, in the types of knowledge they afford. The child's individual highchair retains its overall shape hence its sitting-on capacity over encounters, but Mama does not (you cannot sit on Mama when she is standing). Milk and Mama retain their color, while cat does not. Cat retains its overall shape and rough dimensions, but milk and wood do not. These various subjects of knowledge must be grasped as grouped into rough ontological categories according to the kinds of inductions likely to apply to them.

Even for the very young child, surely, a casual look at a new piece of furniture on the one hand and a new uncle on the other, must indicate which can be counted on to retain its current climbing-up-on affordance and which may grow tired of the sport. Similarly, preschoolers know that what is sleepy might also be hungry, but not made of metal or in need of fixing (Keil 1983). The conception one has of a substance is not merely the ways one knows to identify it, but also the dispositions one has to project certain kinds of invariances rather than others from one's experiences with it. One pole of a substance concept consists of more or less reliable means by which to recognize the substance, the other pole is a rough grasp of an applicable substance template or templates (Section 2.6). An essential part of grasping a new uncle's identity, of acquiring a concept of him, is grasping that he is, at least, a certain kind of physical object (in the broad sense) but better, that he is a human being. This must be grasped not as a set of properties Uncle has but as a sense for things possible to learn about Uncle.

---

2 Some commentators on "More Mama, more milk and more mouse" (Millikan 1998a) did take me to be claiming infants think of Mama and mouse as masses or stuffs.

In the same way that the child differentiates between (My) Highchair and (My) Uncle, both in her methods of keeping track and also in the invariants she projects, she differentiates among individuals, kinds, and stuffs. She has, perhaps, a concept of Mama and also a concept of women. She uses different methods to keep track of these, and projects different invariants over encounters with them. Tracking Mama is one of the means of tracking women. If it's Mama again it's a woman again. But the concepts are entirely separate, not at all confused together. Similarly, knowing what to expect of a connected physical object and knowing to expect something different of a pile of sand (see Blum 1998, and references therein) shows that the child is capable of distinguishing between the domains of application of corresponding substance templates. And obviously the child's methods of conceptual tracking have to be entirely different for objects, kinds, and stuffs. For example, her method of tracking cat will allow her to generalize from the cat on her left to the cat concurrently on her right, whereas her method of tracking individuals, hence Macaffee, will not. Methods of tracking for one ontological category will not necessarily work for another. In this way, the child's concepts of Mama, mouse, and milk do, of course, have to differ.

The child differentiates among individuals, stuffs, and real kinds, yet her concepts of things in these domains have a common structure. Each contains some means or other of tracking its appointed substance and a grasp of how to project some of the invariants defining this substance to new encounters. This is the most important fact about the structure of these concepts because it defines their function. It explains what we have them for. Substances need not be grasped by understanding the principles that structure them and hold them together, but merely by knowing *how* to exploit them for information-gathering purposes. Just as one does not have to be able to describe or even to recognize the conditions required for exercise of one's other abilities, for example, just as a child can swim without understanding Archimedes' principle and ride a bicycle without understanding the laws of dynamics, neither does one need to understand the ontological principles upon which one's successful projections of substance invariances depend. Analysis of the world structures that permit the possibility of human knowing is not the same thing as analysis of the inner psychological structure of the knowing.

Tradition, on the other hand, claims that there is nothing common to the structures of concepts of individuals, kinds, and stuffs, let alone of "here's Beethoven's Fifth again" and "here's white again" (Section 2.5). Throughout the history of philosophy and psychology, the tendency has always been to project the structure of the object grasped by thought into the mind itself. For example, it is thought that concepts of the sort we are calling substance concepts can be grasped only by understanding "criteria of identity" for their ontological kinds. But what would the relevance be, for example, of a "grasp of the criterion of identity for persons over time" to a practical ability to *recognize* the same person again over time? We can't always reidentify persons by following their space-time worms around. Besides, dogs are quite good at recognizing their masters, and babies at recognizing their mothers, even though it is quite certain that neither conceives of a criterion of identity for persons over time. Not that there are no situations in which an explicit grasp of persons, say, as space-time worms might prove helpful. Cross-examination to determine where the accused was an hour before the crime illustrates that. But, for the most part, we employ quite different methods to keep track of one another as substances.

Another venerable tradition argues that it is possible for us to individuate other individuals in our thought only because each such individual is uniquely located relative to us in the same space-time. This is surely a valid point, but not, as this tradition has it, because conceiving of other individuals requires us to *think of* their relations to us, anchoring our thoughts of them beginning with thoughts of ourselves. The valid point is that having a concept of any substance at all involves the capacity to keep track of it, which in turn means interacting with it, actively collecting together various manifestations of it that impinge on our senses or appear in our thought over time. And obviously one cannot collect together manifestations of something not in one's own space-time system. What is true and important is that the activity of collecting and employing knowledge of any individual can be accomplished only in so far as our world has a certain space-time and causal structure in which we too are ingredient and to which we are attuned. That is, for the most part we can find our way about in it. This should not be confused with the idea that knowledge of or thoughts about this structure are required for success in this activity. The capacity to reidentify Mama and learn things about her is a high level skill exercised in the world. Thinking of Mama is not done just in one's head.

The sketch of the structure of substance concepts presented so far has been argued for almost entrely a priori. I have attempted a task analysis for substance concepts and tried to show what follows if they are to perform these tasks. Earlier I compared this project to Marr's first level of analysis in his theory of vision, where he gives a task analysis for visual perception. To fill in higher levels of analysis, explaining exactly how these abilities are implemented, how the various kinds of substances are reidentified across encounters, how skills in reidentification are acquired, how substance templates are acquired and how they operate, is a job, as I understand it, primarily for experimental psychology and for research in child development. But I can try to help make the questions clearer and offer some tentative suggestions about where one might look for answers.

According to various estimates, children acquire from five to nine words daily between the ages of two and six (Byrnes & Gelman 1991; Clark 1991; Waxman 1991) – Chomsky says, "about a word an hour from ages two to eight with lexical items typically acquired on a single exposure . . . " (Chomsky 1995, p. 15). How is this possible? One obvious hypothesis here is that many concepts are developed prior to language, and indeed, at least some must be, for the infant recognizes her mother and the dog recognizes its master. Each has the capacity to re-identify the relevant individual under diverse conditions, thus making it possible to learn how to behave appropriately in their presence.

Some of the skills that are surely essential to reidentifying ordinary substances have traditionally been classified as "motor" and "perceptual" rather than "cognitive." Perhaps the most basic of these is the ability to track objects with the eyes, head, feet, hands, ears, and nose, and so forth. Objects tracked in this way are not merely conceived to be the same but are *perceived* as the same under certain conditions, the perception of sameness bridging, for example, over motions of perceived and perceiver, over changes in properties of the object, and over temporary disappearances of the object behind other objects. The mechanisms responsible for the ability to track and for perceptual "identity-" or "existence-constancy" may well be largely endogenous (Dodwell, Humphrey, & Muir 1987; Nelson & Horowitz 1987; Spelke 1993) and also "cognitively impenetrable" (Shepard 1976, 1983). That is, no matter what you know really happened, under appropriate sensory stimulation, certain illusions of constant identity persist. Even if the perceived object apparently flies right through a brick wall, you still can't help perceiving it as the same object going in one side and coming out of the other. These basic abilities seem to be the bottom layer upon which conceptions of substances are built.

The mechanisms by which infants reidentify individuals perceptually apparently do not rely upon properties of the tracked object remaining the same but upon movement, spatial location, and trajectory (Gopnik & Meltzoff 1996). Xu and Carey (1996) have produced experimental evidence that ten-month-old infants, unlike twelve-month-old infants, are not surprised if an object of one kind apparently turns into an object of another kind, say, a yellow rubber duck into a white Styrofoam ball, though they are surprised if an object they are tracking apparently turns into two objects. Tracking in this property-blind way would make it possible to *observe*, for various broad kinds of objects, what sorts of things tend to remain the same and what sorts may change within a short period, yielding clues for keeping conceptual track of substances. While perceptually tracking a substance you can learn how it looks, how it sounds, how it feels, smells, tastes, the manner in which it moves and changes, and so forth.

Perceptual tracking allows the accumulation of information about a substance over a period of time, information perceived as about the *same* substance. Nor is it only individual objects that are tracked in this way. If I am tracking Fido, I am also tracking the species dog, and also fur and bone. Which of these I am tracking with my mind depends upon which I am learning about or registering information about as I go. And that is determined by which of these substances I identify on other occasions as the one this learning concerns, that is, as being the same substance again. As I dissect my specimen frog in the zoology laboratory, whether I am *conceptually* tracking just the individual Kermit, or tracking frogs, depends on whether I attempt to apply what I have learned from my experience only to later meetings with Kermit or whether to frogs in general.

§5.5 CONCEPTUAL TRACKING USING PERCEPTUAL SKILLS

For the usefulness of your knowledge of a substance to last, however, you must also know how to reidentify the substance after a break, even a lengthy break, in perceptual tracking. And unless the substance is an individual space-time worm, you must be able to reidentify it also over its objective discontinuities in space and time. The substance dog is not space-time continuous, nor is wood. This kind of keeping track of a substance I will call "conceptual tracking." To track a substance conceptually is to understand rather than directly to perceive its being the same one when you encounter it again. Perceptual tracking would seem to be the beginning of conceptual tracking, but conceptual tracking or keeping track must continue over long and wide interruptions in perceptual tracking. Out of what materials are our abilities to track substances conceptually built?

The mechanisms of perceptual constancy for properties are probably the most important. These mechanisms may be fashioned in part through experience and certainly they are tuned through experience, but much of their basic structure may be endogenous (Dodwell et al. 1987; compare Gallistel, Brown, Carey, Gelman, & Keil 1993; Marler 1993). They cause distal qualities to appear as the same through wide variation in proximal manifestations. For example, they allow the same shape and size to be registered as the same despite alterations in angle of observation and distance, colors to appear as the same under widely varying lighting conditions, and voices to sound as the same voice through distortions and extraneous noise. These mechanisms allow one to be sensitive to the objective variances versus invariances characterizing a perceptually tracked object through changes in conditions of observation and in its changing relations to the tracker. And they allow substances to be reidentified via their stable properties under very diverse conditions of perception.

Because the mechanisms of perceptual constancy are involved, however, it should not be thought that *concepts* of properties are always involved in conceptual tracking of substances. Having concepts of properties, I am assuming, would be to *represent* properties, as such, in thought. The thought of a property is not just a reaction caused by a property; it must play an appropriate conceptual role (Section 7.4). Certainly a mere response to a presented property, such as a discriminating reflex response, requires no concepts. The moth turns toward light, but has no concept of light. Similarly, responding, say, to a certain configuration of shape, color, texture, and motion with the thought *squirrel again* is not, merely as such, to have thoughts of these shapes, colors, textures, and motions themselves. Indeed, adults don't seem to have concepts of the particular shapes and motions that are squirrel shapes and squirrel motions except the analytical concepts *squirrel-shaped* and *moves-like-a-squirrel*, these concepts presupposing rather than underlying the concept *squirrel*.

This accords, of course, with the finding that children appreciate holistic similarities before appreciating separate property dimensions such as color and shape, suggesting that concepts of properties and other abstract objects may not be required to have substance concepts. Apparently it also accords with findings in neuroscience:

> . . . more detailed investigation reveals that most sensory neurons respond to complex combinations of stimulus features. For example, visual cells that respond to oriented edges may also respond to color, motion and color disparity (Pribram 1991, pp. 79–81). Moreover, it is not uncommon to find neurons in *visual* cortex that are attuned to *acoustic* frequencies (Pribram 1991, p. 81, citing Bridgeman 1982; Pribram, Speielli, & Kamback 1967). Conversely, it has been reported recently (Calvert, Bullmore, Brammer, Campbell, Williams, McGuire, Woodruff, Iverson, & Davis 1997) that our understanding of face-to-face communication is aided by the response of *auditory* neurons to *visual* stimuli. Finally . . . top–down signals in sensory systems can alter the receptive fields of sensory neurons, that is, their response is context-sensitive (Pribram 1991 pp. 257–8).
>
> Much of the persistence of talk about feature detectors in neuroscience can be attributed to the same descriptivist assumptions that pervade philosophy and cognitive science. If . . . that is what we . . . look for in the brain . . . to a large extent that is what we will find. (MacLennan 1998, p. 78)

MacLennan goes on to claim that cases in which "a stimulus is projected into a very low-dimensional space," are "comparatively rare and secondary to the processing of concrete micro correlations, upon which reidentification rests." Apparently, holistic neural representations are prior to representations of single properties.

Besides perceptual tracking abilities and other perceptual constancies that may be largely built in, there is evidence that infants may have built into them systems designed, specifically, to recognize human faces. It is well known that they have a strong disposition from the earliest days to track and study human faces (e.g., Johnson, Dziuawiec, Ellis, & Morton 1991). Also, many species that recognize individual conspecifics instinctively use smell for this purpose, and in the early months human infants also know Mama by smell (MacFarlane 1977). It appears that the infant may know innately at least two good ways conceptually to track individual conspecifics. Faces and personal odors are indicative of individual identity; clothes, postures, and so forth, are not.

An extension of perceptual tracking through space is a kind of conceptual tracking through space. Even some quite lowly species are equipped with the capacity to keep track of their positions as they move about within their immediate spatial locales. This is the same, of course, as keeping track of where other things are in relation to them.[3] Where something was when you encountered it last is often a clue to where it would or might be when you encounter it again, thus serving as an aid to identifying it.[4] Things that don't move at all can easily be kept track of this way, and things that move slowly or only intermittently can be kept track of this way over short interruptions in perceptual tracking. This extends the period over which other identifying properties can be observed or committed to memory. For example, at the beginning of term I often have concepts of various students that I am not yet able to recognize anywhere outside my classroom. The look of a new face or new kind of animal may take a while to sink in, perceptual tracking and conceptual tracking through space filling in temporarily.

Sometimes, on the other hand, we may find a use for merely temporary concepts rooted in this sort of tracking. Consider the concept you have of your glass at a cocktail party. You keep track of it by keeping it in your hand, or by setting it down somewhere that you remember. But if you turn your back and someone straightens up a bit, that may be the end of the tracking trail for that glass. When the party is over, you lose track anyway, but it doesn't matter. Similarly, concepts of individual dishes in a matching set in one's own cupboard are likely to be only temporary. If these dishes have no individual salient distinguishing marks, and you have no cause to remember special happenings concerning any of them, every time the dishes are done and put away again, all your individual concepts of cups, glasses, and plates disappear, and new concepts of the same old individual dishes must be born again next meal. As an experiment, try to think, right now, serially, of each individual fork in your silver drawer.

§5.6 CONCEPTUAL TRACKING USING INFERENCE

When perceptual tracking and conceptual tracking in space are coupled with exploratory manipulation, probing, and testing, this may reveal properties and dispositions that prove to be better tracers of a substance

---

3 Whitehead is supposed to have claimed that he always knew where he was, but that sometimes he didn't know where the other things were.
4 Compare Gareth Evans (1982, Section 8.3).

than more easily observed properties. An easy example is the tool bag of tests and routines that chemists use in order to identify chemical stuffs. Tests of this latter sort are typically employed with an explicit understanding of the properties one is looking for. One has a disposition, for example, to make an explicit inference from "the stuff has gone green" to "there's copper in it" (Quine 1960). Identifications of this sort generally do presuppose the application of prior property concepts. Further, any explicit knowledge that you have of the properties of a substance can help you to identify it, even if these properties are not unique to it. No, we think, that can't be Sally after all because Sally doesn't know French, or that can't be real gold in the window because real gold would cost more than that.

It is because knowledge of the properties of substances are so often used in the process of identifying them that it is easy to assimilate having a concept of a substance to having knowledge of properties that would identify it, and to assimilate identifying to classifying, to applying a description. But consider: Recognizing Mama by smell certainly is not classifying her nor is it conceiving of her as whatever bears that smell. It is more accurate to imagine it as a tokening of the mental term "Mama" in response to a smell. The thought is of Mama, not of smells, but it arises in response to a smell. Similarly, recognizing copper by the fact that the stuff has gone green is not conceiving of it as being, just, a green-turning stuff. Rather, one tokens a mental term for copper in response to the knowledge it has gone green. What makes it a mental term for copper is not that it occurs in response to knowledge of these or those properties, but the fact that it serves as a repository for incoming information[5] about copper and its tokenings are controlled by previous manifestations of copper in one's experience. These include, of course manifestations by which explicit knowledge about copper has previously been gained (for example, through language – see Chapter 6).

Accurate understanding of the ontological principle or principles that ground a substance can certainly help in tracking it in difficult cases. The psychologists Medin, Gelman, Keil, and Gopnik and Meltzoff, especially, have been interested in tracing the origin and development of children's understanding of these principles, and they have observed that both children and adults appreciate that there must be some such principles underlying their substance concepts. But they have not

5   That is, information derived from natural informationC encountered by the senses. On informationC, see Appendix B.

81

been clear that understanding of this sort is not necessary to having a concept of a substance, and that having or lacking such understanding need make no difference to the extensions of one's substance concepts.

§5.7 DEVELOPING SUBSTANCE TEMPLATES

So much for learning to track substances. But how does the child know what questions she should expect to be answerable about each substance? This requires at least a rough grasp of relevant substance templates. As mentioned in Chapter 2, there is evidence that some preliminary grasp of some substance templates, such as physical kinds, animal kinds, plant kinds, artifact kinds, social kinds and so forth, may be endogenous (Atran 1989; Boyer 1998; Carey 1985; Gallistel et al. 1993; Gelman and Coley 1991; Keil 1979, 1989; Markman 1989; Marler 1993; Spelke 1989, 1993). Mandler (1997, 1998) claims that "the earliest conceptual distinctions infants make is at the level of animal and vehicle, not at the level of dog and cat" (1998, p. 79). If true, this is an interesting contrast to the order in which they acquire the words "dog" and "cat" versus the words "animal" and "vehicle." This makes sense, however, when we consider how few things there are to be learned about either animal or vehicle (as such) on the one hand and how important these are as substance *templates* on the other. What is most interesting about animals, for example, is that they divide into species, and that roughly the same sorts of questions can be asked about each of these species, and answered once and for all after one or a few observations. Since animal is not something there is much to find out about, there also is not much to say about it. So it is not surprising that the word "animal" enters the child's vocabulary rather late. But, since recognizing the substance *template* animal is crucial to learning about the various species of animals, it is equally unsurprising that animals might be recognized as such very early. Indeed, as the various psychologists mentioned above suggest, grasp of such substance templates may have a strong boost from endogenous factors.

However acquired, an adult possesses innumerable substance templates of more and less generality. The ability to recognize substance instances falling under these templates immediately supplies not only answerable questions to ask of these substances but the ability to learn how to track each new instance encountered very efficiently. Things that are likely to vary in posture but not size or color can be tracked using size and color but not posture; things that can be more than one place at once (kinds and stuffs) are not tracked by place, or rather, their tracking can carry over from one place to another, and so forth. Huge numbers of substances are not merely substances, but bring with them templates for more concrete substances falling under them. For example, the ability to identify cats is easily applied to discovering what sorts of questions can be asked about individual cats. What color is this cat (it won't change as with chameleons), is it tame or untamed (not applicable to flies), and does it have feline leukemia (not applicable to dogs) or a loud purr?

Whether we have built in templates and ways of conceptually tracking stuffs or real kinds of any particular sort is clearly a matter for empirical research – research of the sort that the psychologists mentioned above, among others, have been doing, though I am suggesting a somewhat different framework for interpretation of experimental results. Without doubt, the results of more traditional studies of concept formation also cast light on how conceptual tracking develops. Although tradition has pretty single-mindedly taken substance concepts to be classifiers, much experimental work is easily reinterpreted as implicitly addressed to the question how we track substances and how we learn to track them. Examining "the function" from "learning instances plus the target items to categorize" to "the set of possible category judgments," as Billman put it (1992), should help us to discern what kinds of traces are followed as people attempt conceptual tracking, at various ages, and for different domains of real kinds. But I believe that experiments need to be designed and interpreted with it in mind that the cognitive systems are designed by evolution and tuned by experience to find real-world substances, not random logically possible ones. Close attention needs to be paid to the details of real world ontology, to the principles that hold real substances together, and the relevance of experiments using artificial objects and kinds should be carefully justified.

One more fundamental medium through which conceptual tracking is achieved is language. That is what Chapter 6 is about.

6

Substance Concepts Through Language: Knowing the Meanings of Words

As I have described substance concepts, having these need not depend on knowing words. Preverbal humans, indeed, any animal that collects practical knowledge over time of how to relate to specific substances needs to have concepts of these. On the other hand, it is clear that language interacts with substance concepts in vigorous ways, completely transforming the conceptual repertoire. Putnam (1975) argued for what he called "the division of linguistic labor," according to which laymen can borrow on the concepts of experts. Though offering an entirely different analysis, I will conclude similarly, that the public language plays a crucial role both in the acquisition of substance concepts and also in their completed structure.

The story so far about substance concepts seems to collide with the obvious fact that many of these concepts, both for children and adults, have been acquired without encountering the substances "themselves" but only by hearing about them. With regard to these very same substances, moreover, we are often in the position that Kripke (1972) and Putnam (1975) observed, having no unique descriptions of them in mind either, so that descriptionist theories of how extensions are determined also do not fit these cases. I will argue that this entire problem falls away if we view speech as a direct medium for the perception of objects.

It is traditional to assume that gathering information by being told things is a radically different sort of process from gathering information directly through perception. But there is reason to think that this dif-

84

ference has been greatly exaggerated.[1] In fact, uncritically believing what you hear said may be surprisingly like uncritically believing what you see. For example, there is experimental evidence that what one is told goes directly into belief unless cognitive work is done to prevent this, just as what one perceives through other media does. Loading the cognitive systems with other tasks, such as having simultaneously to count backwards by threes, has the effect of facilitating belief fixation regarding whatever one hears or reads (Gilbert 1993).

There are two things that distinguish direct perception quite sharply from the acquisition of information through language, but neither implies a difference in immediacy. In direct perception, the spatial and temporal relation of the perceiver to the object perceived is given, whereas it is not normally given through language. If you see the cat, you normally see also its spatial relation to you, and whatever you perceive it doing is done at the time you perceive it. But if you hear John talking about Xavier, you do not usually hear about Xavier's spatial relation to you, nor is it automatic to know what temporal relation the Xavier-doings that John relates bear to you. There are intermediate cases, however, between ordinary perception and gathering information through language. For example, when watching television, the spatial relation of perceiver to perceived is not given either, nor, unless the program is live, is the temporal relation, yet one perceives that the newscaster frowns or smiles just as immediately as one would in his presence. So this alone is not a reason to distinguish perception sharply from learning about the world through language.

The second feature that distinguishes perception is its near infallibility. It is remarkably difficult to deceive people about what they are actually seeing or hearing. This is why "seeing is believing." On the other hand, given a modern understanding of the mechanisms of perception and a substantial technology it is possible to manage materially to fool the human ear and eye. False appearances can be arranged in the laboratory. And false appearances are now easily arranged using modern communications media. Though generally overlooked in this connection, the latter offer much the most common current illustration of the persistence of perceptual illusion. After seeing her daddy on television, the small daughter of a friend asked him, "Daddy, how did you get in

---

1 Gareth Evans may have had a view similar to the one I present below, though his notion of "information" was different. See Appendix A and Appendix B.

there?" But I mainly have in mind more radical cases such as dubbed films and cartoons.

In a similar way, persistent illusions are easily arranged through language and they are abundant. That is, sentences are often false, and even when you know they are false, they continue to present the same false appearances. They do not shift and appear to say something different. In water, oars look bent and the reflections of the trees show them moving in ripples. We are not, however, tempted to believe that our oars are bent or that the trees are moving in ripples. Similarly, "I'm dying" uttered by a laughing eight-year-old does not tempt us to believe that someone is dying (Gendler 1998). But the appearance is as much of someone dying as the appearance in the rippling water is of rippling trees. Perhaps you will say, but it doesn't *sound* as if the laughing eight-year-old is dying. True, those aren't the sounds an eight-year-old would make if she were really dying. It also isn't the look a tree would have if it were really rippling. Trees don't flex that way. Still, the persistent illusion is that the trees are flexing that way and that the eight-year-old is dying. In sum, hearing sentences may be quite a lot like watching the media, or like watching reflections, which in turn is quite a lot like watching the original.

Think of the matter this way. There are many ways to recognize, for example, rain. There is a way that rain feels when it falls on you, and a way that it looks out the window. There is a way that it sounds falling on the rooftop, "retetetetet," and a way that it sounds falling on the ground, "shshshshsh." And falling on English speakers, here is another way it can sound: "Hey, guys, it's raining!"[2] Nor should you object that it is not rain you hear in the last case but rather "a sentence." Or a sound? Is it then a sound that you hear rather than rain on the roof? Is it a TV screen that you see rather than Bill Clinton? A pattern of ambient light rather than the TV screen? Best of all, perhaps all you see is a visual impression? Which ones of these things are the real or direct objects of perception?

You can, if you like, hear or see any of these things. What you see when you look depends, first, on where you focus your eyes; it depends, second, on where you focus your mind, your attention. True, philosophical tradition, and the psychological tradition following after, has resolutely held that for each of the physical senses there is just one layer of the world that it perceives directly; all other layers are known only through inference. This premise I am denying. There is no single

2 Thank you, Crawford Elder.

"given" layer of perception (again, see MacLennan 1998, quoted in Section 5.5). This, of course, was argued strongly in the broad tradition that includes both Wilfrid Sellars and Willard Quine, so it should not be an unfamiliar idea. Perception, many have held, is "theory laden." Perceptual judgments do not arise through inference, but neither is the content of a perceptual judgment an epistemological given. I would argue that the Sellars/Quine tradition was mistaken in the reasons they gave for this conclusion. Their view was that applying a concept is making a transition from stimulation or sensation into thought, and that the content of the thought produced is defined by the network of inference dispositions (nowadays, the "cognitive role") in which the concept is enmeshed. I am proposing a different theory about the content of a concept and about how its extension is determined. But the conclusion is the same. The substances referred to in perceptual judgments are not epistemological givens but are discovered through a process of fallible construction, fallible learning. They are distal objects, and there is no necessary restriction on their level of distality.

According to the contemporary motor theory of speech perception (Liberman & Mattingly 1985, 1989; Mattingly & Studdart-Kennedy 1991), phonemes are not sounds, not acoustic phenomena, but gestures made by the vocal tract. That is, what you hear as the same phoneme again is not acoustically the same, but is the same movement or same posture aimed at by the vocal tract. Furthermore, the processing of speech sounds, when these are perceived *as* speech, is through different channels than the processing of other sounds. Thus, the end organs of perception, the ears, determine more than one mode of perception. My further suggestion is that when one is listening to speech in order to gain information, the ears hear not just through the acoustics to the speech gestures, but through the speech gestures to the world. What the young child perceives in the presence of speech is not sounds, nor phoneme strings, nor words but, in the first instance, the world. (If a bat can hear that something is square, so can I. It's only fair.)

The child comes into the world without any knowledge of how minds work, without any knowledge of what goes on inside people when they speak (indeed, we ourselves seem to be a bit short on such knowledge). The child does not develop concepts, for example, of beliefs and desires, until several years after the onset of speech. It is clear, then, that children cannot possibly understand language in the way Grice (1957) described, by understanding that the speaker intends them to believe . . . and so forth.[3] But it is also true that the young child has very little phonological awareness. Indeed, contrary to much public opinion, the difficulty of becoming aware of structure at the phonological level is probably the most common first cause of dyslexia (I. Y. Liberman et al. 1984; Lundberg et al. 1988; Morais et al. 1979). Clearly the child has no concepts of phonemes and cannot understand speech by drawing inferences from the patterns of phonemes it hears.

It is also true that children learn very few words by ostentation. They learn them by hearing complete sentences containing them (e.g., Gleitman 1990; Grimshaw 1994; Pinker 1994a). For the young child, language serves simply as another medium of perception, a medium through which to perceive the world – exactly as the child perceives the world through its eyes without knowing anything about light, and through its sense of touch and smell without knowing anything about physical forces or chemicals. How can that be, you may say, since Mama's words are right here while the dog she talks about is way over there? Well, how do you perceive yourself in the mirror? What's funny about language, I have said, is that it does not show your own relation to the things you perceive through it.

§6.2 TRACKING THROUGH WORDS: CONCEPTS ENTIRELY
THROUGH LANGUAGE

But there really is no need to exhaust this point here. In the present context, the part that really matters is that believing what one hears said is a way of picking up information about substances, and that it is by learning a language that a child becomes able to pick up information in this way.[4] It sounds a bit queer to speak of learning a word for a substance as learning a way to identify that substance. But just as the relation of one part of the pattern on the TV screen to another part can manifest the relation of one part of Bill Clinton to another, the relation of a word to other words in a sentence can manifest the configuration of a substance in relation to other substances and properties in the world. The semantics of natural languages is productive; alterations performed upon sentences correspond systematically to alterations in what the sentences represent, just as in the case of pictures, though the mapping functions involved are, of course, far more abstract. So if learning what a substance looks like can be learning how to identify it, similarly,

3 For a critique of Grice, see Millikan (1984, Chapter 3).
4 "Information," in this passage, means informationC as defined in Appendix B.

learning a word for a substance can be learning a way to identify it. In both cases, what one learns is to recognize or understand manifestations of the substance *as* manifestations of it; one learns how to translate information arriving in one more kind of package at one's sensory surfaces into beliefs.

Learning a language is, in part, just learning more ways to pick up information through the senses and put it away in the right boxes. A difference, of course, is that this way of picking up information is much more fallible than in the case of ordinary perception. But no human ability is infallible. Furthermore, just as substances are sometimes look-alikes in the flesh (twin brothers), many substances are sound-alikes in words (John$_{(Doe)}$ and John$_{(Roe)}$). But substances are tracked through the medium of words not merely by means of the same words manifesting the same substances. Like more direct manifestations of substances, words and sentences occur in context, allowing methods of tracking to be used that are analogous to more ordinary tracking, in that they rely in large part on expected spatial, temporal, and causal relations (cf., trajectory) rather than the persistence of properties. How do I recognize that as John's elbow poking out over there behind the lamp? Well, I saw John head that way with a book just a moment ago. Some of these relations are natural, as the natural relation between a speaker's experience plus the context of his speech to the subject of the information he is trying to convey. One will usually know which "John" a speaker is talking about in a way analogous to the way one knows whose elbow that is. Other relations between word and referent are governed more closely by convention, as in the interpretation of certain anaphoric pronouns and certain indexicals.

Recognizing a linguistic reference to a substance is just another way of reidentifying the substance itself. It is identifying it through one more medium of manifestation. Think of this medium as like an instrument that aids perception. Like a camera, a radio, a cat scan, or a microscope, another person who talks to me picks up information-bearing patterns from his environment, focuses them, translates them into a new medium and beams them at me. Or think of living in a language community as like being inundated in one more sea of ambient energy. Like the surrounding light, surrounding people transmit the structure of the environment to me in ways that, barring certain interferences, I can become tuned to interpret.

It is even possible, indeed it is common, to have a substance concept *entirely* through the medium of language. It is possible to have it, that is, while lacking any ability to recognize the substance in the flesh. For most of us, that is how we have a concept of Aristotle, of molybdenum and, say, of African dormice. — There, I just handed you a concept of African dormice, in case you had none before. Now you can think of them nights if you like, wondering what they are like — on the assumption, of course, that you gathered from their name what sorts of questions you might reasonably ask about them (animal questions, not vegetable or mineral or social artifact questions). In many cases there is not much more to having a substance concept than having a word. To have a word is to have a handle on tracking a substance via manifestations of it produced in a particular language community. For the person who remembers faces easily, one look at a new person may be enough to implant the ability to recognize that person again, thus enabling a concept of them. For the person who remembers words easily, one hearing of a new substance through a word for it may be enough to implant the ability to recognize the substance again through that word, thus enabling a concept of it. Simply grasping the phonemic structure of a language and the rudiments of how to parse it enables one to help oneself to an embryo concept of every substance named in that language. It enables one conceptually to track these substances and easily to discover under what sorts of substance templates they fall. That, I suppose, is why it is possible for small children to learn a new word every hour (Section 5.1).

The basic phenomenon here is the same as that underlying Putnam's theory of the "Division of Linguistic Labor" (1975) and Burge's claim that constitution of the very content of one's *thought* sometimes passes through the word usages of a surrounding language community (1979, 1982, 1986). But the explanation I am proposing of this phenomenon is quite different. The image created by both Putnam and Burge is that when I have a concept through language I take out a loan that the experts are prepared to pay up. There are experts out there who "really" have the concept while the rest of us really don't. But even if we soften this just to the claim that some people out there have (or had — consider our concept of Socrates) the concept in a way that was different from ours because focused without reliance on public language, still the image is wrong. My claim is that having a concept grounded only through language is no different than having a concept grounded only through, say, vision. Such a concept is in no way secondary. True, others must help me to have such a concept, just as a television may have to help me if I am to see Bill Clinton. But just as I really do see Bill Clinton on television, having a concept through language is really having a concept. It is really thinking of something.

§6.3 FOCUSING REFERENCE AND KNOWING THE MEANINGS OF WORDS

Words serve in huge numbers as seed crystals around which fuller conceptions of substances are then quickly formed. That is why there can be such differences between the concepts available in cultures not historically related, and why poor Helen Keller was, as she later described it, pretty much unable to *think* until Sullivan taught her some language. Gelman and Coley (1991) are surely right that "a word can serve to stake out a new category, which then must be explored in more depth" (p. 184; see also Gopnik & Meltzoff 1993). Words also are handles to hang onto, helping to stabilize concepts so as gradually to eliminate equivocation in thought, granted that those who speak to us have unequivocal concepts themselves.

Acquiring adequate substance concepts involves learning to focus one's thought, such that all of the incoming information scattered over time about each substance is put into one slot, and the right constancies projected for it. Learning to do this is what Perner called "focusing reference" (Section 4.8). Learning words for substances is in part a matter of focusing reference. Substances are tracked through words and also in other ways. If information about a substance arrives through language and the substance is tracked through a word, but the information culled in this way is put under a concept used also to track a different substance using other means, there will be equivocation in the resulting concept. We say in such cases that the person "does not know the meaning of the word," or thinks that the word means something different than it really does. A perfectly parallel case would be mixing a person known to you only through phone calls with a different person known from glimpses at the beach. One could just as well say, using the same sense of "meaning," that they did not know the meaning of the voice over the phone.

In Chapter 1, I suggested that preschoolers who take tigers to be "kitties" may be confused, not about the meaning of the word "kitty," but about how to identify housecats. From our present perspective, however, thinking tigers are "kitties," that is, putting tiger information away in the same slot as information gotten from observing housecats and from hearing about "kitties," is being confused about tigers as well as about housecats. The child has not yet managed to focus on only one substance. Perhaps the child calls the whole genus *Felis* by the name "kitty." It does not follow that the child means *Felis* by "kitty." Rather, the child's word "kitty" may hover between referring to felines generally and housecats specifically. The child may be putting all information gleaned through language and specific to housecats in the same bin as information gleaned about tigers and lions at the zoo. The child's conception of "kitty" will then be equivocal, part of it tracking felines generally while another part is channeled through the word "kitty," hence is bringing in information much of which is wrong for felines generally. Then the child's referent is not the same as the referent of the English word "kitty," so it is certainly true that child does not yet know the meaning of "kitty." But the public word "*Felis*" is not equivocal, so the child does not mean *Felis* by "kitty." (Suppose, on the other hand, that a foreigner uses the word "kitchen" to refer to chickens. It is very unlikely that she will have gathered in any information through language about kitchens and actually put it in her mental chicken bin, or that she has any disposition to do so. This is an entirely different case from that of the child who calls tigers "kitty.")

Because it is possible for a conception to be channeled completely through language, it is possible to have a substance concept through nothing but a word plus a grasp of its substance template and enough relevant grammar. Many people find this completely unintuitive, and I sympathize. But my point is that filling out the concept into a more and more adequate one happens in degrees. There is no special thing that gets added at some later point that suddenly makes it into a "real concept." It can be filled out more; it can get better and better. But there is no magic moment when it has attained some essence required for true concepthood. There is no magic place to draw the line between merely knowing a word and also knowing what the word means.

Traditionally it is supposed that learning what a word means is coming to exercise the "same concept" in connection with the word that adults do. But, I have argued, a concept is an ability, and there is an ambiguity in the notion "same ability" that shows up also in the notion "same concept." Sometimes what counts as the same ability is what accomplishes the same; other times it is what accomplishes the same by the same means. In the terminology I am using, the organic chemist and the child both have the concept of sugar but they have quite different conceptions of it (Section 1.9). Having the same substance concept as someone else involves being able to reidentify the same substance they can. Identifying a substance the same *way* that someone else does, having the same "conception" of it, is an added frill.[5] Assuming that knowing English requires having the concepts that correspond to English words, an advantage of talking this way is that then Helen Keller gets to know English.

What do we mean, then, when we speak of someone as coming to understand "the meaning of a word"? If the word denotes a substance, there is a sense in which its meaning is, just, its referring to *that* substance. To know what the word means is just to have a concept of the substance that includes knowing to reidentify it by means of hearing that word. But of course the child may not be very good at identifying the substance. The child may make gross mistakes that an adult would not make. Is there then a richer sense in which a child can come to understand "what adults mean" by the word? Is there such a thing as "THE adult conception," of a substance? Given the numerous and diverse methods by which it is possible to learn to identify almost any substance, it seems that there could not possibly be.

On the other hand, for some (how many?) substances, it may be that there are core methods by which nearly every adult (the "nearly" is for Helen Keller) knows to reidentify them. Or there may be certain conditions under which any adult would recognize the substance, or examples of the substance that any adult would recognize given a chance to examine them. There also are occasional words that almost everyone who knows them learns to associate with certain facts about their referents, such as that Hesperus is seen low on the horizon in the evening, Phosphorus in the morning, or that Mark Twain was an author. ("Mark Twain," after all, was a pen name.) Also, occasionally words are passed down from generation to generation along with explicit conventional definitions. For example, every child who is taught the rudiments of geometry in school is taught that all points on a circle are equidistant from its center. Then there may be a sense in which the child does not fully understand "the meaning" of the word for that substance until her competence at identifying the substance has been filled out to match

---

5   There is a further complication, for it is possible for a single person to have two separate concepts of the same substance if they have failed to coidentify these, for example, if they do not understand that Samuel Clemens is the same man as Mark Twain (see Section 12.8).

adult standards. The child must have an adult's conception of the substance. If this is what is to be meant by "knowing the meaning" then knowing how to track a substance only by recognizing its name would not be nearly enough for "knowing the meaning."

The difficulty is that there seems to be no way to draw clear lines around "the adult conception" of a substance. For example, do you, in this sense of "knowing the meaning," know the meaning of the word "molybdenum"? – or "brisket"? – or "African dormouse"? Perhaps your intuition is to say that you *don't* know what any of these words mean? I see no way to avoid a merely verbal dispute at this point if we persist with the question: Who gets to count as *really* knowing the meaning?

7

How We Make Our Ideas Clear: Epistemology for Empirical Concepts[1]

§7.1 THE COMPLAINT AGAINST EXTERNALISM

The view of substance concepts I am offering is an uncompromisingly externalist view. What makes a thought be about a certain substance is nothing merely in the mind, nor any mere disposition of the mind, not even a wide disposition, but the thought's origin — an external causal/historical relation between the concept and the substance (Section 4.8). But meaning externalism has recently come under heavy attack on the grounds that it leaves thinkers in no position to know themselves either what they are thinking about or whether they are genuinely thinking at all. And indeed, the best-known externalist theories all do seem to have this consequence. There is no necessity for an externalist thesis to have this consequence, however, and I propose to show how to avoid it.

What is needed to counter this entirely reasonable complaint against meaning externalism, I believe, is first an adequate account of what would *constitute* knowing what one is thinking of. If you are directly thinking about an external object, knowing what you are thinking of obviously cannot be done as Russell once described it, by having the object of thought literally within or before your conscious mind. Nor, a fortiori, can it be done by simultaneously holding your thought, or a thought of your thought, before your conscious mind, on the one hand,

---

1 This chapter draws heavily on the Tenth Annual Patrick Romanell Lecture (Millikan 1998c), with the same title, delivered to the American Philosophical Association, December 30, 1997.

95

and comparing it with its object, also held before the mind, on the other. What on earth then *could* knowing what one was thinking about possibly be? Gareth Evans devoted much of *The Varieties of Reference* (1982) to this question, and I will devote much of Chapter 13 to comparing his and my views on the matter.

A second thing that is needed to counter this complaint against externalism, I believe, is an adequate empiricist epistemology for empirical concepts, with which one's particular externalist position must, of course, be compatible. The externalism I have described implies, first, that there is no a priori guarantee against reference failure for substance concepts. It is always a priori possible that one's substance conception is not in fact connected to any real substance at all. Second, there is no a priori guarantee against reference duplication for substance concepts, no guarantee against unknowingly referring over again to exactly the same thing with two substance concepts. Third, there is no a priori guarantee against equivocation in reference, against thinking of two substances as if one, merging them together in thought. Elsewhere I have argued at length, moreover, that *any* kind of externalism proposed for *any* kind of empirical concept will necessarily have these three consequences (Millikan 1993a, Chapter 14). If this is so, then it is clearly incumbent on the externalist to show how evidence for the nonemptiness, nonredundancy, and univocity of our empirical concepts can be gathered through experience.

The externalist is obliged to construct an empiricist epistemology of concepts. This epistemology, I will claim, must be different from and prior to traditional empiricist epistemologies, which are all epistemologies either of judgment or of theories taken as wholes. This chapter is devoted to the task of constructing such an epistemology. I will develop it entirely independently of the theses already laid down about substance concepts, as a story about empirical concepts generally. In the end it will be apparent, however, that only a rather special kind of thesis on the nature of externalist meaning would be compatible with such an epistemology. Indeed, the only one I know of is the present one, and a similar theory for concepts of empirical properties presented in Millikan (1984, Chapters 14–17).

The complaint against meaning externalism is often put in a rather different form, however, a form in which it is not legitimate. It is said that meaning externalism deprives us of "incorrigible access" to our own thoughts and that this result is untenable. What seems to be meant is that making the transition from having a thought to correctly representing to oneself that one has that thought is problematic on an externalist view in ways it is not problematic on an internalist view. But this is clearly mistaken. To begin with, it is far from clear that we have "incorrigible access" to our own thoughts, if that means that we can't be mistaken about them. Not only the Freudian tradition but a host of modern experiments on cognitive dissonance attest that we certainly can be mistaken. Nor is it any consequence of externalism that access to knowledge of our own thoughts must be through the same channels as access to knowledge of others' thoughts. Externalism does not prohibit having a different and more direct way of gathering information about your own thoughts. Sellars, for example, held that you could interrupt your dispositions candidly to speak your mind and turn them into dispositions to tell yourself what you believe (1975). Indeed, barring the Cartesian position that mind is epistemically transparent to itself – that the knowing of things mental just equals the being of these things – externalist and internalist would seem to have exactly the same problem of explaining how one acquires concepts of the mental – something that we know small children don't have – and how one successfully applies them to oneself. Even if what thought is about were determined within thought itself, that would not help us with how thought reflects on itself, how it comes to know itself as object (see also Gibbons 1996).[2] Of course, the externalist cannot tell a priori that a second-order thought, a thought about the content of a first-order thought, has content if she cannot tell whether the first order thought has content. But that is a different problem. It is the problem I have already promised to address in this chapter, not something new.

Bill Lycan has reminded me of one more sort of problem that has been posed for the externalist about correctly representing one's thoughts to oneself. Suppose that I have been living on earth but wake up on twinearth one day. After a time, many suppose, what used to be my thoughts of water will metamorphose and become thoughts of twater. Then when I think that last year I thought that twater was wet I will be wrong, for in fact what I believed last year was that water was wet. On the contrary, I suggest, when more than one substance has been

---

2 I am grateful to Keya Maitra for focusing my attention on this point. More generally, it is dismaying how many contemporary discussions of the nature of consciousness, qualia, intentional attitudes, and so forth ignore the question how one gets from the supposed presence of this or that within the mind or consciousness to propositional knowledge of that presence.

tracked under the very same concept, the concept has become equivocal. Equivocation in thought is a very common occurrence, certainly not one that should be ruled out by either internalist or externalist. Each semester when I acquire a new class of freshmen I go through it again, making embarrassing mistakes because I have got Johnny and William or Susan and Jane mixed together in my mind. If they abduct me to twinearth I will soon have an equivocal thought of water/twater and I will be wrong when I believe I used to think that water/twater is wet. My thought did not used to be equivocal. The same thing may happen right here on earth if I know Dr. Peters for some time before meeting, unbeknownst to me, his identical twin, Dr. Peters. It is surely a strength rather than a weakness of externalism if it accounts for this sort of phenomenon.

What really is a problem for externalism, as I have said, is that it implies we cannot tell by a priori means alone (1) when our thoughts are empty of content, (2) when we are thinking double, that is, when psychologically separate thoughts of ours bear exactly the same contents, or (3) when we are equivocating in thought, representing two different contents with only one thought. The externalist owes us an account of how these various things can be discerned empirically – an empiricist epistemology for empirical concepts. Such an account will not be obliged, however, to assuage the insistently bleak Cartesian skeptic. Given naturalist premises, no theory of mind could do that in principle. But in Kantian spirit, we are obliged to show how it is *possible* that our meanings are tested through experience.

§7.2 SIDESTEPPING HOLISM IN THE EPISTEMOLOGY OF CONCEPTS

Traditional empiricism holds, of course, that our abilities to think of external objects and properties are acquired with the help of experience. From this one might think it a short step to the view that ongoing experience is also used in testing and perfecting these abilities. The externalist challenge would then be to develop a theory of the nature of empirical concepts that explains how this testing and perfecting is possible, indeed, how it manages to be highly effective and efficient. Instead, the best-known externalist theories of how thought gets its content make a complete mystery of this matter. To ground our meanings, they seem to suggest, we would need to make prior judgments about causal or historical relations of our thoughts to their objects. Or we would need to judge that the conceptual roles of our thoughts matched corresponding relations among their objects. Such demands are regressive, of course, requiring prior grounded concepts of the same objects – also prior grasp of a true theory of meaning and reference for thought.

Yet I think that a better externalist theory is surprisingly close at hand. With just a tug and a tweak, it falls right out of the central twentieth-century American tradition of philosophy of science and language, beginning with the familiar story about theoretical terms told at mid-century, for example, by Carnap, Hempel, and Sellars.[3] On this story, theoretical terms, such as "mass" "temperature" and "atom," acquire their meanings, first, from the place each holds in (what can be reconstructed as) a formal system containing postulates and rules that fix their intratheoretical relations to other theoretical terms and, second, from their inference relations to observation sentences, or to sentences in a prior theory already anchored to observation. These latter rules correlating theoretical with observational sentences were termed "bridge principles." In opposition to Carnap and earlier verificationists, Hempel then claimed that it was not possible to separate either the intratheoretic laws or the bridge principles of such a theory into two distinct kinds, meaning postulates or matters of definition on one side, empirical postulates or matters of experience on the other. For example, the meaning of the geologist's term "hardness" is determined partly by the intratheoretic law postulating the relation *harder than* as transitive, but also by the bridge principle that if one mineral scratches another it is harder than the other. Together these two principles imply that the relation x *scratches* y is transitive, a fact that is clearly empirical, yet neither principle is more definitional of the geologist's concept *hardness*, nor more an empirical fact about hardness, than the other. "Theory formation and concept formation go on hand in hand; neither can be carried on successfully in isolation from the other. . . . If . . . cognitive significance can be attributed to anything, then only to entire theoretical systems" (Hempel 1950, 1965, p. 113). A more familiar quote is from Quine, who takes concepts of ordinary observable objects to be like theoretical concepts: "Statements about the external world face the tribunal of sensory experience not individually but only as a corporate body" (Quine

---

3 In "Empiricism and the Philosophy of Mind" (1956), Sellars lists among advocates of this view also Braithwaite, Norman Campbell, and Reichenbach. A simple exposition of the theory is in Hempel (1966) Chapter 6.

1953). In Quine, this thesis is again tied to the rejection of a clean distinction between changing your meanings and changing your empirical beliefs, between the analytic and the synthetic.

One result of this midcentury doctrine was a disastrous semantic holism. The meaning of each empirical concept was taken to be determined only through its position in a wide inference network containing numerous other concepts, indeed, perhaps all of one's concepts. But another result was the implicit emergence of the first genuinely empiricist epistemology of concepts. If empirical meanings cannot be disentangled from empirical theories, then if theories can be some more and some less adequate so can concepts, and the adequacy of an empirical concept will be tested through ongoing experience, not a priori. But because of the holism, this empiricist epistemology of concepts is not useful against current attacks on meaning externalism. It suggests that we would need to arrive at the end of Peircean inquiry before knowing whether any of our concepts are adequate, hence before knowing whether we are genuinely thinking about anything at all. We need, I suggest, to take the baby from the bath, keeping the thesis that meanings are tested empirically but discarding the holism. Another look at the classical theory of theories suggests how this can be done.

The paradigm bridge principle bridging from observation to theory was taken to correspond to an operation either determining a theoretical property or measuring its numerical value. As a theory matures, it was supposed, typically it accumulates more and more operational bridge principles of this sort. For example, one would expect geologists to accumulate more ways of determining hardness than by scratching, as there are numerous different ways to measure temperature, distance, volume, pressure, and mass. Given the Hempelian position, none of these operations will be more central than others in determining the meaning of the theoretical concepts they collectively define. Take, then, any such set of operational bridge principles helping to define a single theoretical proposition and consider it in isolation from the rest of its encompassing theory. Consider, for example, all the known ways of determining that a certain thing's temperature is 40° centigrade. Surely the convergence of all these ways to the same result when applied to the same physical object attests to the reality of the property *temperature 40° centigrade* quite independently of our knowing any intratheoretical laws about temperature. The objectivity of concepts such as temperature or mass or length is strongly evidenced quite separately from theories employing these concepts. Or better, one's readiness to judge the same proposition true on multiple observational bases itself constitutes a sort of *minitheory*, namely, the theory that *if p then p*, for exactly that one proposition. The minitheory is confirmed when a variety of empirical methods consistently converge on this single result.

It will be objected perhaps that new operations determining interesting physical properties typically are known to determine them only through the application of theory. But surely, *here* it does help to distinguish the context of discovery from the context of justification. How a measuring method is discovered and how it is explained are neither of them relevant to confirming its accuracy. That the measure is good, that it correlates with other measures, is fully compatible with failure of the theory that predicts and attempts to explain this fact.

For nontheoretical concepts, the ability to make the same perceptual judgment from different perspectives, using different sensory modalities, under different mediating circumstances such as different lighting and acoustic conditions, offers similar evidence for the objectivity of the concepts employed in these judgments. Holism is easily avoided in the epistemology of concepts so long as there exist empirical propositions, each of which can be judged by a variety of independent methods not employing prior empirical concepts, making possible an independent test of the concepts contained in that particular proposition. It is not the job of empirical concepts to help predict experience. We do not predict our experience. We predict what we will read off our experience, namely, that since p then p. We do not predict the appearances of things. We could not possibly do so, for we cannot predict the ever-changing conditions under which we observe them. We predict only the truth of distal facts.[4]

§7.3 SEPARATING OFF THE EPISTEMOLOGY OF CONCEPTS

It is important in this context not to entangle the epistemology of concepts with the epistemology of judgment. Consider, for example, the following passage from Wilfrid Sellars:

. . . if [having the concept of green] presupposes knowing in what circumstances to view an object to ascertain its color, then, since one can scarcely determine what the circumstances are without noticing that certain objects have

---

4   On this particular point, Quine (1960) seems to have had it the right way around: "Our prediction is that the ensuing close range stimulations will be of the sort that vigorously elicit verdicts of stonehood. Prediction is in effect the conjectural anticipation of further sensory experience for a forgone conclusion" (p. 19).

certain perceptible characteristics – including colors – it would seem that one couldn't form the concept of [such things as] being green . . . unless he already had them. It just won't do to reply that . . . it is sufficient to respond when one is in point of fact in standard conditions to green objects with the vocable "This is green." Not only must the conditions be of the sort that is appropriate for determining the color of an object by looking, the subject must know that conditions of this sort are appropriate . . . one can have the concept of green only by having a whole battery of concepts of which it is one element." [Sellars 1956, p. 275.]

Sellars' basic concern here is not that one couldn't in point of fact learn to respond discriminatively to green objects with the vocable "This is green" in standard conditions without already having a battery of concepts. Rather, it is that one couldn't *know* that anything was green without this. His concern is to ensure that suitable observation judgments indeed express "knowledge" in the sense that they can be "placed in the logical space of reasons, of justifying and being able to justify what one says" (Sellars 1956, p. 299). But there is no cause to suppose that the process of fashioning and honing adequate concepts presupposes the ability to justify the judgments that use these concepts. Knowing about the conditions under which one's perceptual and cognitive systems will work properly is not required for learning how to use them properly any more than knowing about the atmospheric conditions required for breathing properly is required for breathing properly (compare Section 4.3). The epistemology of concepts is prior to and not the same as the epistemology of judgments. Nor is it a criterion of adequacy for an epistemology of concepts or, more broadly, for a theory of mind, that it can lever a person out of skepticism. There is no compulsion to suppose that human minds are so built that we can't possibly fall into epistemological black holes that can't subsequently be reasoned out of. The question we need to answer about our concepts is *how* we do it, *how* we make them clear (cf. how we focus our eyes) not how we can *know that* we have succeeded in making them clear. Recognizing when one's thoughts are clear is not making a judgment about one's thought, nor is it knowing how to justify one's thought.[5] Sellars' final conclusion that "one can have the concept of green only by having a whole battery of concepts" does not follow from the premises he offers.

---

5 In Chapter 13, I will argue, likewise, that knowing what one is thinking of is not making a judgment about one's thought.

The mechanisms of perceptual constancy that enable us to perceive, for example, the same color, shape, voice, or moving object as being the same one through diverse proximal stimulations, diverse intervening media, and various kinds of distortions and static, exemplify our ability to make the same perceptual judgment in a variety of ways. So does our ability to use different senses to confirm the same judgment perceptually. Given a variety of ways to observe the same state of affairs, none of these methods is definitional of the concepts employed, just as on a Hempelian view, no bridge principles leading from observation into theory are more definitional of the theory's concepts than others. None of our ways of making the same judgment is distinguished as a or the infallible method of judging its content. Each is but a practical ability, more or less reliable, to identify the perceptually presented situation correctly. Each relies either on historically normal conditions obtaining for correct use of one's perceptual mechanisms, or on historically normal conditions for observing that these normal conditions obtain. Or better, being more careful, the most usual reliance is on normal conditions obtaining for the support of successful epistemic action. One knows how, physically, to maneuver oneself into conditions normal for making accurate perceptual judgments of a given kind.

Highly consistent convergence of independent methods to the same judgments serves as strong testimony to the objective univocal sources of these judgments. For example, I check my perception by moving in relation to the object, by employing others of my senses, by manipulating the object, to confirm a constant result. In so doing I not only verify my original result, but also confirm the more general abilities that constitute, in part, the subject and predicate concepts on which my judgment rests. I confirm them again when I find that another person has arrived at the same judgment as I, another way of making judgments being to believe what one is told (Chapter 6). Emptiness in empirical concepts shows up characteristically in lack of variety in the perspectives from which they can be applied. Equivocation shows up in the emergence of contradictions systematically correlated with perspectives taken. Redundancy shows up, just as Leibniz said, with the accumulation of coincident properties and the absence of contrary ones.

In *Word and Object*, Quine defines stimulus meaning as having two parts, "affirmative" and "negative," and he claims that "[t]he affirmative and negative stimulus meanings of a sentence (for a given speaker at a given time) are mutually exclusive" (Quine 1960, p. 33). This exclusivity results naturally from the fact that "stimulus meaning" is defined by reference to overt affirmations and denials of a sentence coupled with the assumption that a speaker won't affirm and deny the same sentence at the same time. Quine also remarks that "many stimulations may be expected to belong to neither" the affirmative or negative stimulus meaning. Notice that this "neither" category will, technically, cover cases of total confusion as well as more ordinary "can't tell" cases such as those Quine explicitly includes as "poor glimpses." The effect is that Quine overlooks the most interesting cases relevant to concept formation, namely those in which contradiction bypasses theory and appears directly at the level of observation. These are the cases having the most leverage for testing meanings, but they are invisible given Quine's tools of analysis.

How can contradiction bypass theory and appear directly at the level of observation? Easy cases are two thermometers, whether of the same or different construction, placed in the same medium but reading different temperatures, or an object that shows different weights when placed on different scales, or on the same scale, one minute from the next. So, you say, something must be wrong with at least one of the thermometers, or with the scale. Apparently they are not good measures of temperature and weight. But the only evidence we have that there are such objective properties as temperature and weight at all is that there exist ways of making thermometers match consistently and ways of making scales that weigh consistently. We can, of course, turn to our theories about the causal properties of temperature and weight to explain why thermometers and scales agree when they do and why they don't agree when they don't. We also may turn to theories when it is necessary to repair or calibrate our thermometers and scales. But having adjusted the thermometers and scales, whether by employing a theory, or by trial and error tinkering, or by sheer accident, no theories are implicated in the use of these instruments to confirm the objective adequacy of our concepts of temperature and weight. Similarly, making a prediction that a certain proposition will come true as a result of performing an experiment and later judging perceptually that it has indeed come true is a way of testing not only the theory but the objectivity of the concepts involved in the judgment. And these two are independent tests. That the concepts have been reaffirmed as objective does not depend on the theory itself being true. The method of prediction used may work for a reason independent of the particular theory, as ancient astronomical predictions often proved accurate for good reasons but not for the reasons the astronomers thought at the time.

Most people purchase their thermometers and weight scales knowing nothing of the principles of their construction and operation. This does not make these people's concepts of temperature and weight less well epistemologically grounded than those of the scientist. It does not give them less reason to place trust in the objective meanings of these concepts. Similarly, all of us were natively endowed with perceptual systems whose principles of operation scientists are barely beginning to fathom. Trust in the objective reference of judgments made using these systems is warranted in so far as we agree each with ourselves in these judgments: *if p then p*. What feels cubical looks cubical, and continues to look cubical from different angles and distances. What sounds as if in front of me looks to be in front of me and can be attained by reaching in front of me – like measuring temperature with a mercury thermometer, a gas thermometer, and a bimetallic strip. Nor are even the most basic perceptual self-agreements logically necessary. Müller-Lyer arrows measure the same length but look different lengths. After watching a waterfall closely and continuously for a minute or two, if the eyes are then fixed on a stationary object it will appear to be at once moving and stationary (Crane 1989). There is a way of focusing one's eyes on a pair of spots, one red and one green, such that there appears to be only one spot that is both red *and* green all over. A and B can appear to be the same color, B and C can also appear to be the same color, while A and C appear to be different colors (Goodman 1966). That the affirmative and negative stimulus meanings of any perceptual judgment are mutually exclusive is not a necessary truth but a matter of experience, and a continual reaffirmation of the objective meaningfulness of the empirical concepts used in making the judgment.

§7.4 REMAINING INTERDEPENDENCIES AMONG CONCEPTS

That concepts are tested and honed in ways that do not entangle them with theories does not imply, in general, that they can be tested singly or one by one. Adequacy in concepts is tested by whether their employment makes stable judgment possible. But no judgment employs only one concept. To make the same judgment again, one must recognize its subject or subjects as being the same again and also the properties or relations it attributes as being the same. Both subject and predicate terms must be adequate if stable judgment is to result. Equally important, that a judgment is stable implies that it might have been unstable, that one might have fallen into contradiction instead. Adequacy in concepts can be tested only if one can recognize contradiction in judgment. And this requires the capacity to recognize the complements or contraries of predicates. Let me explain.

Consider Quine's observation that many stimulations may be expected to belong neither to the affirmative nor negative stimulus meaning of an occasion sentence. One important reason is that the mere absence of affirmative stimulation does not constitute negative stimulation. Most obvious, I cannot make either an affirmative or a negative perceptual judgment if I fail to recognize its subject. If I don't see the rabbit at all, I can't judge it to be white or not to be white. Less obviously, failing to perceive that the predicate of a proposition applies to its perceived subject does not warrant judging it not to apply. I may feel the apple in the dark, know it is an apple, even know which apple it is, but I cannot judge its color by feeling. I may strike a match and look at the apple, but still not be able to see its color clearly or at all. Not observing that the apple is red does not equal observing that it is not red. To tell that it is not red I must be able to tell what other color it is instead, that it is some contrary of red or, more generally, that it is non-red, the complement of red. Having concepts of the contraries and complements of predicates is required if negation in judgment is to be possible, hence if contradiction in judgment is to be possible. To judge that it is not blue, you must be able to judge that what you are seeing is its being grey, not, say, its being in shadow. To judge that it is not round you must be able to judge that what you are seeing is its being elliptical, not, say, its being at an angle.

It follows that subject concepts can be tested and honed only along with at least some applicable predicate concepts and also complements of these. It also follows that Quine was at least close to right about the empirical status of at least one law of logic, the law of noncontradiction applied to empirical judgment. It is an empirical matter that we can carve out concepts of objects along with concepts of properties and their contraries such that the object concepts are suitable to be subject terms for empirical judgment, each consistently taking just one contrary from each of a series of predicate contrary spaces. Just as it is an empirical matter whether anything real has Euclidean structure, it is an empirical matter that there exist objects to judge about that have properties discernable as stable over a variety of perspectives. It is an empirical matter, that is, that there exist any "substances" as these were described in Chapter 2.

In Sellars' famous myth of the necktie shop, Jim teaches shopkeeper John to use the language of "looks" and "seems" after the installation of electric lights has caused John to misjudge the color of one of his neckties:

> "But it *isn't* green," says Jim, and takes John outside.
> "Well," says John, "it was green in there, but now it is blue."
> "No," says Jim, "you know that neckties don't change their colors merely as a result of being taken from place to place."
> "But perhaps electricity changes their color, and they change back in daylight?"
> "That would be a queer kind of change, wouldn't it?" says Jim.
> "I suppose so," says bewildered John.
> (Sellars 1956, pp. 270–1)

Here Jim convinces John to recalibrate his ways of judging color contraries, of making negative color judgments, by appealing to stability of judgment across change in perspectives and conditions as an ideal. Still, his argument for misperception rather than change of color seems rather weak. What really is the evidence that the necktie does not itself change when placed under incandescent light, that the distal stimulus is constant despite the proximal variation? Isn't that a matter of stability in distal causal properties, hence a matter of law, hence of theory? But the evidence against distal change need not digress through theory. Unless other ways can be found of observing this supposed change, unless other perspectives can also reveal it, there is no evidence for it's reality. Evidence for the objectivity of objects and properties can only be obtained by triangulation, triangulation in that there is variety in the kinds of evidence for them. I have argued that triangulation can be achieved through variety in perception taken alone, and it can also be achieved by the use of theory. Presumably neither route is possible in the case of the necktie's change of color.

The myth of the necktie shop raises another and broader question, familiar to us from the earlier discussion of conceptual development (Section 5.7). How does one know what kinds of properties can be expected to be stable over what kinds of perspectives and for what categories of objects? Animals regularly change their shapes over short stretches of time whereas most other physical objects do not. The material gold, as discovered in different places, has any of innumerable shapes and sizes, but is stable with respect, for example, to density, color, malleability and resistance to corrosion. The frog species *Rana pipiens*, as observed in different places and different times, is quite stable with respect to adult size, with respect to the variety and placement of its inner organs, and pretty much all of its behavioral dispositions, but not, say, with respect to shape (postural attitude) or the contents of its stomach. Acquiring concepts of these various substances must involve some understanding of which predicate contrary spaces are correlative to them, that is, of the "substance templates" under which they fall (Sections 1.8 and 2.7), such as person, animal, animal species, plant, plant species, mineral, and so forth. Thus the claim that theories need not be involved in the development and testing of empirical concepts does not imply that no concepts are interdependent.

On the other hand, the ability to reidentify substances is required to guide practical as well as theoretical activities. The practical use of the capacity to reidentify important individuals, kinds, and stuffs probably long predates theoretical conception, ontogenically as well as phylogenetically. In order to accumulate knowledge over time of how to deal with any individual or kind or stuff, also in order to apply what has been learned, an animal must be able to reidentify it over various encounters under a wide variety of circumstances. Practical tests of the adequacy of substance concepts are independent of other concepts, thus providing a certain sort of foundationalist base for the conceptual abilities later employed in theoretical knowing.

8

Content and Vehicle in Perception[1]

§8.1 INTRODUCTION

I have tried to show that the ability to reidentify things that are objectively the same when we encounter them in perception is the most central cognitive ability that we possess. It is an extremely difficult task, deserving careful study by psychologists and neuroscientists as well philosophers. But in order to study how a task is performed one must begin, of course, with some understanding of what that task is. We have not yet asked in what the act of reidentifying consists.

The question is made more difficult by a tradition we have all been trained in, philosophers and psychologists alike, that takes the answer to be obvious. Answers to various other questions have then been constructed on this implicit foundation, so that challenges to it have become both hard to understand and anxiety producing. This traditional answer is that reidentifying an object or property in either perception or thought consists in being able to discriminate it, and that this ability is manifested in sameness of one's reaction to the object, or sameness of one's treatment of it, or sameness of the mental term or concept one applies to it. That is, reidentifying is repeating some kind of response. Call this "the repetition view of reidentifying."

One familiar doctrine constructed on the repetition view is that when sameness in the referential content of two perceptions or thoughts fails to be transparent to the thinker, this is because the content is not thought in the same way both times. It is because one

---

1 Portions of this chapter were revised from "Perceptual Content and Fregean Myth" (Millikan 1991), with the kind permission of Oxford University Press.

does not repeat one's way of thinking of it, because the referential content is not thought of under the same mode of presentation. To fully describe the content of a person's thought thus requires indicating in what way, under what modes of presentation, the various objects of their thought are grasped. A second familiar thesis is that wherever identity of referential content fails to be transparent, this identity can only be grasped by making an identity judgment correlating the two modes of presentation. In the following chapters, I will try to show that these views are mistaken. I will argue for another view of the act of identifying, and supply other tools with which to understand the phenomena that modes of presentation and judgments of identity were introduced to explain.

The point to be made about grasping sameness is a very abstract application of a more general point that pertains to all varieties of mental representation. It will be easiest to explain using quite concrete examples taken from the realm of perception. In Chapter 5, I tried to show how perception of substance sameness was in certain ways similar to or even continuous with cognitive understanding of substance sameness. The basic lesson to be learned about cognitive grasp of identity, also, is applicable to the theory of perception. So here I will temporarily broaden the focus, beginning with points that may at first appear to concern perception alone, only later applying them to cognition. The chapter will be mainly negative. It is no help to introduce a new theory of what grasping sameness consists in unless a need for it has been shown.

§8.2 THE PASSIVE PICTURE THEORY OF PERCEPTION

In its most general form, the confusion that produces the repetition theory of identifying is found also in classical representational theories of perception. It consists in a confusion or mingling of the intentional contents of a representation with attributes of the vehicle of representation. For a starting intuition, compare Kant's suggestion in the Analogies that Hume had confused a succession of perceptions with a perception of succession. In the case of the repetition view of reidentifying, I will later argue, the error consists in confusing sameness in the vehicle of representation with a representation of sameness.

Classical representational theories of perception typically were motivated by an argument from illusion. Verbs of perception all are, in the first instance, achievement verbs. In the primary sense of "see" you cannot see what is not there to be seen, you cannot touch what is not there to be touched, and so forth. If there is perception at all, there must be a real object that is perceived. Add to this the fact that perceptual illusion is possible. Straight oars look bent in the water, and the same bucket of water may be perceived as cold by one hand and hot by the other if one hand is first heated and the other first cooled. A simple step takes us to the conclusion that what is directly perceived is never the real world, but merely an inner representation or picture of it. The representation really is bent, or cold at one hand and hot at the other.

In part, the temptation to make this move results from missing words in the language. In the realm of conception we have the term "know," an achievement verb, but we also have another term "believe," which is a verb only of trying. If you know something, it has to be true, but if you merely believe it, it may or may not be true. Missing are verbs of trying that contrast in this way with the achievement verbs of perception. Suppose then that we introduce a general term for what stands to perceiving as believing stands to knowing. I will coin the term "visaging" for this purpose. Let it stand for apparent hearings and touchings and smellings and so forth, as well as for apparent seeings. There is little temptation to conclude from the fact that you can undergo illusions of knowing that what is known is never what the world is like but only what one's representations of the world are like. The parallel conclusion in the case of perceptual illusion is equally easy to refuse if we allow ourselves to speak of visaging things we are not actually seeing. Believing wrongly about things in the world is not knowing about an inner realm that mediates between me and the world. Visaging things in the world wrongly is not perceiving an inner realm that mediates between me and the world either.

But classical theories of perception claimed otherwise. Clearly there is nothing that we know when we believe falsely. But according to classical theories of perception, there is something that we perceive when we visage falsely. The intentional object of a visaging is always something real, but not, of course, something in the ordinary world. Just as primitive peoples take dreams to be knowledge, though knowledge of another realm, classical theories of perception take illusory visagings to be knowledge, though knowledge of another kind of object.

Visagings were taken to be graspings of, awarenesses of, a realm of representations, and representations, on nearly all the classical views, are likenesses. Visagings were taken to involve items appearing before the mind that are similar to what they represent, hence that *have* the properties that they represent. The properties claimed by visagings to characterize the world exist in "objective reality" (Descartes), or they, or doubles of them, are true of sense data, or percepts, or phenomenal objects, or visual fields, and so forth. Not exactly the same properties, perhaps, but at least properties having something like the same "logical form." When the world resembles the inner picture, then the visaging is veridical, showing how things really are. But like pictures drawn with the purpose of showing how things are, visagings can also misrepresent.

Gareth Evans calls this sort of move "the sense datum fallacy," and then says, "[i]t might better be called 'the homunculus fallacy' . . . when one attempts to explain what is involved in a subject's being related to objects in the external world by appealing to the existence of an inner situation which recapitulates the essential features of the original situation to be explained . . . by introducing a relation between the subject and inner objects of essentially the same kind as the relation existing between the subject and outer objects" (1985a, p. 397). He thus suggests that the main problem with this sort of view is that it invokes a regress. How will the inner eye then perceive the inner picture? In the same way that the outer eye does?

I think this is a mistaken analysis, that regressiveness is not really the problem. Nothing forces a regressive answer to the question how the inner eye works. After all, the purpose of introducing inner representations was to account for error, but there seems no reason to suppose that the inner eye would have the problems the outer eye does of sometimes misperceiving what was there before it. So there would be no need to suppose that it must use additional still-more-inner representations in order to see. What is wrong with this classical view, I submit, is the story that it *does* tell about how the inner eye works. Having projected the visaged properties into the direct presence of the mind, the classical assumption is that there can be no problem about how these properties manage to move the mind so as to constitute its grasp of what they represent. Their mere reclining in or before the mind constitutes the mind's visaging of them and their contents. They are before the mind, hence the mind is aware of them, hence of the properties they embody and represent. That's all there is to the story. Call this the "passive picture theory" of inner representation.

The passive picture theory produces a facade of understanding that overlooks the need to give any account *at all* of the way the inner understander works, any *account* of the mechanics of inner representation, any account of what kind of reacting is comprehending. Clearly it must be the mind's *reaction* that constitutes its understanding of the content of an inner representation. The mere being of the representation cannot by itself constitute an appreciation of it. Rather, the inner eye or mind must understand the representations before it by reacting to them appropriately, by being guided by them appropriately for purposes of thought and action. But once you see that it must be the mind's reaction that constitutes understanding of an inner representation, you see that the picture part of the passive picture theory is also suspect. Why would a picture be needed to move the mind appropriately? At least, wouldn't something more abstractly isomorphic do as well?[2]

Perhaps no philosopher explicitly holds quite the passive picture of perception today. But there are vestiges of this way of thinking in many modern discussions of perception. The passive picture theory has left its mark in arguments that implicitly move from the fact that certain properties are visaged to the conclusion that the vehicle of the visaging must also have these properties. Or they move from the assumption that the vehicle of visaging must have certain properties to the conclusion that these properties must be ones that are visaged. Let us look in detail at some of these moves.

§8.3 INTERNALIZING, EXTERNALIZING, AND THE DEMANDS FOR CONSISTENCY AND COMPLETENESS

The passive picture theory projects properties claimed in or by the visaging onto the inner vehicle of the visaging. Call this move "content internalizing." It also projects properties of the vehicle of the visaging into the visaging's content. Call this move "content externalizing." The illusion is thus created both that one directly apprehends aspects of the nature of the vehicle of perception in apprehending the visaged object, and also the reverse, that one can argue from the nature of the vehicle of perception to what must be being visaged.

One result of these moves is to make it appear problematic how inconsistencies could occur in the content of a visaging. Inconsistencies in content would have to correspond, per impossible, to inconsistencies in the actual structure of the representation's vehicle. We can call this the "demand for consistency" in content. The demand for consistency in a

---

2   I have taken the position that thinking and perception probably both involve inner representation and that representation involves abstract mappings by which representation are projected onto representeds (Millikan 1984 and elsewhere). See also Sections 14.2–4 below. But this claim does not entail that any particular concrete properties and relations are shared by representation and represented. Nor is it likely to be open to merely philosophical demonstration which abstract mathematical relations are shared.

113

visaging's content is what makes it seem problematic how something could appear at the same time both red and not red, or to be both moving and not moving, or to be the same color as, yet a different color from something else (Section 7.3).

A sister result is that there could be no visaging that does not visage also all logically necessary or internal features of what is visaged. For example, there could be no visaging of properties without a simultaneous visaging of their internal relations. Contents lacking, failing to claim, logically necessary or internal features associated with their contents would have to correspond, per impossible, to vehicles lacking logically necessary or internal features of themselves. We can call this the "demand for completeness" in content. Examples of submission to these various demands will be given below.

Internalizing and externalizing moves are enormously interesting, for in certain forms these moves can survive the contemporary turn that explicitly denies the phenomenally given, substituting neural representations for phenomenal ones. Indeed, there are forms in which these moves can survive even the turning of inner representations into mere cognitive dispositions and capacities, or into the states that account for these. I will soon argue that in the case of Fregean senses these moves also can survive turning from perception to cognition, a mode generally thought of as very unpicturelike. For example, the demand for consistency and the demand for completeness each finds subtle expression in Frege's views on conceptual content. Because the confusions that I wish to discuss cut in this way across both theories that postulate experienced and those that postulate nonexperienced inner representations or other nonphenomenal states, I propose to ignore such distinctions entirely. Sense data, percepts, sensations, neural states and acts of grasping Fregean senses, even when the last are interpreted as mere capacities or as states that account for these, are none of them exempt from internalizing and externalizing moves. I will speak indiscriminately, then, of moves covering postulated "intermediaries." Let me emphasize this: I am counting as "intermediaries" even capacities and the states in which they are grounded when these are understood to account for the intentional contents of mental episodes.

The move that I am objecting to is not, of course, that of positing intermediaries. Postulation of intermediaries of some kind is essential to understanding perception and thought. The error is that of projecting, without argument, chosen properties of what is visaged or conceived onto these intermediaries, and vice versa. The error is equally that of taking this sharing of properties to constitute an explanation of mental representing. The passive picture theory causes the underlying nature of the vehicle of thought to disappear from (the theoretician's) view as an agent. The nature of the actual intermediaries for perception or thought, the actual mechanics of these, retires, leaving in its place a frictionless substitute that translates meaning directly into mental action and *vice versa*.

§8.4 INTERNALIZING AND EXTERNALIZING TEMPORAL RELATIONS

Now for examples from perception. No one supposes, nowdays, that visaging colors or shapes requires that any similarly colored or shaped intermediaries should appear either before the mind or in the brain.[3] But have we assimilated the parallel truth about temporal visagings? Daniel Dennett and Marcel Kinsbourne (1992) have spoken to the multitude of confusions about this that persist in the psychological and philosophical literature, citing experiments that show clearly that the order in which one perceives events is not the same as the order in which one perceives the events to occur (see also Jarrett 1999). A succession of impressions does not necessarily produce the impression of succession. But here are two leftovers that are still worth examining.

In "Molyneux's Question," Gareth Evans (1985a) discusses the classic view that the blind cannot perceive space, this because the parts of an object can only be touched in succession, and because successive touchings could not yield a perception of the object's simultaneous spatial layout. Evans' counter is that one cannot argue "from the successiveness of *sensation* to the successiveness of *perception*" and that there is no reason why "the information contained in the sequence of stimulations" might not be "integrated into, or interpreted in terms of, a unitary representation of the perceiver's surroundings" (1985a, p. 368). So far, so good, were he to mean by "unitary representation" only a representation of something unitary. But Evans proceeds to call such representations "simultaneous perceptual representations of the world" (1985a, p. 369), thus expressing his basic agreement with the assumption behind the classic

---

3   Recall, however, this passage from Strawson's *Individuals*, Chapter 2: "Sounds . . . have no intrinsic spatial characteristics . . . [by contrast] . . . Evidently the visual field is necessarily extended at any moment, and its parts must exhibit spatial relations to each other" (Strawson 1959, p. 65). The *visual field* is itself extended?

115

view, that a representation of simultaneity can only be accomplished by simultaneity among elements in the vehicle of representation.[4]

In a similar vein, Evans answers with a confident but unargued "yes" the question "whether a man born deaf, and taught to apply the terms 'continuous' and 'pulsating' to stimulations made on his skin, would, on gaining his hearing and being presented with two tones, one continuous and the other pulsating, be able to apply the terms correctly" (1985a, p. 372). The assumption behind Evans' confidence seems to be that continuousness and pulsatingness in whatever medium must be represented by continuousness and pulsatingness, hence will always be recognized again. Yet first Evans, and then I, have just now represented pulsatingness and continuousness to you without using the pulsatingness or continuousness of anything in order to do so. Evans' assumption illustrates first "content internalizing," then "content externalizing." Perception of pulsatingness both in pressure on the skin and in sound must be represented by pulsatingness in the vehicle of representation, and if these two vehicles possess the same property, pulsatingness, this sameness in properties must produce a visaging of sameness to match.[5]

§8.5 INTERNALIZING AND EXTERNALIZING CONSTANCY

A second example concerns the perception of change *versus* constancy. Consider one of Christopher Peacocke's arguments (Peacocke 1983) for the existence of an intermediary called "sensation."[6] Ironically, his argument is presented in support of the view that the properties of sensation are *not* derivable as mere correlates of the intentional contents of perception. The argument concerns the "switching of aspects" that occurs as one fixates on a neckar cube (or, say, a duck-rabbit). "The suc-

---

4   That this is indeed what Evans intends comes out very clearly in his discussion of "simultaneous" *vs.* "serial" spatial concepts in Part 4 of Evans' "Things without the Mind" (1980).
5   But see also McDowell's footnote in Evans (1985a, p. 373), suggesting that Evans may later have rethought this issue.
6   I am grateful to Christopher Peacocke's challenging work on perceptual content (Peacocke 1986, 1987, 1989a, 1989b), in which he introduces "manners" of perception (1986, 1989a), and contrasts these with Fregean modes of presentation, for leading me to investigate the possible roots of Frege's senses to be discussed here. Although we disagree on some quite fundamental points, without Professor Peacocke's help I should never have thought of looking at Frege in this light. My ungrateful choice of a couple of Peacocke's claims and arguments to use as negative examples in the text that follows reflects that these happened, thus, to be on my desk at the time of first writing, not that they are unusual in any other way.

cessive experiences have different representational contents," Peacocke says, yet "the successive experiences fall under the same type . . . as Wittgenstein writes, 'I *see* that it has not changed' " (Peacocke 1983, p. 16). Peacocke's conclusion is that beneath the change in representational content lies a constancy in properties on the level of sensation. Now assuredly, "that it has not changed" is something that I see, but that *what* has not changed? My visaging has as part of its content that the *world* has not changed – that is where the constancy lies. Peacocke has internalized this content to yield an intermediary, a sensation, that has not changed. Compare a man looking through a perfectly ordinary window who erroneously believes he is watching a 3D movie. He quite automatically takes it that whenever he sees a change or a constancy, that is because the movie screen image has changed or been constant. Analogously, Peacocke's assumption seems to be that a perception of constancy can only be accomplished via an inner intermediary that is itself constant.

This particular assumption, call it "constancy internalizing," which both philosophers and psychologists routinely fall into, has pervasive and far-reaching effects. It produces the illusion of constancy at an intermediary level, not just as shifts in aspect occur, but more devastating, as shifts in attention occur, and even over episodes of perceptual learning. Shifts of attention are, of course, routinely coincident with perception of constancy in the object perceived, indeed, coincident with perception of constancy in the very properties upon which attention focuses and then withdraws. This is true also for episodes of perceptual learning. Learning to perceive, for example, learning to distinguish major triads or learning to see what's in the field of the microscope as microbes, is simultaneous with the perception that what is perceived is not itself changing or undergoing reorganization over the interval. When these constancies are internalized, the illusion is produced that there is a background intermediary corresponding to the whole detailed scene before or around one in perception, an intermediary that changes only when caused to change by changes in the world outside, or by shifts in the perceiver's external relations to that world. This intermediary is traditionally labeled "the sensory field," for example, "the visual field." Nearly everyone still believes in it.

The constancy of the hypothesized sensory field may then be externalized again. If the intermediary that supposedly stays the same is projected to become a constant intentional content for the visaging, we arrive at a backdrop of continuing content from which there emerges a

117

varying foreground as learning or attention switches occur – perhaps as connections are made into conception. Peacocke calls such contents, which in the case of vision determine (densely grouped alternative sets of[7]) complete spatial configurations of objects or surfaces around one, "scenarios" (Peacocke 1987).[8]

Internalizing and externalizing of constancy threatens to produce inconsistency. What is visaged – the intentional object – changes yet the visaging also claims that the world has remained constant. But how could the intermediary of perception remain constant so as to account for the perception of constancy, yet change so as to account for changes in content over changes in attention or over learning? When inconsistency threatens, distinguish levels. Peacocke distinguishes two levels of properties for his intermediaries, "representational properties," and "sensational properties," the first of which concern content, the latter of which do not, although "experiences with a particular sensational property also have, in normal mature humans, a certain representational property" (1983, p. 25).[9] As we will see later, Frege, in a related sort of bind, distinguishes two levels of content so that differences can be projected from one level that are not found on the other.

What would it be to refuse to internalize constancy? Perhaps the perceptual-cognitive systems manufacture perceptual intermediaries piece by piece, only as one needs them, each expressing only a fragment of the content that would be available for expression given other needs. The question whether this is how it works surely turns on empirical evidence, perhaps on neurophysiological evidence, rather than a priori arguments.

§8.6 IMPORTING COMPLETENESS

If some aspect of content, taken by itself, is merely internalized and then externalized again, this will not result in any change of content. But if an aspect of content is internalized and then filled out so as to make

---

7 This feature allows for indefiniteness or indeterminacy due to lack of perfect visual acuity.

8 I had much the same view in mind when I wrote Millikan (1984). There are passages there on perception that may be uninterpretable if one declines to take this view – and with it another relative of Peacocke's views, namely, that perception involves some type of analogue intermediaries. What I claim here is that at least certain arguments for this don't go through.

9 Drawing the distinction between these two kinds of sensational properties is not always easy. See Peacocke (1983, pp. 24–6).

consistent the hypothesis of its inner reality before it is externalized again, the result may be an apparent change in content. This changes the scope of the visaging operator in a way Quine called "importation" (Quine 1956). For example, any property or relation that is internalized from a visaging to an intermediary demands to be filled out and made determinate. For if the intermediary really has the visaged property or relation it must have it in determinate form. Nothing real has indeterminate properties, being, say, rectangular but neither square nor nonsquare. This is how Berkeley argued against abstract ideas. Contents that have been internalized cannot be abstract. But when they are first made to be concrete and then externalized again, the result is a change of scope for the visaging operator. Using a familiar example, if my visaging claims that there exists a large number that is the number of speckles on a certain hen, then there must exist a definite large number that the visaging claims to be the number of speckles on the hen. If V:[(Ex)(x is a number and x is large and there are x spots on a hen)] then (Ex)[x is a number and x is large and V:(there are x spots on a hen)]. There may not be anything wrong with exporting the existence of a number, but the result here is also to import determinacy to within the scope of the visaging operator. That this move is in error becomes clearly evident when one applies it to the visagings of imagination. There the result is that I should not be able to imagine a speckled hen without imagining that it has a certain definite number of speckles. But of course I can easily do so.

Call the move that first introduces determinacy at the intermediary level, then externalizes it as part of the visaging's content, thus moving the intentional verb's scope brackets over, "importing determinacy." This move illustrates the demand for content completeness (Section 8.3), the internal feature required for completeness in this case being determinacy.

A significant form of completeness importing imports determinate relata. Any internal relation between properties, such as *larger than* or, for tones, *a fifth higher than*, that is internalized from a visaging to an intermediary must be provided with appropriate relata, for real relations can't be instantiated, of course, without also instantiating their relata. If the relation *larger than* is actually exemplified, there must be two things having definite sizes for it to be between. If a visaged concrete relation were to be internalized directly, its intermediary being taken to embody that very relation, then the intermediary would be thought, most implausibly, to contain things literally having, say, determinate sizes or pitches. Of course most forms of internalizing for concrete properties and relations are more subtle than this, not the very content itself but an analogue being taken to characterize the intermediary. The intermediary is taken, implicitly, to have properties existing in a logical space isomorphic to that of the visaged. For example, the intermediaries for colors and shapes are taken to "stand to one another in a system of ways of resembling and differing which is structurally similar to the ways in which the colours and shapes of visible objects resemble and differ" (Sellars 1956, p. 193). In either case, determinate relata must be introduced at the level of the intermediary. Externalizing, it then appears that the original visaging must have been of determinate relata. Again, the result is to move scope brackets over for the intentional verb involved. From the fact that my visaging claims that there exist relata related by a certain relation, it is concluded that there exist relata that the visaging claims to be related by that certain relation.

An easy example of the importing of determinate relata is found in Evans' "Molyneux's Question" (1985a). Molyneux's question concerned a man born blind who much later regains his sight. Molyneux asked whether, lacking any prior visual experience, such a man would immediately be able to distinguish a square from a circle by sight. Evans has a contender, B, who gives the question an affirmative answer, use the "very familiar" argument that there could not be an experience of something rotating "in the visual field" without there being "four sides" to the visual field, "a, b, c, d, which can be identified from occasion to occasion" (1985a, p. 386). That is, the experience of rotation requires four determinate "directions" for the rotation to occur from and to.

The importing of determinate relata is implicit in Peacocke's claim that a "matching profile" can be described, for example, for the visual experience of the direction from yourself in which the end of a television aerial lies (Peacocke 1986, 1989a). This matching profile is the area within which the aerial must lie if your experience of its direction is veridical. It is described as a solid angle with yourself at the vertex, and it is determined by seeing how far in space the aerial can be moved without your noticing a difference. But the fact that you can perceive a discrepancy when a certain magnitude has been introduced between direction A and direction B would be evidence that you are discriminating the *absolute* directions of A and B within that range only if visaging a discrepancy required one to visage a direction or range of directions for A and a different direction or range for B. And this would be necessary only if visaging a discrepancy required that the intermedi-

120

aries for the visagings of A and of B be discrepant, thus having different absolute values.

To appreciate that something has gone wrong here, compare pitches. If I can tell there's a difference between two pitches when these are as little as 2 Hz apart, does it follow that I can visage pitches taken separately each within 2 Hz? I don't have absolute pitch. So either I don't hear absolutely – I don't "visage" absolutely – within any such narrow range. That is, I don't definitely visage C# and definitely visage C#-plus-2 Hz in order to visage a discrepancy. Or else I can visage exactly the same content, say the C# content, twice without being aware of the sameness – a possibility to which I will turn a bit later. Certainly it is not clear that my visagings of absolute pitch are in fact so accurate. Indeed, notice that there is no reason to think that there is even any natural information present in me to represent the absolute values of the pitches I hear, for the phenomenon of adaptation is very deep-seated in the structure of the nervous system. Quoting Oliver Selfridge (unpublished), "the range of stimuli that can be distinguished is greatly increased by the power of adaptation [of the nervous system], although the ability to signal absolute intensities is lost."

Peacocke also remarks on "what you can learn about the size of the room by seeing it" that you cannot necessarily learn by measuring it (1989a, p. 299). But my absolute sense of distance is not too good. What I can learn is mostly relative, it seems to me, and will help me only if I know independently something about the sizes of other relata involved. Suppose that I wrongly perceive two items on opposite sides of the room as different in length. In fact they are just the same length. Does it really follow that one or the other of my absolute distance perceptions is wrong? How then is it determined which one is wrong? – Or can one, perhaps, grasp wrongly that the intentional contents of two perceptions are different? In the case of the Müller-Lyer arrows, for example, do you perceive one, or both, as having the wrong length? Or do you perceive each as having its correct length but fail to grasp that this length is the same in the two cases, as one might think of Cicero and think of Tully, that is, think of the same, without grasping the sameness? Similarly, if I perceive things of different length as being the same length, which of the two lengths am I perceiving them both to have?

Another change in scope produced by internalizing and externalizing moves imports internal relations. Any relata that are projected from a visaging to an intermediary must then be provided with all necessary internal relations. If an intermediary really embodies the relata (or analogues of them) it must also embody these relations. Externalizing, it follows that the visaging was also of these relations. Thus, from the fact that A and B bear an internal relation R to one another, and the fact that I visage A and also visage B, it is concluded that I visage R. For example, I could not truly visage middle C and then orchestra A without visaging one as higher in pitch than the other, or visage a square and a triangle without visaging one as having more sides than the other. Or, using the example just above, I could not perceive each of the Müller–Lyer arrows as having its correct length but fail to grasp that this length is the same length. The demand here is for content completeness (Section 8.3).

A final alluring example of importing completeness found in many places is warned against in Lorenz (1962). Animals, presumably, do not represent the world in the same respects that we do. They represent those aspects of the world that are of practical significance to them. There are narrow limits on what they represent. From this it may be concluded that animals represent the world as having narrow limits, or as having only the aspects they represesnt it as having. Similarly, our own understanding of the world has limits, though different limits. So we represent the world as having different limits. It follows that our representation of the world conflicts with that of the animals, indeed, the representation of the world by each type of animal conflicts with the representation by each other type. Every animal's representation of the world, including ours, is necessarily a distortion of the world. Each animal lives in its own world, and none of these worlds are objectively real.

The mistake here involves importing and exporting the limit of a representation. If there is a limit to what is represented, there is a corresponding limit to the vehicle of representation, and a limit to the vehicle of representation is then exported to be a representation of the limits of the represented. But the limit of a representation is not a representation of a limit. Representing only part of the world is not representing this as the only part.

9

Sames versus Sameness in Conceptual Contents and Vehicles[1]

§9.1 SAMES, DIFFERENTS, SAME, AND DIFFERENT

For certain purposes sameness can be treated as a relation.[2] So treated it is of special interest because, although there is only one kind of real sameness relation, hence only one kind of sameness in the real world, and only one kind of sameness on the level of intermediaries (intermediaries are, after all, supposed to be real in their own realm) there are two separate relations corresponding to sameness on the level of intentional content. A visaging might involve (1) two or more presentations of what is the same content in fact or (2) two or more presented contents visaged *as being* the same. Call the first of these a "visaging of sames," the second a "visaging of sameness." Either can occur without the other — as I will slowly try to make clear — or they can occur together. Compare other internal relations. One might visage a tone, say, middle C, and also visage a different tone, say, A above C, but not visage one being a fifth higher than the other though of course it is. Or one might visage that one color was brighter than another without visaging either of these as a definite brightness or even as very definite hues. Imagine, for example, that the lighting is poor and peculiar, so one can't really tell "what the colors are." The passive picture theory of perception (Section 8.2), however, with its projection of properties of the

---

1 Some portions of this chapter were revised from "Perceptual content and Fregean myth" (Millikan 1991) and "Images of Identity" (Millikan 1997b), with the kind permission of Oxford University Press, and from "On unclear and indistinct ideas" (Millikan 1994), in *Philosophical Perspectives, 8, Logic and Language*, with the kind permission of Ridgeview Publishing Company.

2 It is not in fact a relation, as I argue in Millikan (1984, Chapter 12).

visaged onto the intermediaries of the visaging, requires that visaged sameness should correspond to real sameness in intermediaries, that is, that sameness should be represented by sameness. This is what I have called the "repetition" theory of the act of reidentifying (Section 8.1).

Similar remarks go for real difference versus visagings of difference. Although there is only one kind of difference that is real, we must distinguish "visaging differents" from "visaging difference." Consistently held, the passive picture theory of perception would imply that visaged difference should correspond to difference in intermediaries, that is, that difference should always be represented by difference. When coupled with the above thesis that sameness must be represented by sameness, it would imply that no mistakes could ever be made concerning identity versus difference in visaged contents. Let us look at these moves now in more detail.

§9.2 MOVES INVOLVING SAME AND DIFFERENT

Because there are two possible kinds of visaging for same and two for different, there are two kinds of internalizing and two kinds of externalizing moves (Section 8.3) for each. One can internalize sames, or one can internalize sameness, in either case positing both sames and corresponding sameness on the level of intermediaries. One can internalize differents or internalize difference, in either case positing both differents and corresponding difference on the level of intermediaries. One can externalize sames or externalize sameness, projecting assumed sameness of intermediaries into visaged content in either of these ways. One can externalize differents or externalize difference, projecting the assumed difference of intermediaries into the visaged content in either of these ways. Externalizing sames is equivalent to internalizing differents, for if the same vehicles always produce visagings of the same contents then visagings of different contents can only have been produced by different vehicles. Similarly, externalizing differents is equivalent to internalizing sames. But we must be careful, for externalizing sameness is not the same as internalizing difference, nor externalizing difference the same as internalizing sameness. These would be equivalent only on the assumption that visagings are always consistent. In that case, if sameness of vehicle produces a visaging of sameness, assuming it is impossible to visage identity and difference as both obtaining between two things, sameness of vehicle will not be compatible with a visaging of difference, so a visaging of difference would have to have been produced by a difference in vehicle.

The following four simple importation moves (Section 8.3) are possible for same and different.

- One can import sameness. First internalize sames, yielding sames in intermediaries hence sameness in intermediaries, then externalize this sameness. The result is
  (1a) what are the same contents are always visaged *as* the same contents.
  It follows that
  (1b) if you don't visage contents as being the same it must be different contents that are being visaged.
- One can import sames. First internalize sameness, yielding sameness in intermediaries hence intermediary sames, then externalize these sames, yielding
  (2) what are visaged as the same contents always are determinate contents that are indeed the same.
  (For example, you could not hear that two pitches are the same without hearing what pitch they are.)
- One can import difference, yielding
  (3a) what are different contents are always visaged as being different contents.
  It follows that
  (3b) if you don't visage contents as being different they must be the same.
- One can import differents, yielding
  (4) what are visaged as different contents always are determinate contents that are indeed different.
  (For example, you cannot see that two things are different colors without seeing what colors they are, these visaged colors being different.)

Each of these moves yields to a different demand for content completeness, that is, a demand to fill out content with logically necessary aspects so that what is envisaged is a fully determinate state of affairs. But no one of these moves strictly implies any of the others.

If we also apply the demands for determinacy and consistency to visagings of same and different we get the strong result mentioned earlier (Section 9.1) that no mistakes can ever be made concerning sameness or difference among contents of visagings. The demands for determinacy and consistency arise from the necessity that intermediaries, being real, must themselves be determinate and consistent, and from projecting this back into the intentional world of the visaging. By the law of non-contradiction, intermediaries are never both the same and different in any respect, hence that two things are both the same and different in some respect cannot be visaged. By the law of excluded middle, two things are always either the same or different in a given respect, hence intermediaries must be determinate in all respects, hence are always visaged as being either the same or different. For example, if my visaging is of two colored items, it must either be a visaging of them as same in color or else as different in color. ("They all look the same in the dark" – because they don't look different.) Thus when either the demand for consistency or for determinacy is added in, various of the four content-completing moves listed above will imply various of the others, even though when taken merely in pairs, the moves are logically independent. For example, there is no logical connection between content-completing move (1) (what are the same contents are always visaged *as* the same contents) and move (3) (what are different contents are always visaged as being different contents) because there is none between externalizing sameness and externalizing difference, nor between internalizing sameness and internalizing difference.

§9.3 SAME/DIFFERENT MOVES IN THE LITERATURE

Nelson Goodman (1966) attempted to exploit dissociations between internalizing and externalizing different and same in defining identity for qualia. Goodman began by calling attention to an apparent paradox concerning the nontransitivity of identity over appearances. One thing, A, can appear to be the same color as a second thing, B, and the second appear the same as a third, C, yet A appear to be a different color from C. The paradox will result from conjunction of these two internalizing moves. (1) Internalize sameness: If B is visaged as remaining the same while being compared first with A and then with C, it corresponds to an intermediary that remains the same over the comparisons. (Alternatively, this might be treated as an example of internalizing constancy – Section 8.5.) Also, if A is visaged as the same as B, then their intermediaries are the same; likewise for A and C. (2) Internalize difference: If A and C are visaged as different, their intermediaries are different. Goodman calls his intermediaries or their relevant qualities "qualia." A clarification is needed here, however. Qualia are not external objects or their properties, but recline before the mind. And on classical views, what reclines before the mind should not have any part of its nature hidden from mind. Nor can something real lying before the mind have a contradictory nature. Clearly Goodman is conceiving of his qualia here as themselves dividing into two aspects, the real qualia and the appearances of the qualia, only the appearances of the qualia being transparent to mind. The appearances of the qualia are thus the visagings of qualia and the qualia themselves are the vehicles. (Amazing!)

Goodman does not, of course, explicitly analyze the paradox the way I have. But he tries to avoid it, in effect, by now internalizing difference but not sameness and then externalizing sameness but not difference. Qualia α and β are identical just in case every quale γ that matches either α or β also matches the other (Goodman 1966, p. 290), where " . . . to say that two qualia are so similar that they match is merely to say that on direct comparison they appear to be the same" (1966, pp. 272–3). (Notice that qualia, quite explicitly, can appear to be other than they are.) Being very careful, it is not merely difference that is internalized here but lack of sameness, that is, sameness is also externalized. The assumption is that "on direct comparison" qualia that are the same never fail to produce visagings of sameness, so that not appearing the same on direct comparison – not matching – can be a criterion of qualia difference.

Now the sorts of things Goodman calls "qualia" originally were conceived in the tradition to be intermediaries explaining the intentional contents of perceptions of ordinary external objects. Just as Peacocke had to split perceptual intermediaries into two levels with two levels of properties (Section 8.5), if we opted not to be phenomenalists, Goodman's reflections would tempt us to make the same sort of split. The level that contains the appearances of Goodmanian qualia, these being the intentional contents projected by qualia themselves, is the same as the level that acts as intermediary for the perception of the external world. In a moment I will discuss a similar dissociation between the handling of same and different in the Fregean tradition, and a similar split between levels of intentional content engendered.

It is easy to produce paradox by combining internalizing of constancies with internalizing of visaged samenesses and differences. Suppose, for example, that between two identically colored objects a colored band is inserted, one that is subtly graded in color from side to side. The effect may be that while it appears that nothing has been changing color, still what started out looking like two samples of the same color now look like samples of different colors. Or suppose while you are watching, someone draws arrow ends on each of two equal parallel lines, turning them into Müller-Lyer arrows. While appearing not to grow or to shrink, the lines will begin by appearing the same length and end by appearing different lengths. Again: those trees in the distance looked the same size until I noticed the men standing beside them. Now they appear to be quite different sizes, yet things appear not to have changed. If we internalize constancy, sameness, and difference, such visagings would appear to be impossible. The demand here, of course, is for content consistency.

An entirely explicit externalizing and internalizing of the sameness relation occurs in Peacocke's discussion of manners of perception (1986). Using perception of distances as his example he writes "if μ is the manner in which one distance is perceived and μ' is the manner in which a second distance is perceived by the same subject at the same time, and $\mu = \mu'$, then the distances are experienced as the same by the subject (they match in Goodman's sense)" (1986, p. 5). Granted that modes of presentation are supposed to be some kind of real thing, real abstract object, real disposition, real process, real adjectival or adverbial property, real relation, or whatever, as opposed to being merely intentional objects, this externalizes sameness. Next, " . . . the same manner can enter the content of experiences in different sense modalities. You may hear a bird song as coming from the same direction as that in which you see the top of a tree: we would omit part of how the experience represents the world as being were we to fail to mention this apparent identity" (1986, p. 6). That is, a visaging of sameness of direction is produced by some kind of sameness in real intermediaries (sameness in "manner") responsible for these visagings, regardless of the differences between these intermediaries with regard to modality. This internalizes sameness. Thus, Peacocke claims, there are cross-modal manners of perception. I believe that Peacocke intends these moves to be stipulative, defining what *constitutes* sameness of perceptual manner. But such stipulations do not come for free. That there is any such correlated sameness *existing on a nonintentional level* must be argued. What is the argument that the appearance of sameness can only result from the presence of some kind of real sameness? For example, is the appearance of sameness necessarily transitive, as would be required if the appearance of sameness is always associated in this way with the same real manner of perception?

Another way of externalizing sameness is suggested when Evans (1985a) gives a tentative "yes" answer to Molyneux's question. His reasoning is that if perceptions of shape by sight and by touch produce parallel behavioral orientations in the space surrounding one, hence constitute perceptions of space for the same reason, then they are understood to be perceptions of the same. Because "[t]here is only one behavioral space" (Evans 1985a, p. 390) within which grasp of visual and felt shapes are manifest, there could be no problem about identifying across these modalities. Again, relevant sameness in relevant intermediaries – the intermediaries here are dispositions to orient oneself in space or the states in which these are rooted – is externalized to yield a visaging of sameness. Behaving the same in response to visual and tactual perceptions is grasping content sameness.

§9.4 SAME AND DIFFERENT IN THE FREGEAN TRADITION[3]

Now perhaps we are warmed up enough to discuss sameness and difference in the more abstract context of theories of thought or conception.

Frege's senses (or more accurately but awkwardly, "graspings" of these) are his "intermediaries," given our gloss, for beliefs about the world. Graspings of senses of the kind Frege calls "thoughts" are what stand between mind and world, making errors in thought possible when harnessed by mental acts of assertion. Also, senses are what move the mind, as vehicles should. Differences among various grasped senses account for differences in mental movement if the mind is rational. Senses also actually *constitute* a level of intentional content – they *are* intentional contents – just as Peacocke's intermediary for perception has not only "sensational properties" but also "representational properties" (Section 8.5), and just as Goodman's qualia, if freed from phenomenalism, would serve both as vehicles for visagings of the ordinary world and as things that are themselves visaged (Section 8.7). But let us put the latter feature of Fregean senses aside for the moment and consider them merely in their role as vehicles for reference to the world.

Frege certainly did not explicitly intend to project properties of things as thought of – call these "conceptually visaged properties" – upon his intermediaries. Contrast Hume, who took thoughts to be copies of impressions, themselves clearly picture-like. Frege's senses are modeled, very abstractly, on sentences and sentence parts, not pictures. Given this model, the only internalizing/externalizing games that can still be played are with sameness and difference.

---

3   I am no Frege scholar. I speak here to the understanding philosophers have mostly had of Frege, not to his texts.

First, Frege externalizes sames, hence internalizes differents (Section 8.7). That is, he assumes that if the vehicles are the same − that if the senses grasped are the same − then the referents are the same. Grasping a sense is a way of conceptually visaging something. And the way of visaging is not separable from the thing visaged. One cannot visage two different things in the same way. Repeating a way of visaging also repeats the thing visaged.

Is any alternative to such a view possible? Is it possible not to externalize sames in the case of thoughts? In Chapter 10, I will argue that there are many alternatives to externalizing sames. Here let me suggest just an analogy. In natural language, sames are not always externalized. The pronoun "he" might stand for any male person. Also, there are lots and lots of people named "Jane." But the issue is complex. I will discuss it in Chapters 10 and 11.

If sames are externalized as Frege does, and then senses or ways of visaging are taken to be transparent to mind, the immediate result is internalism concerning thought content. Thus Frege's senses determine their own referents, each distinguishing its referent from all other things, and nothing external to what is grasped within the mind is relevant to this determination. This view contrasts sharply with the thesis of this book. Suppose that Frege is right to externalize sames. Suppose that it is a psychological fact that human conceptual systems are designed to use the same vehicle again only to represent the same content again. Still, what the human cognitive systems were designed to do and what they in fact manage to do would be two separate things. Mistakes in reidentification are surely possible, in which case the same vehicle again may not represent the same content again.

Frege externalizes not only sames but also sameness. If senses are the same, then the corresponding referents are necessarily conceptually visaged as same, or necessarily available to the rational mind as same. That is why the rational mind cannot take contrary intentional attitudes toward referents conceptually visaged under the same mode of presentation. And that is why identity judgments are uninformative when the sense of subject and predicate terms is the same. It follows, of course, that whenever referents are not conceptually visaged as same, the corresponding senses are always different. And in accord with the demand for consistency in content, when referents are visaged as different they are not also visaged as same, hence, senses are again different.

The thesis that grasped senses' merely *being* the same is equivalent to visaging their referents *as* the same is the passive picture theory of cognitive grasp of identity and a form of the repetition view of the act of reidentifying. I will discuss alternatives to this view in the next two chapters. Here let me merely note that if one adds to the externalization of both sames and sameness the assumption that senses or ways of visaging are transparent to mind, the result is that where senses are the same, sameness of reference in thought is known a priori and with certainty. This particular Fregean thesis might be viewed as the central target of this book. If I accomplish nothing else, I should like at least to make clear that this thesis is a substantive claim, not a necessary truth.

Frege externalizes sames and sameness but, like Goodman, he does not externalize either differents or difference. Referents may be taken to be the same even though the grasped senses are different. For example, this is how the thoughts *Cicero* and *Tully* are related for one who knows that Cicero is Tully. Where senses are different, their referents may be conceptually visaged either as same or as different, or neither visaged as same nor as different. Since difference is not externalized, failure to visage difference is not internalized nor, in accord with the demand for consistency in content, is sameness internalized. Conceptual visaging of sameness can be accomplished actively through identity judgments as well as passively through sameness in grasped sense. Identity judgments can visage sameness of reference despite difference in sense.

On the other hand, Frege introduces a second level of content (like Peacocke and our nonphenomenalist version of Goodman) onto which he projects sames, sameness, differents, and difference, indeed, on which no distinctions at all are drawn between content and vehicle. The sense contents in Ayer's *Language, Truth and Logic* were like Frege's senses in this way. They were their own intentional objects, lying passively within awareness and being visaged (intended) by mind in the same act. For Frege, differences in vehicle, differences in sense, become differences in content on this second level. Senses are intentional contents. On this level, thought forms an ideal vehicle, nonredundant and unambiguous, one thought one content, one content one thought. The fact of sameness or difference in content can be read off the sameness or difference of thoughts and vice versa. Thus for the rational thinker no misidentifications of thought content should ever occur. Contradictions show up right on the surface of thought so that no inconsistencies should occur either. The relation between thought and its content is perfectly transparent, indeed, it entirely disappears. There is no vehicle moving the mind but the very content itself.

Why does Frege introduce a second level of content onto which *differents and difference* can be projected in this way? What happened in *Frege's* mind is clearly documented. First, he saw that in the case of differing definite descriptions referring to the same there *was* a way in which they did, but another in which they didn't, have "the same content." They referred to the same thing, but they got there by different routes and from different starting points, from initially different visagings of referents. They made their contributions to truth values in different ways. But this does not give us a distinction among levels of content for the starting points, or not without regress. It does not give us a difference in content between the thought *Tully* and the thought *Cicero*, for example. Why then did Frege generalize? Why did he project two levels of content upon apparently *simple* thoughts?

Frege's second move is continually rehearsed in the literature. *Cicero is Tully* is an informative thought whereas *Cicero is Cicero* is not, so these thoughts must have different contents. But, quite transparently, that begs exactly the question at issue. Of course the thoughts corresponding to "Cicero" and "Tully" are *different*, at least for some people, or they couldn't move these people's minds differently. Their causal action on these people's minds is not the same, so clearly they are mediated differently. The question is whether their *contents* must be different in order for this to be so. Might they not differ instead, as it were, merely in notation, in vehicle?

One has to assume same–different transparency, in particular, one has already to have externalized differents, for this Fregean argument to go through. One has already to believe that only different *contents* could correspond to, that is, either determine or be determined by, different movements of the mind. But it is perfectly possible that even though the same movements of the mind always corresponded to the same contents again, different movements sometimes corresponded to the same content as well. Sames can be externalized without externalizing differents. One needs an argument that different movements of the mind always correspond to semantic differences, to different ways of helping to determine truth value. One needs an argument that only content can affect movements of the mind, that there is no vehicle moving the mind but the very content itself. Or one needs an argument that different movements of the mind result in different contents, different ways of helping to determine truth value, if that is the direction in which the determination goes.

In confusing the content of thought with its vehicle, I believe the passive picture or repetition theory of the act of reidentifying is surely mistaken. This point needs to be made very generally. For example, no matter what kind of description is given of "modes of presentation," say, as words or descriptions in a language of thought, or as graspings of abstract objects, or as presentations of Kaplan-style character types, or applications of concepts with certain possession conditions (Peacocke), or ways that the thinker knows which object it is he thinks about (Evans), and so forth, still, the repetition of such a referential mode of thought would not, simply as such, *constitute* an act of reidentifying content. Reciprocally, there can be no direct argument from the fact that a certain sameness of content is or is not grasped to a conclusion about identity or difference for corresponding "intermediaries" (Section 8.3). There can be no direct argument from the necessary visaging of sameness (by a rational or well-oiled mind), say, from the impossibility of taking opposing attitudes toward contents, to a conclusion about repetition of aspect in the presentation of these contents, that is, to a conclusion about sameness of mode of presentation as this notion is usually understood.

Supposing that identical intermediaries always possess identical contents (that is, suppose we externalize sames), then sameness in intermediaries will be an *indication* of sameness in content, perhaps it will contain the fact of this sameness as natural information and so forth. But compare: Two bee dances danced side by side may jointly be an indication, or between them contain the natural information, that two sites of nectar are forty yards apart. It does not follow that the bees can read this information off the pair of dances. Not everything that falls out of a representational system is necessarily read or readable even by its primary interpreters. If we have rejected the passive picture theory of inner representation we should also be able to see that the mere being the same of two thoughts or percepts does not accomplish anything all by itself even when the fact of this sameness is a natural indication of sameness in content, or when this sameness is an implication of the content represented. The fact of sameness must be *read* somehow if it is to represent, rather than just be, a sameness. This sameness must appropriately interact with or *move* the thinking system in some way if it is to represent itself.

Nor should we fall into this nearby error: The way that the system must move or be moved in order to be grasping a sameness is just in-the-same-way-again. Given the same context, having the same effects may be secured, of course, just by being the same. Having the same effects is merely a part of being the same, and does not add anything to it.

Consider the story of Zak, a patient at the Bell Neurological Institute, a victim of stroke, suffering selective amnesia. Each morning, Dr. Helm comes in to see Zak, wearing a white coat and a name tag that says "Dr. Helm, MD." Each morning Zak greets him with "good morning, Dr. Helm," and when asked if he knows who Helm is, being no fool, Zak unhesitatingly answers "my doctor." The appearance is thus that Zak always identifies Helm the same way and correctly. Nor, we suppose, does Zak have problems articulating a theory of the identity of persons over time; he used to be a philosophy professor. Upon further questioning, however, each morning Zak reveals that he does not remember ever having seen Helm before, nor does he show any signs of familiarity with the routine Helm puts him through each morning. That is, it appears that Zak does not recognize Helm after all. Though he appears to have an individuating idea of Helm, even what Gareth Evans would call a "fundamental Idea" of Helm (Section 13.3), he is incapable of reidentifying him. He has no concept of this person that lasts over time.

Compare a much simpler case. The frog that reacts the same way each time its optic-nerve bug-detector fires does not thereby cognize a sameness among the bugs it eats. Something rather like the opposite is true, I suggest. A creature's perception that it is encountering the same thing again shows up, characteristically, in its reacting *differently* this time, differently according to what it learned last time. That the baby recognizes you is exhibited not in its crying again – that is how it reacts to strangers – but in its smiling, or exhibiting other behaviors apparently based on its earlier experience with you. And, of course, the notion that reidentifying a thing involves "applying the same concept again," say, attaching the same thought or mental name to it, is precisely the central version of the passive picture theory we have been discussing all along.[4]

As mentioned in Section 9.3, there is a passage in which Evans answers Molyneux's question by externalizing sameness, taking behaving the same in response to visual and tactual perceptions to constitute visaging of sameness in content. It would be odd to call this an application

---

4 But see also Section 10.3.

of the "passive picture theory" of the act of identifying. But the general principle is exactly the same. It is another kind of example of the repetition theory of the act of reidentifying. Surely, merely effecting the same connection with "behavioral space" again is not to manifest a grasp of anything's sameness.

In what kind of way *does* one's thinking have to move then, or in what kind of way *does* one have to behave, in order to grasp an identity? That is what Chapter 10 is about.

10

Grasping Sameness[1]

§10.1 INTRODUCTION: IMAGES OF IDENTITY

In *Subject and Predicate in Logic and Grammar*, Strawson (1974) offers "a picture or model" of what happens when a man learns that two things formerly thought to be separate are in fact one and the same. "We are to picture a [knowledge] map, as it were" on which all those individuals the man knows of are represented by dots, and the predicates the man knows to apply to each are written in lines emanating from these dots or, if the predicate is relational, lines joining two dots.

Now when [the man] receives what is for him new information . . . he incorporates [this] by . . . making an alteration on his knowledge map [for example,] he draws a further line between two dots. But when it is an identity statement containing two names from which he receives new information, he adds no further lines. He has at least enough lines already; at least enough lines and certainly one too many dots. So what he does is to eliminate one dot of the two, at the same time transferring to the remaining one . . . all those lines and names which attach to the eliminated dot. (Strawson 1974, pp. 54–5.)

On Strawson's picture, the identity of a particular is represented in the mind by the identity of another particular.[2] So long as you haven't

---

1 Portions of this chapter were revised from "Images of Identity" (Millikan 1997b), with the kind permission of Oxford University Press, and from "On unclear and indistinct ideas" (Millikan 1994), which appeared in *Philosophical Perspectives, 8, Logic and Language*, edited by James E. Tombelin (copyright by Ridgeview Publishing Co., Atascadero, CA). Reprinted by permission of Ridgeview Publishing Company.

2 I will move back and forth between idioms appropriate to traditional thinking about minds, and idioms more appropriate to thinking about brains, on the assumption that the structural forms we will be comparing are abstract enough to justify this. Theories of

made any mistakes, everything you know about your mother is attached to the same *particular* mental representation of your mother, to the same token. Your understanding that all these facts are facts about the same woman consists in the representations of the logical predicates of each of these facts being attached to numerically the same "dot" in your mind or brain. Call this the "Strawson model" of how identity or sameness is thought.

A more familiar model pictures thoughts each as a separate sentence token in a mental language. On this model the identity of a particular is represented by the identity of a mental word type rather than the identity of a token or particular. What Strawson would model using a single dot and two lines, a language of thought model renders as two different sentence tokens containing a word type in common, say, <Tom is married> and <Tom is harried>. Generalizing this to any system in which sameness is represented by duplication of form, we can speak of the "duplicates model" of how identity is represented. The use of this model should be carefully distinguished from the repetition view of the act of identifying, scouted in Chapter 9. The duplicates model is a model of how identity is represented. The repetition view from Chapter 9 concerns what constitutes the act of reidentifying, that is, what constitutes that the mind understands a certain representation of identity *as* a representation of identity. Compare: I can represent a dog by drawing a picture of a dog or by writing down the word "dog" or by saying "dog." The question what it is for me to understand any of these *as* a representation of a dog is another matter entirely. It might be claimed, for example, that although the appearance of identical representational vehicles does not actually *constitute* an act of identifying, still a reasonable hypothesis about the mechanics of human conception is that our conceptual mechanisms have a compulsory disposition to perform acts of identifying *over* identical representational vehicles.

Another model of how identity might be represented, one also taken from language, is the "equals" model. Here a second marker, a mental equals sign, rides piggyback on the duplicates marker, indicating *examples* of two different duplicatable types. The effect of this "identity

thought inevitably proceed on the assumption that there are abstract analogies between how thoughts work and how more mundane things work or might work. Think, for example, of Plato's *Theaetetus* with its mind that talks to itself, its wax imprints and its birds, or to the classical tradition that ideas are "like" their causes or that ideas are "associated" in the mind, and so forth. My talk about "the Strawson model," "the Christmas lights model," "the synchrony model," and so forth, should be understood in the same spirit.

belief" is that all tokens of either exemplified type are then treated as representing the same.

An absorbing contemporary discussion among cognitive neurologists concerns the "binding problem." Neurological evidence indicates that various kinds of sensory information arriving from the same object, such as information about form, color, and direction of motion, are not processed in the same area of the brain but filtered through "widely disseminated feature detecting neurons located even in different areas or cerebral hemispheres" (Engel 1993). How then is it represented that these various features belong to the same object, and not to entirely different objects merely copresent in the perceptual field? One hypothesis is that synchronous spiking in neural firing patterns on a millisecond time scale indicates which sets of neurons are responding to the same object. Roughly, cells that fire together purport to talk about the same object; identity is represented by synchrony. If identity might be represented this way in perception, why not also in thought? Call this the "synchrony model" of how identity is thought.

Connectionist explorations suggest as a crude model that units representing the same object might be strongly connected so that they tend to be activated together like Christmas tree lights on the same string. Then a certain causal connection would represent identity. Call this the "Christmas lights model" of how identity is thought.

Anaphoric pronouns, which occur in all natural languages, suggest a model according to which each representation of the same object bears some kind of pointing relation to prior representations of that same object. Call this the "anaphor model" of how identity is thought.

And so forth.

Now it is strongly emphasized in the Fregean tradition that representing the same referent twice, representing it once and then again, must be carefully distinguished from representing it *as being* the same referent again. If someone represents Mark Twain to herself and then represents Samuel Clemens, she represents the same thing twice, but it does not follow that she represents or understands that these are the same. Reflection on the above models, combined with the reflections in Chapter 9, shows that we should be equally careful to distinguish between representing the same thing twice *in the same way*, that is, duplicating a representation of it, and representing it *as being* the same thing again. If someone represents Mark Twain to herself in a certain way and then represents Mark Twain again in exactly the same way – if she duplicates a representation of Mark Twain – it does not follow that she represents or understands that the two referents are the same. To assume this would be either to embrace the passive picture view of the act of reidentifying, or else to beg the question how the mind or brain represents identity. If the latter, it would assume that *duplication* is used by the mind/brain as a sameness marker prior to any evidence that this is the case. There is no reason to suppose in advance that it is sameness – likeness – that represents sameness.

Employing an example from perception, suppose that you observe the same individual apple in exactly the same context from exactly the same angle under exactly the same lighting conditions on two different occasions, and make exactly the same perceptual and cognitive response to it each time. Merely as such, this fact neither constitutes that you recognize the apple as being the same apple again, nor need it trigger or produce such a recognition, either perceptually or cognitively. On the other hand, there are relations other than duplication among percepts that mark object identity across time straightaway for the human perceiver, namely, the right continuities in perceived place and time. Given the right continuities, one's perception may be of an object as being the same one over a period of perceptual tracking despite its apparently changing in every one of its observed properties. This sort of tracking of an object, say, with the eyes, does not involve *repeating* some particular way of perceiving or thinking of the object, or repeating some way of recognizing it over and over. It is not repetition that constitutes or triggers perceptual grasp of identity.

What I have been saying about mental markers for identity of individuals also applies, of course, to markers for other kinds of sameness. Just as representing the same individual twice in the same way is not representing it *as* the same individual, representing the same property twice in the same way is not representing it *as* the same property – not unless duplication happens to be what the system uses as its sameness marker for properties. We cannot assume without evidence, for example, that whenever the same color, shape, or distance are represented in perception the same way twice, once on the left, say, and once on the right, one ipso facto recognizes these properties *as being* the same. Also recall, for example, the identifying of a heard with a seen direction. Although this kind of identifying is automatic, even compulsory, it is implausible that an identity in vehicles triggers it. Recall also that we can *learn* to perceive hitherto unrecognized identities directly or compulsorily via perceptual learning. It seems implausible that the vehicles of perception are somehow changed accordingly so that they now match.

A system of thought might also use different sameness markers for different kinds of identities. As Strawson described his own model, the sameness markers for predicates were not what I have called "Strawson markers," but were duplicates markers.

In this chapter, I propose to address the question what would *constitute* that a mind or a brain was using one method of marking sameness rather than another.

§10.2 LOCATING THE SAMENESS MARKERS IN THOUGHT

Suppose that the cognitive neurologist – or God – looks down into the mind/brain with an eye to deciphering which of its various states or events are the ones representing identities. How is the neurologist or God to tell, given a mind in motion, *how* it is thinking identities?

First, we might ask, on what evidence do neurologists *in fact* suppose that synchrony may be the brain's marker of identity for perceived objects? The evidence they give is that synchrony is in fact found (in monkeys and cats) among cells responding to the various properties of numerically the same visually presented objects. At least within the more accessible visually involved layers of the brain, information about one and only one individual object feeds into one synchrony, information about others into other synchronies.

Generalizing the neurologist's method suggests that evidence for some feature being the sameness marker used by a system is that information derived from the same thing in the environment systematically shows up marked by this marker. Thus, evidence for Strawson's model would be that all and only structures bearing information derived from numerically the same environmental source showed up attached to numerically the same something-or-other in the brain or mind; evidence for the duplicates model would be that all and only structures bearing information derived from numerically the same source showed up attached to structures alike by some specified principle of likeness, and so forth.

There is an obvious problem with this method, nor has it escaped notice by the neurologists (e.g., Singer 1995). Synchrony among neuronal firings caused by the same object may be only a byproduct of the brain's perceptual activities. That these neurons fire synchronously may have no connection with any cognitive work done by the brain. That a bit of natural information about sameness of source resides in the brain does not prove that the brain *uses* or *understands* this information, any more than the presence of natural information in the sky carried by

140

black clouds proves that the sky thinks it will rain. Compare the hypothesis that certain neurons in the visual system are "feature detectors." The circuitry that produces firing of such neurons may seem to be intricately specialized to support this function, but the final proof must demonstrate that the firings are *used as* feature detectors, that is, that the information collected by them actually guides the organism to take account of the features apparently detected. Similarly, for whatever is found in the brain or mind that appears to be a sameness marker. What the neurologists would like to show is that synchrony is not just a natural indicator of sameness, but is effective in guiding thought and action to take account of the indicated sameness. It appears then that we must start further back. We must ask, what is involved in *using* a marker *as* a sameness marker? What does a mind have to do in order to manifest understanding of its own sameness markers? In what kind of way does one's mind have to move in order to grasp an identity?

Begin by asking, what is the point of grasping identity? What does one *do* with a knowledge of identity? Why should it matter to any organism whether or not various pieces of information that it has acquired are about the same object or about different objects? Suppose that I recognize for the first time that Cicero is Tully. What am I able to do that I was not able to do before? Well, if I knew before that Cicero was bald, I now also know that Tully was bald. And how does that change anything, that I now know that Tully was bald? After all, I already knew that Cicero was bald and that was exactly the same thing to know. Why not be satisfied with knowing some things about Cicero under one idea of him, other things under other ideas of him, even if I don't know that these ideas grasp the same? So long as I pack all the right information in one way or another, why does it matter (putting things in familiar duplicates-model terminology) what notation I use? Why does an organism need to have sameness markers in perception or thought?

It matters because if I don't recognize the identity of Cicero with Tully, then I cannot combine the various things that I know about this man, Cicero/Tully, so as to yield anything new. I cannot perform mediate inferences using the thought of Cicero/Tully as a middle term. Taking a mundane and more general example, suppose that I perceive that α is orange and that β is round and that γ smells sweet and that δ is fist-sized and that ε is within reach. Why does it matter whether $\alpha = \beta$, or whether $\delta = \varepsilon$, and so forth? Because if $\alpha = \beta = \gamma = \delta = \varepsilon$, but only then, probably this is a reachable orange, hence can provide me nourishment. Only by using these various bits of information *together* can this understanding be reached. But these bits can be used together legitimately only if they all carry information about the same. Suppose that I believe that A is smaller than B and that C is smaller than D. Only if I also grasp both that B = C, and also that the thought *smaller than* has the same content in both beliefs, can I make an inference: A is smaller than D.

Some middle terms are predicative (A *is smaller than* B and B *is smaller than* C . . .) and some are propositional rather than denotative (if P then Q, and P, therefore Q) but there is always at least one repeated element involved in an amplificatory inference. Again, suppose that I believe that Cicero is bald but that Tully is not. Only if I also understand both that Cicero = Tully and that the thought *bald* has the same content in both beliefs can I discover that I am involved in a contradiction. Consider a person manipulating symbols to derive theorems in a logical system. In such a system, identity is marked, primarily, by duplication. Does such a person do the same thing again whenever the same referential symbol is encountered again? The reaction depends, rather, on the context in which the representation is found, reactions being, paradigmatically, to pairs of strings, which the reader combines to yield a third. Such combinings invariably require an overlap in the two strings, a "middle term." The middle term has to be duplicated in the two premises for a rule of mediate inference to apply.

Nor do we need the image of a language of thought in order to grasp the role that reidentifying plays in amplifying information. Imagine a creature that carries mental maps of various places it has been about in its head. It has a map of the locale in which it last found water, and another of the locale in which it last saw lions. On each of these maps its den is marked. Now imagine that it overlaps these maps, using its den as a pivot, and arrives at a third map showing the proximity of lions to the source of water. Guided by this new map, it seeks a new source of water rather than going back to the lion-infested source on its map. As is characteristic of all mediate inference, two vehicles of information have been combined, pivoting on a middle term, an overlap, so as to produce a third vehicle containing new information. Thus our creature exhibits a grasp of the sameness in content of the two representations of his den that were on the two original maps.

More basic even than the involvement of identifying in theoretical inference is its involvement in practical inference, action, and learning. It is

142

only through recognizing the identity of an item currently perceived with an item known or perceived earlier that what was learned earlier can be joined with what is perceived now to yield informed action. Suppose that I wish to congratulate A on his engagement and that I see that B is in the lounge talking to C. This seeing will be of no use to me unless I grasp whether A = B or A = C. Consider learning. Suppose baby has noticed that A scolded her when she cried but that B, C, and D kindly picked her up. Whether she learns anything from this will depend on which if any of these four she takes to be the same person again.

Returning to Evans' speculations on Molyneux's question and behavioral space (Section 9.3), it is not a person's ability to be motorically guided *in the same way* by perceptions from different sensory modalities that would manifest grasp of sameness of content represented through these modalities. Rather, such a grasp would be manifested in the ability to combine information obtained through these different modalities to yield behavior or thought guided by both put together. Or, taking a different sort of example, consider a duckling that has imprinted on its mother. The result of imprinting is that whenever the duckling sees its mother, a certain set of behavioral dispositions emerges. The duckling has stored away a "template" matching its mother's appearance so as to "recognize" her. Despite our natural use of the term "recognize" in this context, it does not *follow* (though it may of course happen to be true) that the duckling reidentifies its mother (for example, that it has a substance concept of her). Only in so far as the duckling is capable of learning things *about* its mother on some encounters to apply on other encounters with her does it identify her. Just reacting the same to her time after time does not indicate identification.

Every mediate inference, every recognition of a contradiction, everything learned either from perception or inference and applied in action, every belief or behavior issuing from coordination among sensory modalities, for example, eye-hand coordination, even such subpersonal activities as the use of images from two eyes in depth perception, depends upon recognition of content sameness. Grasp of identity is the pivot on which every exercise of perception and thought must turn that collects together different pieces of information from different perceptual modalities, or from different contexts, or over time, and effects its interaction. Every act of identifying is thus implicitly an act of *re*identifying, consisting in the use of two or more representations or pieces of information together. Described on the level of content, on the level of the visagings or believings-that involved, we call these "acts of identifying" or "reidentifying." Described on the level of the vehicles or mental bearers of information involved, we can call them acts of "coidentifying." In an act of coidentifying, two representational vehicles are employed together in a manner that assumes, that is, requires for correctness, an overlap or partial identity in content, thus effecting an act of reidentifying of content.

§10.3 SUBSTANCE CONCEPTS AND ACTS OF REIDENTIFYING

The thesis of Section 10.2 can be put as follows:

For a perceiver or cognizer to reidentify something JUST IS to be disposed, or for some subsystem of theirs to be disposed, to pair representations of that thing in perception and/or thought as a middle term for mediate inference, or other amplificatory information-processing, and/or for guiding action.

That will do for a first pass over the phenomenon of recognizing sameness.

A second pass must take into account that where valid mediate inferences are made, or correct content-sameness pairings or groupings are made for other information-using purposes, this result must follow from some kind of indication in the initial or "premise" representations of where sameness of reference is occurring. It must result from a system or systems of sameness marking in perception and thought – perhaps using Strawson-style markers, and/or duplicates markers, and/or Christmas light markers, and so forth.

What makes a marker a sameness marker is that the perceptual/cognitive systems use it to control the mediate inferences and other content pairings that they make in guiding amplificatory information-processing and action.

Derivatively, then, the mere occurrence of an appropriate sameness marker connecting two perceptions or thoughts can count as an "understanding" that the marked representations are representations of the same. It is, as it were, a "first act understanding of sameness," where a "second act understanding" is an actual process of mediate inference, amplificatory information processing, or action guidance controlled by these markers. First act identifications, sameness markings, prepare for second act identifications.

Suppose that in the case of thoughts of substances, we were to take first act identifications to be "applications of substance concepts." That is, "applying a substance concept" would be marking incoming information in such a way that its bearers will be ready for coidentification with certain other information bearers. "Applying a substance concept" will be readying bearers of incoming information for interaction with a restricted set of other information bearers – those bearing information about the same substance. Then there will be, after all, a sense in which "applying the same substance concept" counts as an act of identifying or recognizing sameness. But this sense of "substance concept" will be that in which the abilities that are substance concepts are counted or individuated by their ends, not their means. Substance concepts must be scrupulously distinguished from *conceptions* of substances (Sections 1.9, 4.8, and 6.3) in this context.

A third pass over the question what it is for content sameness to be recognized in thought should take error into account. Under unfavorable conditions, even simple perceptual identification tasks can be mismanaged. For example, there is a way of crossing your fingers so that the identity markings that bridge between tactile and visual percepts become mixed. The finger one sees being touched does not seem to be the finger one feels being touched. When looking through a stereoscope your visual systems misidentify portions of two pictures as portions of the same, thus producing the illusion that you are looking at a three dimensional scene. The skill of sleight of hand artists depends largely on their ability to fool your visual systems into failing to track objects correctly, thus inducing perceptual misidentifications.

Such misidentifications do not occur commonly, and may require specially designed apparatuses or other circumstances of perception to induce them. Conceptual responses to the data of sense, on the other hand, are more tenuously correlated with affairs in the world than are perceptual responses. Failure to mark sameness correctly in thought is quite common. We often fail to recognize a thing, or we confuse two things together, say, mistaking Jim for Bill or failing to distinguish between mass and weight. Consider, then, a mediate inference that is made over two premises containing information in fact derived from different sources. The premises do not carry information concerning the same thing, and as a result, let us suppose, the conclusion arrived at is false. Should such an erroneous move count as a mistake in inference? Or should it count merely as a mistake in data collection and labeling?

Which internal moves should count as valid inferences would seem to depend on how sameness of origin is marked during data collection. But how sameness of origin should be marked during data collection surely depends on what sameness markers the inferencing systems will recognize. There will be nothing wrong, for example, with representing two different objects with identical representations so long as duplication is not the identity marker. Does it follow that which structures really are the sameness markers is well defined only for a system that never makes mistakes?

This kind of problem is classic, of course, for theories of naturalized thought-content. These theories typically take cognitive abilities to be some kind of dispositions (Chapter 4), or to rest on *ceteris paribus* laws. The problem is then taken to concern "idealization." How far away from a certain ideal can a system's actual practice or actual dispositions be while still counting as an example of a given ideal type? What do we say about content when the system hovers indeterminately between or among alternative ideal types?

My own preference is to refer instead to evolutionary design on this sort of question (Millikan 1984, 1993a, in press b). There will be ways that our perceptual-cognitive systems worked when they operated such as to be selected for by natural selection. There will be a way or ways, that is, that they were "designed" to mark and to recognize sameness. With enough knowledge of the internal mechanisms controlling cognition, what these normal ways are should be no harder for us to distinguish than, say, how the human eye is designed to work, even though many human eyes function poorly. The distinction between having gone wrong in collecting the data and having gone wrong in inference may then be a perfectly objective distinction.

Thus there is room to distinguish two kinds of error, either of which might be called an error of misidentification. There could be error in performing a first act identification, that is, an error in the labeling of incoming data. Or there could be an error in second act identification, an error in mediate inference, or an analogue, of the general sort traditionally labeled "the fallacy of the fourth term." The first would be an error in the fixation of belief, the second an error in inference or an analogue of inference. I will not try very hard to keep these possibilities distinct in the chapters that follow, though occasionally it will be helpful to recall their difference.

11

In Search of Strawsonian Modes of Presentation[1]

§11.1 THE PLAN

There are many alternative ways that a mind or brain might represent that two of its representations were of the same object or property – the "Strawson" model, the "duplicates" model, the "equals sign" model, the "synchrony" model, the "Christmas lights" model, the "anaphor" model, and so forth (Section 10.1). In the last chapter I discussed what would *constitute* that a mind or brain was using one of these systems rather than another in order to mark identity. In this chapter, I discuss the devastating impact of the Strawson model of identity marking on the notion that there are such things as modes of presentation in thought. I will then argue that Evans' idea that there are "dynamic Fregean thoughts" has exactly the same implications as the Strawson model. In Chapter 12, I will claim that, in fact, all of the other models of identity marking we have discussed are strictly isomorphic to the Strawson model, hence have exactly the same devastating results for modes of presentation. There is no principled way to individuate modes of presentation such as to achieve any semblance of the set of effects for the sake of which Frege introduced them.

§11.2 NAIVE STRAWSON-MODEL MODES OF PRESENTATION

Suppose that our minds/brains used Strawson markers for marking identity. Keeping clearly in mind that the project here is neither exegesis of Strawson's text nor exegesis of Frege's, let us ask what, on this

---

1 Portions of this chapter are revised from "Images of Identity" (Millikan 1997b) with the kind permission of Oxford University Press.

model, would correspond most closely to the Frege-inspired notion that the same object can be thought of by a thinker under various different "modes of presentation."

Gareth Evans tells us that different modes of presentation are, just, different ways of thinking of an object (e.g., Evans 1982, Section 1.4). Suppose that we take this statement completely naively. On a Strawson model it appears that, so long as we always recognized when we were receiving information about the same object again, each of us would end up having only *one* way of thinking about each object. No matter what attributes the Strawson-style cognitive system thinks of an object as having, as long as it does not fail in the task of reidentifying, it always thinks of the object the same way, with the same dot. Two modes of presentation of the same might occur, for example, as the system collected information about a person seen in the distance prior to recognizing them, or about a person being discussed by gossipers before finding out about whom they were talking. But this sort of situation is usually temporary. Either the person seen or discussed is soon identified, or the information collected about the unknown person is easily forgotten. For example, we do not usually retain memories of people we pass on the street unless we recognize them. On this model, it would usually be so that all your beliefs concerning the same object were beliefs entertained under precisely the same mode of presentation.

On this naive reading of "modes of presentation," moreover, no two people could think of an object under the same mode of presentation. To do so they would have to have numerically the same dot in their heads! On a Strawson model, there is no kind of similarity between two minds, either in internal features or in external relations, that would constitute their thinking of the same "in the same way." There might be relevant similarities between the ways you and I think of a thing, conceivably we might even have exactly the same beliefs about a thing, associate with it all the same identifying descriptions and so forth. But on this interpretation this would not bring us any closer to thinking of it under the same mode of presentation.

Interpreted this way, "modes of presentation" obviously would bear scant resemblance to Fregean senses, the very first job of which was to correspond to shared meanings of words and sentences in public languages. For example, Frege supposed that the very same senses are grasped first by the speaker and then the hearer when communication is effected through language. Also, on the Strawson model the different identifying descriptions that you attach to the dot representing a given man are not different ways of thinking of him, but merely various things you know about him, some of which *might* sometime come in handy in helping to reidentify him as the source of some incoming information. Correspondingly, the differences between various kinds of referring expressions – descriptions *versus* proper names *versus* indexicals – would not parallel differences between various kinds of thoughts. On this model there are, for example, no indexical thoughts or ideas, although there would, of course, be times when the thinker used perceptual tracking abilities to collect various bits of incoming information together next to the same dot in his head.

And, of course, sentences expressing nontrivial identities could not be analyzed Frege's way on the naive Strawson model. Accordingly, Strawson's description of the semantics of identity sentences (Strawson 1974) differed radically from Frege's. The public meaning of the identity sentence does not correspond to a particular sharable thought. It concerns what the sentence conventionally *does* to hearers' heads. What it does is not to impart information but to change the mental vocabulary, altering the mental representational system. As such, its function is different, in one important sense, for every hearer. Both the affected dots and, barring weird coincidences, the information in the structures attached to these dots, will be different for each hearer.

Perhaps most critical of all, on this model, should the thinker make a mistake in identifying, the result will be the creation of an equivocal mode of presentation, one that has two referents at once. Nor will the subject who grasps the equivocal mode of presentation have direct access to this flaw. Suppose that you are confused about the identity of Tweedledum, having mixed him up with Tweedledee, so that whenever you meet either you store the information gathered next to the very same dot. Which man does this dot represent? Which man is it that you misidentify, thinking he is the other? Rather, the dot must stand for Tweedledumdee, an amalgam of the two. Further, if systematic misidentifications occurred, or if misidentifications were frequent and random, it seems that a dot's reference might focus on no object at all, hence reasonably be considered quite empty. Similarly, it seems that a dot might undergo massive yet invisible shifts in reference. Consider, in this light, the suggestions offered on the epistemology of substance concepts in Chapter 7.

An interesting corollary would be that negative identity sentences have no determinate meaning, not even for individual persons. For example, on this model you have no separate ideas *Cicero* and *Tully*, nor even *the man called "Cicero"* and *the man called "Tully."* Your way of thinking of the referent of each of the four corresponding public terms merges them irretrievably together. They are different for you only in that they are recognizably different packages in which information about the same thing can enter when you are among speakers speaking a language you know. Suppose then that a historian now informs you that there has been, in fact, an unaccountable confusion among philosophers and that Cicero was *not* in fact Tully. How are you to understand this negative identity claim? What you've got in your head is one dot, attached to which is a variety of (presumed) information, including the information . . . *is called "Cicero"* and . . . *is called "Tully."* But how will you divide the rest of the information into two piles? This could only be accomplished through a major job of reconstruction, as you tried to remember or to guess how you had acquired each separate bit of information, hence from which of these separate men it was most likely to have originated.

It is hard to imagine anything further from Frege's intention than these various results. What has gone wrong? Later (Section 12.4–6), I will tease apart several strands that are woven together to produce the peculiarities of this "naive" Strawson-inspired image of "modes of presentation," and I will try to articulate the underlying principles that divide it from Frege's own vision. But there is also another interpretation possible of what modes of presentation might be for a mind that used Strawson markers.

§11.3 STRAWSON-MODEL MODES OF PRESENTATION AS WAYS OF RECOGNIZING

In our "naive" image above, Strawson's dots are taken to be modes of presentation because they are "ways of thinking of things," a phrase most easily interpreted in this context to mean kinds of mental representations of things. In interpreting modes of presentation this way, we parted from a very important strand within, anyway, the contemporary neo-Fregean tradition. Gareth Evans, for example equates the way one is thinking about an object with the way in which the object is identified (Evans 1982, p. 82, McDowell's formulation for Evans). Similarly,[2] Dummett takes Fregean sense to be a method or procedure for deter-

---

2 Similarly *enough* that is. Evans is at pains to distinguish his views from Dummett's here, but not in ways that affect what is at issue for us.

mining a *Bedeutung*, paradigmatically, for determining the presence of the *Bedeutung* (e.g., Dummett 1973, pp. 95 ff). Evans and Dummett agree, for example, that grasp of a particular way of recognizing a referent encountered in perception corresponds to a mode of presentation of the referent. Now the Strawson image of sameness marking seems to pry apart the way one thinks of a thing from the various ways one knows to recognize it. Perhaps, then, if we identify modes of presentation with the latter instead of the former we will find them to be more as Frege intended.

Suppose then we take modes of presentation, on the Strawson model, to be not ways of *thinking* about a thing but ways of *identifying* it, in particular, ways that a thinker knows to recognize incoming information, arriving via perception, language (Chapter 7), or inference, as being about that thing. That is, given the terminology developed in earlier chapters of this book, we take modes of presentation to correspond to various aspects of the *conception* that a person has of an object, rather than to the concept itself. Modes of presentation will thus describe people's conceptual reidentifying abilities by their means rather than by their ends (Section 4.5).

On this reading, it seems that a person might grasp not just one but many modes of presentation for a given object. Also, perhaps different people might grasp the same mode of presentation, for they might be able to recognize the object in the same way. Moreover, suppose that understanding a certain sort of linguistic expression as referring to an object is, just, grasping a particular way to reidentify the object, through its manifestations in the speech of others (Section 6.2) and/or, in the case of definite descriptions, through prior identification of certain of its properties. Then it might seem that some modes of presentation would correspond directly to meanings of referring expressions. Certainly many philosophers have supposed something like this to be true. The results look much better at first than on the "naive" interpretation of Strawson-model modes of presentation.

But trouble is not far away. On the Strawson model, the terms in the various *beliefs* that a person has will not then be characterized by determinate modes of presentation. Characteristically, each dot will be coordinated with multiple ways of identifying, multiple ways that the thinker would be able to recognize incoming information about that referent. But the various pieces of information attached to a given dot are not associated with any one of these ways more than another. True, each bit of information may have found its way to the dot by just one

151

path of recognition. But the Strawson system keeps no record of which information entered by which path. Besides, on this model modes of presentation are not supposed to be just ways a thing has *historically* been recognized by the thinker, but ways s/he *knows* to recognize it. Many modes of presentation grasped for it may never have been used in the forming of particular beliefs. Certainly these will not be modes under which anything is believed about it. Note also that if the terms of a thinker's belief are not each characterized by a determinate single mode of presentation, but by many modes at once, and if these various modes should happen not, in fact, all to determine the same object, then, as before, it seems that the thinker's thought might in all innocence be equivocal.

A more serious problem with taking Strawson modes of presentation to be merely ways of identifying things so as to channel information about the same arriving in different packages to a single focus or "dot," concerns the difficulty of *individuating* ways of identifying a thing, such as to form distinct modes or senses. Such a view is implicit, I believe, in Gareth Evans' discussion of "dynamic Fregean thoughts," so I will use his analysis to exemplify its weaknesses. Evans' view that there are dynamic Fregean thoughts, if pushed to its limit, yields exactly the same paradoxical results as does the naive Strawson model of modes of presentation.

§11.4 EVANS' "DYNAMIC FREGEAN THOUGHTS"

Evans (Evans 1981, 1982, pp. 174–6, pp. 194 ff) proposed that when you are tracking an object perceptually, say, keeping it in view as it moves and you move, if you continue to believe over this period of time that the perceived object has a certain property, this should not be considered to be a sequence of similar beliefs that you have, but a single belief that persists over time.[3] You continue to think of the object under the same mode of presentation, as long, that is, as you haven't unknowingly lost track of it. Evans calls this sort of thought a "dynamic Fregean thought," and he says that in such cases the relevant "way of thinking of an object" is a "way of keeping track of an object" (p. 196). Now, if you do not merely persist in the same belief about the object over the tracking period, but continue to collect new information about it from perception, noting, say, its way of moving, what it looks like from the back, what it sounds like, how large it is, and so forth, pre-

3   See also John Campbell (1987/88).

sumably this will not change the fact that you continue to think of it under the same mode of presentation, as long as you don't lose track. Note the isomorphism with the Strawsonian analysis of the same tracking event. You continue to keep many old predicates attached to the dot while you funnel in various new bits of information to attach to the very same dot.

And what if you should unknowingly lose track of the object? You thought it was one little minnow – you named him "Primus" – that nibbled first your toe then your ankle, but there were actually two. In that case, Evans claims, "we have not a case of misidentification but a case where the subject has no thought at all" (Evans 1982, p. 176). For in the absence of "an ability to keep track" of the object, "it is not possible for a subject to have a thought about an object in this kind of situation at all" (p. 195).

But an ability, I have argued, is not, in general, something one either has or has not. Most abilities come in degrees. One of my surest abilities is my ability to walk, but there are still times when I trip. Hence there seems another response possible for Evans. You do have an ability to keep track of things like minnows, only this time you tripped (Chapter 4). This particular dynamic mode of presentation of yours is indeed part of a thought, but the thought happens to be equivocal. It hovers between the two minnows, presenting both as if one. Taking another example, imagine a person losing track and apparently, but wrongly, perceiving the same squirrel eating first six and then seven more Brazil nuts. The result is an indelible memory of the squirrel who ate thirteen whole Brazil nuts at a sitting. Surely this is not a case of no thought at all, but a case where two contents have been blended, a case where thought is equivocal.

True, Evans is wedded to "Russell's principle" – "that a subject cannot make a judgment about something unless he knows which object his judgment is about" – and he interprets this to mean that the subject "has a capacity to distinguish the object of his thought from all other things" (Evans 1982, p. 89). But Evans gives no argument anywhere for the soundness of this principle used this particular way. I am happy to agree that if a dynamic mode of presentation were sufficiently equivocal, not just mixing little minnow Primus with Secundus, but also rolling in, say, Sextus, Septimus, and Octavius, indeed, a large random sample of other minnows in the school, it would be odd to consider it as determining a thought of any minnow at all. It should probably be considered "a case where the subject has no thought [anyway, of individual minnows] at all." In earlier chapters, I, too, have argued that some ability to track them individually is necessary to having thoughts of individuals. This is parallel to the result we got on the naive Strawson-inspired model: If enough mistakes in identifying were made, the resulting thoughts would be effectively empty. But I have never heard an *argument* anywhere that *no equivocation at all* is ever possible in thought.

Whatever one decides about that, however, surely the case of error-infected naive Strawson-inspired modes of presentation and the case of error-infected Evans-inspired dynamic modes of presentation must be decided in the same way, for the parallel is exact. The parallel can be shown, indeed, to be a structural identity.

Consider the dynamic mode of presentation involved as you perceptually track a person, Kate, to whom you have just been introduced at a party. For a brief moment – not much longer, suppose, than a saccade – you divert your eyes to the face of a friend, but immediately pick up Kate's face again. Then a large fat man, excusing himself, passes between you and Kate, but again you immediately pick up the track. Looking at Kate and hearing her voice, you perceive these as having the same source, as locating the same person. Now Kate passes for a moment into another room, but you continue to hear her voice – though of course there are spaces between the words – and she soon emerges again. By now she is beginning both to look and to sound quite familiar, so that after stepping outside for a moment, you immediately find her again. The time interval was longer this time than between her words, but short enough for her voice still to be "in your ears." Compare this, for example, to the way a bloodhound tracks a person by smell, at moments losing but then picking the scent up again, or the way one tracks an object visually, seeing it as the same object as it emerges after passing behind a tree. You should not think of the bloodhound as merely *repeating* a particular way of recognizing the person over and over as the scent is lost and regained. Nor do you merely repeat a way of recognizing the visually tracked object. You keep track of it by tracing and anticipating its natural projectory in space.[4]

Now suppose that Kate looks and sounds familiar also an hour later and then a day later when you meet her again, first in the lobby, then on the street. Probably you would not have recognized her, however, had you met her in Singapore – in some radically disjoint context. Similarly, Evans tells us in his chapter on recognition that though by using your

---

4 Compare Evans: " . . . demonstrative Ideas will shade off, without a sharp boundary, into Ideas associated with capacities to recognize objects" (1982, p. 176).

154

recognitional ability alone you might not be able to tell a certain sheep you are thinking of from every other sheep in the world, still, because you can keep track of the neighborhood in which the sheep is likely to be and you can also keep track of where you yourself are, you can maintain an ability to reidentify the sheep (Evans 1982, Section 8.3). Further now, suppose that Kate's name has become familiar, and as more time goes by you often pick up information about her from friends. Again, you usually know which "Kate" they are talking about from the context, from anticipating her possible projectories, and the possible projectories of various kinds of information emanating from her.

When did you stop tracking Kate? When did you stop following her spoor, the trail she left of ambient energy structures bombarding your sensory surfaces? When did the original mode in which she was presented to you come to an end?

A dynamic mode of presentation that never came to an end would be, functionally, exactly the same as a "naive" Strawson-style mode of presentation. Each of the peculiar, distinctly unFregean traits that I have described for the latter modes would characterize the former as well. Whether Evans' dynamic modes really differ from Strawsonian modes in function depends, then, on whether a clear principle of individuation – of sameness and difference – could be drawn for ways of tracking or abilities to track. When did you leave off one way of tracking and start using another ability to track, or some different kind of ability to "know which object you are thinking about," as you collected information over time about Kate?

§11.5 MODES OF PRESENTATION AS WAYS OF TRACKING

The concept of a substance consists, in part, of an ability to reidentify its object or to track it conceptually. One's *conception* of a substance, I have said, concerns *how* one is able to do this. To describe someone's conception of a substance is to tell how they would go about reidentifying or tracking it. If modes of presentation of substances were ways of tracking substances, then when the same substance is presented to a person through a variety of different modes of presentation and they understand these as presenting the same substance, their conception of the substance would have to be divisible into subconceptions, or discrete means of tracking. Each of these means would then be a distinct sense, capable, by itself, of uniquely determining that substance as referent.

First is the problem of division. The general method used for reidentification of every substance is the same. One relies on certain expected, that is, projected, continuities over times or occasions of encounter, for example, continuity in spatial projectory, in color, in shape, in odor, in general arrangement of parts, in manner of motion. Or one may rely on continuity in identity of parts or other associated features. Perhaps it is the shape of your face, or just your eyes that I recognize immediately as indicative of you, or your voice, or your signature, or your walk, or your humor, or your name, or your pocket watch with its distinctive pop-up cover (see Preface), each given the right context. The means employed to recognize a substance thus embed prior or more general means, not means that are unique, usually, to this substance. I follow the object's projectory, granted I can do this for objects generally, under a certain variety of conditions. My ability to track with my feet as well as my eyes and head may be involved here, hence my ability to walk over rough ground or to avoid slipping on ice. I can recognize blueberries partly by their color because I can reidentify colors generally under these and those sorts of conditions. I recognize squirrels by their shapes and characteristic motions, granted I can reidentify shapes and motions generally, big shapes, small shapes, motions in the open, motions partially obscured, shapes and motions close at hand, shapes and motions in the distance. I recognize many people "by their voices," where this means catching the same regional accent again, along with the same vocal quality. I recognize individual old fashioned pocket watches by their shapes and markings, such as initials engraved on them. I identify individuals and kinds by their names, or by descriptions of them, where this requires recognizing the same word again, recognizing the same description put in different words, or put in a different regional accent, or a different language. Recognition by one such complex means or another of enough of these sorts of continuities, all reinforcing one another, often suffice for the practical act of reidentifying a substance. But that the various methods, actually or possibly employed, making up my ability to reidentify some particular substance, might be divided nonarbitrarily into discrete, countable "ways of identifying" simply is not coherent. Just as many integrated skills go into even an act of playing "Twinkle Twinkle Little Star" on the violin or, catching a ball, many integrated general skills, added to specialized bits of knowledge, go into any particular act of recognition or particular act of keeping track of a substance.

That a person's various means of recognizing a substance cannot be divided and counted does not imply, of course, that they cannot be described, or individually designated. Means are like places. There is no answer to how many places there are in London, but I can describe where I am, with greater or lesser exactness, and I even can designate this place entirely exactly, as, just, the place I am now in. Similarly, I can describe my means of identifying Kate on some occasion more or less exactly, as by sight, say, or as by noticing the shape of her nose, or I can refer to a way of having identified her as the way I used last Thursday in the park.

The second problem with identifying ways of recognizing with modes of presentation concerns the requirement that each mode of presentation be capable, by itself, of uniquely determining its referent: one mode yields one referent. What would it be for a way of identifying a substance to determine that substance uniquely? This would require that it be an infallible method of determining that particular substance, never catching another substance instead. But a second traditional requirement on modes of presentation is that the rational thinker always *grasp* the sameness when employing the same mode of presentation again, for the rational thinker must never make contradictory judgments about the same grasped through the same mode of presentation. We would need then to individuate ways of recognizing such that (1) each cannot fail to net always the same object and (2) this fact is guaranteed a priori. But ways of recognizing are always in principle fallible, or at the very least cannot be known a priori to be infallible, because they depend on certain external conditions being in place. This is because "ways of recognizing," in this context, are not ways of holding an object up before the mind, but ways of knowing when one is receiving information about an object. And there is no such thing as an ability to interact in a given way with a distal object that isn't in principle fallible. That is the infamous Achilles heel of verificationism.

Perceptual evidence never guarantees its sources. Perceptual tracking is always fallible. There cannot be an a priori guarantee that one has kept track, or even that there is anything actually there to keep track of. The same is true for conceptual tracking. You are surely able to identify each member of your immediate family in myriad ways, some ways of which — a long look full into your spouse's face in full daylight, for example — may (barring removal of your brain to a vat) actually be infallible. But if that is so, it is because the world, not anything in your mind, is constructed so as to make it so. It is because there is not in fact any other person in the world who looks just like that in the face (and no one *actually* able, and desirous of, putting your brain in a vat) — a convenient fact but not one guaranteed a priori.

Similarly, recognition using identifying descriptions is never infallible. First, that the description is unique is always contingent. There might always be, within limits of discernability, two tallest or two oldest, for example, so that neither is really tallest or really oldest. And one can always make a mistake about which one *is* tallest or oldest because one perceives wrongly, or because one infers wrongly, or because one is informed wrongly by others. True, it has seemed to many that an identifying definite description is the surest sort of tool one could use to make fixed what one was thinking about. But the job that must be done by a method of recognition for incoming information is not to fix a thing before the mind. It is to effect *actual* reidentifications, to direct *actual* incoming bits of information about the same to a focus, so that they will interact with one another in inference. Used for this purpose, most definite descriptions are of severely limited value.

I conclude that given Strawson's model of sameness marking, there is no way to salvage the notion that there are such things as modes of presentation that will do all, indeed perhaps any, of what Frege wanted them to.

12

Rejecting Identity Judgments and Fregean Modes[1]

§12.1 INTRODUCTION

I would like to understand what the basic principles are that distinguish the vision of thought we have generated using the Strawson image of sameness marking from Frege's original vision of thoughts as exemplifying modes of presentation. The first conclusion I will reach is that, surprisingly, the way the Strawson markers mark identity plays no role in determining this difference. The interaction of Strawson's image of sameness marking with Frege's vision of modes of presentation yields strikingly unFregean results. Yet these results are not merely an artifact of the Strawson model. They follow given any model of sameness marking. Strawson's way of marking identity highlights a general feature implicitly present in all other models as well. It will take a while to argue for this conclusion. I will place particular emphasis on the equals marker, and on the image of thoughts as sentencelike, in which the equals-marker model is embedded. For initially it is quite unintuitive that this particular model is isomorphic to the Strawson model. Such is the hold that the mental sentence image of thought has on all of us, with its careful but, as I will argue, illusory distinction between duplicates markers and equals markers, that is, between graspings of necessary identity and contingent judgments of identity.

Further search is thus needed to understand the division between the vision of thought we have generated and Frege's original vision of

1   Parts of this chapter are revised from "Images of Identity" (Millikan 1997b), with the kind permission of Oxford University Press, and from "On Mentalese Orthography" (Millikan 1993b), with the kind permission of Blackwell Publishers.

thoughts as exemplifying modes of presentation. What exactly is the source of the difficulties we have encountered in trying to interpret what a mode of presentation might actually be in a thinking mind or brain? I will argue that the classical notion of modes of presentation rests on two assumptions, both of which are mistaken. One classical source is an implicit denial that the way the mind uses the thoughts or ideas that it harbors has any bearing on their intentional contents. In particular, as suggested in Section 8.7, the Fregean model invokes the passive picture theory of the act of understanding sameness of content. What the mind does with the pictures is not involved in determining their contents, or in determining whether they are thought of as same or different in content. The second source is an internalist view of thought content, that is, a denial that the natural informational content carried by a thought has any bearing on its intentional content.

§12.2 DOES IT ACTUALLY MATTER HOW SAMENESS IS MARKED?

Begin by considering duplicates markers. How will a system consisting, say, of mental sentences, and that uses only duplicates markers, come to realize that Cicero is Tully? It must put all the Cicero and Tully information into sentences using the same mental name, either "Cicero" or "Tully," choose which. Just as one of the dots has to go on the Strawson model, one of the mental words has to go on the duplicates model. So if it should turn out later that Cicero is not in fact Tully, whichever mental name got chosen will be equivocal, nor will the news that Cicero is not in fact Tully represent, for the system, any definite instructions for separating the information again into two piles. Duplicates markers do not differ from Strawson markers in function.

A moment's reflection shows that the synchrony model, the Christmas lights model, and the anaphor model of sameness marking also have this result. Each merely binds all the things known about an object into one bundle. Each performs acts of identifying merely by merging bundles, so that no particular information about any subject has a particular or different mode of presentation from any other. The only method of marking we considered that does not obviously have this effect is the equals model of marking. We find this last model illustrated, implicitly, in Frege himself.

Frege might be interpreted as having supposed that the mind uses, in part, a duplicates system of sameness marking. For although senses were not supposed to be psychological entities, *graspings* of them surely are dated, psychological occurrences, and Frege seems to have held that it is awarenesses of duplicate graspings-of-sense that keep us from contradiction and govern the performance of rational mediate inferences (Chapter 9). If so, this constitutes, I have argued, a substantial psychological claim. A perverse deity might have made our minds otherwise. Imagine, for example, the same sense coming into mental view twice simultaneously as subject term of contradictory judgments, but the demon has determined that only synchronously vibrating viewings of the same sense will move the mind to visage sameness of reference.

It is clear, however, that Frege did not view the result of an identity judgment to be the elimination from use of one of the two kinds of senses grasped, nor did he suppose any senses were equivocal. Rather, he took there to be two kinds of identity judgments, the "informative" ones such as "Cicero is Tully," and those such as "Tully is Tully," which are not. We might suspect, then, that it is the introduction of this new way of marking identity, used for identities not known a priori, that allows the Fregean thinker to identify referents without merging his thoughts of them together. This second identity marker, we suppose, functions like a mental equals sign. It marks two thoughts as being thoughts of the same, not by merging or destroying either, but simply by flagging them for use together in mediate inference.

The suggestion that there is something like an equals sign in thought which marks identity comes, more generally, from modeling thoughts on sentences, and it deserves very careful study. The sentence model is so deeply ingrained both in our everyday and our philosophical thought about thought that we will do well to understand it very explicitly. Otherwise it may mislead us in important ways. A way to begin to explore this model is to examine it in its most naked form, namely, that in which discursive thinking is analogized to the unfolding of a formal system.

§12.3 FORMAL SYSTEMS AS MODELS FOR THOUGHT

A formal system is usually laid out in the following way. First you say what elementary symbols will be used: ps and qs, say, or As and Bs, and xs and ys, wedges, horseshoes, parentheses, and so forth. Next you explain how to construct well-formed formulas (WFFs) from these ingredients, typically with the aid of recursion. Then you may (but need not) lay down axioms. And last, you lay down rules (this in the metalanguage, of course) that will move you from WFFs already laid down or derived to new WFFs. This laying down of symbols, well-formedness rules, axioms, and inference rules, is traditionally done by displaying tokens of symbols, using these as examples of the types of symbols to be put down and manipulated in accordance with the system's rules.

But how are other tokens of these same symbol types to be recognized? By what criterion will they be tokens of the same types? Typically, nothing is said about this. One supposes, traditionally, that some understood but unmentioned parameter on sameness of shape is what binds the tokens into types. For our purposes it will be important explicitly to recognize this implicitly designated part of a formal system. Formal systems have, I will say, besides (1) basic WFFs and rules for constructing more WFFs, (2) axioms or postulates, and (3) rules of inference, also (4) "symbol-typing rules" or just "typing rules," that is, implicit rules telling what is to count as the same symbol or WFF again.

It is well known that in developing formal systems, rules can in general be substituted for axioms or postulates and also, axioms or postulates can be substituted for rules, though the latter (since the tortoise's historic conversation with Achilles – Carroll 1894), it is supposed, not without residue. Typing rules have generally been ignored. But in fact, as I will illustrate, typing rules also can sometimes replace axioms or inference rules.

A very simple interaction among axioms, inference rules, and typing rules happens to be the interaction of the axiom, say, "B = B," with the two inference rules "replace . . . B . . . with . . . B . . . " and "replace . . . B . . . with . . . B . . . ," and with the typing rule "B and B count as symbols of the same type." Now it is usually supposed that although one can trade off rules and axioms to a degree in this way, still the difference between the systems that result from these swaps is objective. Certainly, it is not so that there is really no difference between an axiom and a rule or no difference between a rule of inference and a typing rule. It is just that in some cases one can substitute one for another to determine the same set of theorems. What I will be urging, however, is that distinctions among these three categories break down in crucial ways when we hypothesize representation in the mind or brain. My conclusion will be that there is no difference in this context between a mental equals-sign marker, an identity rule and a duplicates marker.

To quell the suspicion that identity is somehow a special case here, let me first illustrate the trade off between typing rules and axioms and/or inference rules with a completely different kind of example.

Consider, first, laws of commutativity. Standard renderings of the propositional calculus require that the equivalence of A&B to B&A and of A∨B to B∨A be either introduced as axioms, derived as theorems, or (aberrant but possible) given as special rules of inference. Suppose, however, that one were to construct a system in which the difference between left and right on the paper is ignored when grouping symbol tokens into types. No distinction is drawn between "p" and "q," or between "b" and "d," and so forth. Similarly, "A⊃H" is the same string as "H⊂A." More interesting, "A∨H" is the same string as "H∨A," and, if we use the traditional dot instead of "&," "A·H" is the same string as "H·A." Here a symbol typing rule does duty for one or a couple of axioms, theorems, or rules.

For another example, suppose we read right-left distinctions as usual and play instead with up and down. We read "p" as a symbol of the same type as "b" except that it has been turned upside down. Then we use turning upside down for the negation transformation. We negate propositional constants and variables by turning them upside down; we negate strings by turning the whole string upside down. Double negation elimination now no longer appears as an axiom, theorem, or rule. It can't be stated, or can't be differentiated from *p implies p*. Of course, we have to be terribly careful. We must not use any symbols that are symmetrical top to bottom, or we won't be able to tell whether they have undergone the negation transformation or not. On the other hand, suppose we use the traditional symbol "∧" for conjunction. The effect is that De Morgan's laws need not be stated, are indeed unstatable, being mere fallout from the symbol-typing rules. For example, suppose that you turn "p" and "q" each upside down, put a wedge between them, and then turn the whole string over, thus saying that it is neither the case that not-p nor that not-q. The result, "p∧q", is a string that is more naturally read straight off as saying, simply, that p and q. The possibility of swapping symbol-typing rules for axioms or rules of inference is not then an artifact resulting merely from the peculiarities of identity.

Next, I would like to argue that when we turn from a representational system written on paper in a public language to a representational system in the mind or brain, both the distinction between axioms and inference rules and the distinction between typing rules and inference rules tend to break down.

Consider first the apparently nearly self-evident truth that although it is possible to build a logical system that has no axioms but only rules, it is not possible to build a system with no rules but only axioms. The rules of a system cannot all be represented explicitly (Carroll 1894). In a traditional formal system, each axiom or hypothesis is written down on a separate line of paper. The system unfolds as new sentences or formulae are derived from these by rule and written down below. In such a system, adding axioms – writing down more sentences at the top of the page – won't by itself determine how these axioms will be *used* in order to guide derivations within the system. Rules telling how the axioms, as well as the other strings, are to be manipulated must be given in a metalanguage which the system builder reads and, if appropriately inspired by them, then performs the appropriate transformations.

But if the system is unfolding not on paper but in the head, the "user" is just another part of the head. Since representations in the head are just head-structures designed to vary according to how the world varies, this user part may itself constitute a representation. Taking a childish example, imagine an inference machine designed to perform inferences using universal categorical sentences as major premises and constructed in the following manner. Premises representing that All As are Bs are entered by constructing a sliding board between two ports, the top port being an A-shaped hole, the bottom a B-shaped hole. Sentences ascribing predicates to individuals consist of pieces of putty the colors of which name individuals and the shapes of which ("A," "B," "C") ascribe properties to them. These pieces of putty are gently pushed across the tops of the constructed slides, where they enter the ports through which they fit, proceeding to the bottom where they are pressed down through the lower ports and change their shapes accordingly. They thus become conclusions. *All As are Bs* and *a is an A* thus yields *a is a B*.

Surely this image could be improved on, but the principle should be clear. There is no reason why one premise has to lie passively beside the next in a representational system in the mind or head. There is no reason why the structure, the mechanism, that operates upon a representation during inference may not itself be a representation that has been molded or tuned to perform its appointed tasks, reflecting something in the dynamics, uniformities, or logic of some aspect of the environment, for which aspect it stands. Ways that various individuals' inferencing systems are put together can themselves be representations, so long as they are determined by learning under the influence of individuals' environments, such that variations in ways of being put together correspond, systematically, to variations in environments, according to the design of the learning systems.

If the difference between rules of inference and premises of inference in a cognitive system is not clearly marked, the difference between typing rules and identity axioms or rules for a cognitive system is altogether chimerical. To see exactly why this is so, two more failures of parallel between formal systems and the way representations are used by cognitive systems need to be recognized. One concerns the conventional and public nature of symbol typing in formal systems. The other concerns the use of duplicates as the sameness markers in formal systems.

Earlier I remarked that, typically, nothing is explicitly said about the symbol typing rules when a formal system is laid down, but that it is assumed that these unspoken rules concern parameters or limits on variation in physical form. Better, we *pretend* that these unspoken rules concern sameness, that is, concern duplication, of physical form. The rules we actually employ are derived, at the start, from irregular rather disjunctive conventions for determining what is the same symbol type. There are, for example, numerous conventional styles of writing the same letter by hand, and numerous type fonts, across which the shape of a particular letter may vary in a rather irregular way. Compare this, for example, with the typing of words, where practices can be quite disorderly. The rules may be quite disjunctive and may include many exceptions. For example, in English, contrasting pronunciations of "schedule" (s-k-e-dule versus sh-e-dule) count as tokens of the same word type while exactly the same contrast between the pronunciations of "mask" and "mash" or "skin" and "shin" produces different word types. Moreover, the methods we use in practice to determine what counts as another token of the same symbol type concern not just shape but how the person who wrote the symbol intended it to be taken. Recall that most actual formal systems are originally developed in somebody's handwriting on paper and that a typical way of passing them on is by writing on a blackboard. What counts as an "a" or as an "~" then is what was intended to be an "a" or a "~," having been purposefully copied, carefully or carelessly, competently or incompetently, with or without consciously added style, on the model of earlier "a"s or "~"s.[2] Why do we keep up this pretense that formal symbols are typed by nondisjunctive exceptionless rules on shape?

There is one innocent reason and, I believe, one lingering guilty reason why we do this. The innocent reason is that proofs of consistency

2   For fuller discussion of this etiological principle in grouping words and other symbols into types, see (Millikan 1984, Chapter 4, in press c; Kaplan 1990).

and completeness in formal systems work, exactly, by treating systems as if their symbols and WFFs corresponded to well-defined simple physical shapes and well-defined configurations of these. This assumption makes the proofs easy, indeed, possible, and nothing is distorted thereby. The guilty reason is that it is implicitly assumed that the only *true* marker of sameness in content, the only way sameness of content can be *directly* represented, is by *duplicating* representations. That is, the passive picture theory of the act of identifying hovers over. Or it may be assumed that identifying is reacting the same way to what is identified, so that the same physical form will be needed to produce the same reaction again.

But ease in proving consistency and completeness is clearly irrelevant to how cognitive systems work. And the passive picture theory, and the repetition theory of identifying, I have argued, are mistaken. If we keep clear on these issues it becomes evident that there is nothing different in principle going on in a mind that uses "sameness of form" to mark identity if that mind happens to define equivalence classes for these forms disjunctively, or with numerous exceptions, dividing up its space of forms in as gerrymandered a way as you please. All that is needed is that the typing rules used remain consistent with one another. Should the brain mark sameness by equivalence classes of physical type, there is no distinction in principle between systems that mark neatly by perfect duplication of some aspect of form, and systems that mark messily with lists and disjunctions and exceptions. There is nothing magical about simple nondisjunctive typing rules where classes of physical forms mark samenesses.

Now in a public symbol system, *which* similarities determine that two symbol tokens are of the same type depends on the conventional practices of the language community. That "*defence*" is read as the same word as "*defense*" and also as the word "DEFENSE," for example, is a matter of public convention. That "Cicero" is not read as the same word as "Tully" is equally a matter of public convention. Certain physical forms and not others are grouped into the same representational type because someone, in this case the general public, reads them that way. And if an individual user of the public language comes along who happens to, or learns to, read "Cicero" and "Tully" as equivalent in type – these produce thoughts of exactly the same type – that doesn't change the conventional typing rules for words used by the community. It doesn't change the typing rules for the public language.

But for *mental* representations, there is no distinction like that between public convention and private response. Whatever the individual mind/brain treats as the same mental word again IS the same word again. For mind-language there are no conventions – there is only the private user. Nor is there any reason why mental typing should not *evolve* in an individual mind or brain over time. If the private user changes her habits, then the typing rules for her mental representations will change. This is because the typing rules ARE nothing but her dispositions to coidentify.

For the mind, there also is no distinction like that between an identity axiom or postulate, A = B, written at the top of the page, and a typing rule. For there is no distinction like that between what is written on the paper and what is written in the structure of the reader – in the structure responsible for conforming the reader's reactions to a certain typing rule. One structure responsible for brain coidentifying patterns is on a par with any other; all are equally "written" in the brain. Write an identity sentence, that is, a structure responsible for producing certain coidentifications, in neuronal patterns instead of in graphite, and the distinction between identity sentence and interpreting mechanism vanishes. Whether the mechanism in the mind effects only that the mental *Cicero*s get coidentified with the mental *Cicero*s, or also that the mental *Cicero*s get coidentified with the mental *Tully*s, this mechanism is no more or less of an extra postulate one way than the other. What is the alternative? That to be an identity postulate it would have, literally, to be physically shaped like this: "Tully = Cicero"? Marking sameness, however that's done, and fixing identity beliefs is exactly the same thing.

Thus if we think carefully about the effects of an equals marker on the system that understands it, the distinction between it and a Strawson marker collapses. What effect are we to imagine mental *Cicero* = *Tully* to have if not, precisely, that it changes the mind's dispositions to mental typing? Henceforth, mental *Cicero* and mental *Tully* will behave as representational equals. They become the same mental word, that is, they are ready to be coidentified. But if this is so, the mental equals marker behaves exactly like a Strawson marker. It merges two thought types into one, threatening equivocation in thought, and doling out to each thinker just one mode of presentation per object.

We must conclude, I think, that the peculiar effect of the Strawson markers was on us, on our understanding, not on the operation of the cognitive systems modeled. Systems that use Strawson markers grasp identities by *explicitly* changing their mental vocabularies, replacing two representations with one. Systems that use equals markers do exactly the same thing but implicitly, changing merely the typing rules for their mental vocabularies, that is, merely the *functions* of the symbol forms.

§12.4 NEGATIVE IDENTITY JUDGMENTS

One possibility concerning negative identity judgments and the undoing of identity markings hasn't been dealt with yet. Imagine a system that keeps a log of the various changes made in the representational system as identities are marked, and keeps a log of mediate inferences that pivot on these marked representations. Compare the way modern word processing programs can keep track of the last two or three hundred commands carried out. Then if a mistake is discovered, the "undo" button can be pressed until the system is returned to the point where the original false coidentification was made. Different pieces of information that were attached to the same Strawson dot at different times then have different statuses in case of emergency. Indeed, might we say that they represent predicates attached to the same subject but under different modes of presentation? How many of the various purposes of Frege's modes of presentation could differences of this sort serve?

I have not explored these questions because I think such a model is completely lacking in psychological plausibility. Imagine keeping such a log on all the times you have ever reidentified or made inferences about your husband or mother! Of course it is true that were I seriously to suppose, say, that Mark Twain was not Samuel Clemens, I might have some idea how to guess which of my beliefs about this double person should be attached to which name. Certain facts would cohere with Twain's role as an author, others perhaps with his role as public speaker or builder of the Twain house in Hartford. But this untangling would certainly not be done on the basis of a *memory* of when and in what order I had discovered or inferred what about Twain. It would be done using a *theory* about how I had got two men so mixed in my mind, and by *speculating* about which items of information are most likely to have come from which source.

§12.5 THE FIRST FREGEAN ASSUMPTION

How then *does* the Fregean avoid the Strawson image with its threat of equivocation in thought and its frugal offer of just one mode of presentation per object? The trick is to imagine that how a thought *functions* has no effect on its content. One assumes that how the mind *understands* its thoughts is irrelevant to their significance. Throughout I have assumed, on the contrary, that use does affect representational

168

value. I have assumed that what marks content sameness in thought is whatever the cognitive systems *read* as marking sameness, or what they are designed to read as marking sameness. I assumed that if thought tokens are marked to function as representing the same, this will affect their representational value. In particular, if this marking conflicts with other factors relevant to representational value, say, with the information content of the tokens so marked, or with other ways their associated referents may be determined, then there will be equivocation in content. Sameness is represented yet different things are represented. Visagings of conceptual contents need not be consistent, nor is inconsistency in conceptual content discovered by a priori inspection.

The Fregean view assumes, on the contrary, that insertion of a sameness marker (an identity judgment), hence change in the employment of the marked terms, has no bearing on content. Placing a mental equals sign between mental *Cicero* and mental *Tully* has no effect on the representational value of either, even if Cicero is not in fact Tully. Similarly, if duplicated thoughts are in fact thoughts of the same, each token of *Cicero* referring again always to the same (rather than acting, say, like the English word "he"), this depends in no way on the fact that duplication is what is *read* by the mind as marking identity. Thought typing is determined independently of thought use.

This Fregean assumption implies, I believe, that thoughts are not mental representations. For we cannot suppose that a representation could be a *mental* representation, a representation *for mind*, yet that its representational value was independent of its effect upon mind, independent of how the mind reads it. And, of course, Frege himself did not hold that thoughts are mental representations. Fregean senses are abstract entities that bear their contents quite independently of whether or how a mind "grasps" them. The conclusion that classical Fregean modes of presentation are not compatible with a representational theory of mind is not then a criticism of Frege. But if *we* propose to defend any sort of representational theory of mind, we cannot also keep Fregean modes of presentation.

§12.6 THE SECOND FREGEAN ASSUMPTION

According to Frege there are informative and also uninformative identity claims. Uninformative identities are so called because they do not inform us of anything not already immediately known *a priori*. Presumably these claims also cannot be false. Frege is not supposing that there might be false identities that we cannot help but affirm. The Fregean senses that figure in uninformative identities function psychologically as would thoughts marked with duplicates markers. But on Frege's view this way of functioning is not, of course, what determines that duplicate graspings of duplicate Fregean senses always have the same content. Function has no effect on content. On a representationalist view, sameness markings do force both marked thoughts to refer to the same thing, hence if the markings are wrong, forces both to refer equivocally, but on a Fregean view, the referents of duplicate thoughts are determined independently of the mind's way of being governed by them. That the thinker identifies the referents as one and the same is in no way responsible for them being the same. What is the guarantee, then, that the referents of duplicate thoughts actually ARE the same? (Or if what you mean by "duplicate thoughts" *includes* that they have the same referent, what is to guarantee that the mind that grasps two thoughts can *tell* whether these thoughts are indeed duplicates?) How can there be uninformative identities that are at the same time certain to be real identities and not merely false appearances of identity?

This line of questioning highlights the internalist assumption built into the Fregean position. What is duplicated when "the very same thought" is repeated must be something that is simultaneously (1) compelled always to bring with it the same referent and (2) capable of being unmistakably known by the mind, when the mind duplicates its entertainment, as being the very same thought. That, I take it, is one role of a Fregean sense: it always determines the same referent regardless of the context, the grasper (understander), or the use, and its identity is transparent to mind.[3] More generally, that which completely determines the referent must be exactly the selfsame as that which, when duplicated, constitutes a grasp of same*ness*. Otherwise the appearance of sameness might not be veridical.

It follows that whatever determines the reference must be entirely internal to mind. Reference cannot be affected at all by, say, the external causes of thoughts, or their natural informational content, for there can be no certain internal or a priori mark proving the external causes or the informational contents of two thoughts are really the same.

---

3 If it were not transparent to mind, then that one cannot think a contradiction about a thing while thinking of it under just one mode of presentation could not be criterial of sameness of sense, nor could it be assumed that uninformative identities are never false identities. (If Frege's position is not that identity of sense is transparent to mind, certainly this is what many have thought his position to be. The purpose here is not, of course, Frege exegesis but clarification of where certain incompatibilities of position lie.)

I have been arguing in this book for an externalist and representation-alist position on thought, but it is crucial that we not rely on a lan-guage-of-thought model of mental representation. This misleading model offers an image of thought as having two levels of sameness marking, on one of which sameness of content for concepts is not an empirical issue but a matter of mere inner form. It pictures errors about identity as impossible on this level and, correlatively, pictures the differ-ence between valid and invalid mediate inference as though it were dis-tinctly marked from within. But on externalist grounds, no distinction can be clearly marked in thought between valid inference that relies on false identity premises and invalid inference. There is no analytic/syn-thetic distinction for identity as grasped in thought.

It follows, for example, that the Quinean distinction between tau-tologies and merely analytic sentences and, similarly, the distinction cus-tomarily drawn between inferences valid due to logical form and those whose validity depends on the meanings of nonlogical terms, cannot be drawn for thought. In a similar vein, we have a linguistic convention that any adjective grammatically marked as comparative – in English, for example, by adding the suffix "-er" – expresses a relation that is transi-tive. This gives the appearance that thoughts expressed in the argument form "A is φer than B and B is φer than C, therefore A is φer than C" are valid a priori. But, as Hemple showed us clearly, using the geologist's "harder than" as his example (Section 7.2), particular applications of this form are not valid a priori. They are valid only in case the English lan-guage happens to conform, in particular cases, to the convention, and conformity cannot be guaranteed, exactly because the transitivity of an empirical relation cannot be known a priori. The linguistic form of the argument makes it valid by linguistic convention, but there can be no guarantee that the convention is manifested in particular cases. Similarly, Whitehead claimed that it is always an empirical matter, in the particu-lar case, that one plus one equals two. One raindrop plus one raindrop sometimes equals one raindrop, and one quart of water plus one quart of alcohol equals less than two quarts. The convention is to use num-bers and numerical operators only where number theory applies, but that it applies in particular cases is known empirically.

Putting the inevitably aposteriori nature of our grasp of sameness in John Campbell's terms (1987/88), there is no such thing as completely "manifest sameness of reference." The mental sentence image causes us to overlook the most central fact about cognition, namely, that its most difficult job is to get the empirical identities right, to create a coherent, nonredundant and nonequivocal mental representational system. Without such a system, or something sufficiently close, there can be no conceptual thinking at all.

There can be no representation of sameness in thought without sameness marking, and there are no substance concepts without representings of sameness. Indeed, what substance concepts are initially *for* is grasping, which requires somehow marking, sameness in substances. But since there also is no difference between marking sameness and fixing identity beliefs, it follows that there are no representations of substances that are free from the possibility of empirical error. It is always contingent that a substance concept represents univocally, or represent at all. We must proceed very carefully here, however. It does not follow that substance concepts somehow make claims, or that they are "theories," or that they really are identity judgments in disguise.

There are lots of ways to do things right rather than wrong without making claims or holding theories. You don't make claims when you stand up to walk just because it's possible you could trip and fall. Similarly, you don't make claims when you develop substance concepts or when you mark identities in thought. Erroneous identification is not failure on the level of know-that but failure on the level of know-how. It is failure in an activity. Standing back from a failed activity it is often possible to explain its failure by pointing to some proposition that, had it only been true, would have prevented the failure. Had that wrinkle in the rug not been there, I would not have tripped. It doesn't follow that my attempt to walk involved a judgment that no wrinkles were in the rug. Similarly, when representations carrying information about different substances are wrongly coidentified, it is true that had they carried information about the same they would not have been coidentified wrongly. It does not follow that the act of coidentifying, or of identity marking, is a judgment that they carry information about the same. It is not a judgment about sameness of content.

Rather than substance concepts being implicit judgments or theories, it is better to say that, as distinguished from an identity sentence or assertion, there is no such thing as an identity *judgment*. It is not the job of an identity sentence to induce a belief. Its job is to induce an act of coidentifying. True, an identity sentence has a grammar superficially like that of ordinary subject-predicate fact stating sentences. It has traditionally been recognized, however, that it does not have a logical subject and a logical predicate. Only if we insist on modeling thought on language should there be a temptation to assimilate what an identity sentence produces – an act of coidentifying – to what a subject-predicate sentence characteristically produces – namely, an intentional attitude.

Grasping an identity is not remotely like harboring an intentional attitude. Similarly, mistaking an identity is not harboring a false belief. It is an error of its own kind. Misidentifying is not, in central cases, an innocent act of false judgment, but an act that tends to muddy the very content of the thought involved, corrupting the inner representational system. The development and maintenance of relatively clear and distinct ideas is a substantive ongoing activity. Descartes was quite right that not all ideas are clear and distinct, indeed, that some are materially false. He went astray only in failing to see how much more than mere armchair reflection is involved in the activity of clarifying our ideas (Chapter 7).

§12.8 REJECTING MODES OF PRESENTATION

Where Frege drew one distinction, between sense or mode of presentation and reference, there seem really to be two distinctions, or anyway two phenomena, confused together. First, there is the distinction between concept and conception, that is, between designating conceptual abilities by their ends only and designating them by their means (or by certain of their means) as well. Second, there is the possibility of having more than one concept of the same, these concepts being separate and not marked as of the same.

This second possibility gives rise to an embarrassment in terminology. I have spoken of two different ways to understand the notion "same ability" hence "same concept," depending on whether "the same" means the same end achieved or whether it means the same end achieved by the same means (Sections 1.9 and 6.3). But it appears now that there is also a third way to interpret the notion "same concept." If concepts can be called "the same" when they involve abilities to identify the same, thus allowing you and me to have many of "the same" concepts, then it will also be possible for me to have two different *tokens* of the "same concept" because I have failed to coidentify two concepts of the same thing. "The same" concept *token*, is identified neither by its end alone nor by its end plus its means. If a person harbors two different tokens of the same concept these will, of course, be governed by different conceptions, by different means, but that is not what makes them two.

Similarly, someone might be said to have two separate abilities to achieve the same end, where the point is not merely that they know several ways to achieve that end. Suppose, for example, that before it was known that scarlet fever is the same disease as rheumatic fever but in a different form, there was a doctor who knew how to cure scarlet fever by one means and knew how to cure rheumatic fever by another. Such a doctor might be said to have two different abilities to cure strep infections, two tokens of the same ability.

In sum, we should distinguish, first, among concept tokens, and second, among two different sorts of concept types, types distinguished by ends and types distinguished by ends plus means. It is also possible to classify concepts more abstractly, according merely to *some* of their means. But here we should proceed very cautiously

One of the things we have put in place of Fregean modes of presentation is conceptions. I have described conceptions as the "means" by which the thinker knows how to reidentify a substance. Is the word "means" in this usage a singular noun, a plural noun or a mass noun? Can we, for example, sensibly speak of "some of the means" of a concept? In Section 11.5, I argued that in the case of recognitional abilities, the means actually or possibly used to reidentify a substance cannot be divided into discrete countable "ways of identifying." "Means," in this context, seems to be a mass noun. Conceptions don't for the most part divide into discrete parts. The individual recognitional abilities that any two people have have, allowing them to reidentify the same substances, are very unlikely to be identical in means, nor are they likely to be describable in a readily available way.

On the other hand, some features of these means may be describable. For example, I might be able to recognize Xavier by sight but not by his voice on the phone, or recognize lemons by smell but not by their name in Russian, or recognize Jon Jones by the fact that he is the one chairing the meeting but not by scanning his face. Of course, that I recognize Xavior by sight does not tell *how* I recognize him by sight, nor does my recognizing Jon Jones by his chairing the meeting tell *how* I recognize which person is chairing. Mentioning certain features of the conceptions I use is not telling the whole story about how I recognize, even the whole story on some specific occasion. Still, it is possible, sometimes, to describe conceptions by aspects of their means in this rough sort of way, and this allows us to give certain kinds of psychological explanations.

174

Where a person's reidentifying abilities have proved fallible, descriptions of intentional attitudes referring only to the objects and properties these concern, that is, purely referential descriptions of them, can be misleading. Where it matters to psychological explanation, the normal assumption is that relevant identities have been correctly recognized. If they haven't, or easily might not have been, we describe thoughts by reference to rough aspects of the conceptions involved. Thus we explain why Paul didn't speak to the woman he admires, even though she was present and he very much wanted to, by the fact that he didn't know what she looks like. Similarly, we may refer to identifying knowledge that forms part of a person's conception of an object, or make reference to a name by which they recognize an object. In this way we may move back and forth between purely "transparent" descriptions of a person's intentional attitudes and somewhat more "opaque" ones. Consider, for example, a case with which I opened this book. It would certainly be misleading to say, *without further explanation*, that someone at the Yale Alumni Association headquarters wished to know whether I knew where I was, but not misleading to say that they wished to know whether Mrs. Donald P. Shankweiler knew where Ruth Garrett Millikan was. From the fact that the conceptions governing the two different concepts of me could be described individually in this manner it does not follow, however, that the entire conception governing either concept could be described. Nor does it follow that there could be a description of an intentional attitude that was entirely opaque, making no transparent reference to any objects or properties outside of the thinker.[4] Even knowing someone merely by their name is not having a conception of them describable in completely opaque terms. "The ability to recognize the name X" is a transparent description of that ability. So-called opaque descriptions of conceptions and intentional attitudes are never more than semiopague.

Besides semiopaque descriptions of various means supporting real substance concepts, there also can be, of course, semiopaque descriptions of various "would-be" means but that fail to support real substance concepts. That is, unbeknownst to their possessors, they are not the means for any real recognition abilities. These substance concepts are "empty" or, more accurately, they are not substance concepts at all. An

4 Various different ways of describing intentional attitudes are discussed in Millikan (1984, Chapter 13).

ability that is not an ability to do anything is not an ability at all. Empty substance concepts result from failures of the mechanisms designed to develop substance concepts. They are "concepts" only in that their biological purpose was to have been concepts. Nor should they be confused with concepts we merely pretend to have, such as the concept we pretend to have of Santa Clause after we are grown. Semiopaque descriptions can also be given of pretend concepts, of course, but that is another matter.

Opaque descriptions characterize aspects of conceptions, that is, aspects of ways of identifying substances. They do not describe ways of thinking of substances. "Via a definite description" and "via a proper name" are not ways of thinking of things. Nor, of course, is "by recognizing her face" or "by recognizing her voice" a way of thinking of a person. A neo-Fregean tradition has it that perceiving a person is a sort of way of thinking of them, indeed, it is supposed, an indexical way of thinking of them – thinking of them via an indexical mode of presentation. This, I believe, is a serious confusion. Suppose that you see Alice and track her perceptually, picking up information about her as you proceed but without recognizing her as Alice. Then for the moment you have two concept tokens of Alice that you have not coidentified. Your current tracking ability supports a "naive Strawson mode of presentation," if we may still use that terminology, which is separate from the naive Strawson mode in which your prior knowledge of Alice is stored. As we saw in Section 11.2, however, this mode is no Fregean mode of presentation. Furthermore, once you have recognized Alice, no distinction of "modes" of any kind remains.

To be sure, your current perception of Alice yields, in part, a special kind of information about Alice, namely, information about her current spatial relation to you. But that it yields information about her relation to you has nothing to do with indexicality. This is a subject I have already addressed at length elsewhere, and will not pursue further here. There are, I have claimed, no mental indexicals at all, least of all any (so-called) essential indexicals (Millikan in press a).

13

Knowing What I'm Thinking Of[1]

... for it is scarcely conceivable that we can make a judgment or entertain a supposition without knowing what it is we are judging or supposing about. ... the meaning we attach to our words must be something with which we are acquainted ... [but] Julius Caesar is not himself before our minds.

(Russell, *The Problems of Philosophy*, p. 58)

The difficulty with Russell's Principle has always been to explain what it means.

(Gareth Evans, *The Varieties of Reference*, p. 89)

§13.1 INTRODUCTION

In Chapter 7, I offered an answer to the question: How do we know when we are thinking of a substance, and thinking of it unequivocally and nonredundantly? But I did not answer the question, equally urgent: What, on an externalist account, could possibly constitute that one knows what substance one is thinking about? In this chapter, I will try to answer that question.

I will agree with Evans that grasping the identity of the object of one's thought requires having a concept of that object. I have already agreed with him, throughout this book, that a (substance) concept is, in part, an ability to reidentify its object. But abilities, I have said, can be

---

1 Parts of this chapter are revised from "On unclear and indistinct ideas" (Millikan 1994), which appeared in *Philosophical Perspectives, 8, Logic and Language*, edited by James E. Tomberlin (copyright by Ridgeview Publishing Co., Alascadero, CA). Reprinted by permission of Ridgeview Publishing Company, with the kind permission of Ridgeview Publishing Company, and from "Knowing What I'm Thinking of" (Millikan 1993c), reprinted by courtesy of the Editor of the Aristotelian Society © 1993.

better or worse (Section 4.3). Especially, one can know how to do a thing only under very restricted conditions or under a great variety of conditions. Knowing what one is judging about is thus a matter of degree. One can come to know better what one is judging about.

Also, as I have emphasized (Chapter 4), one can know how to do a thing but still fail. The conditions required for successful exercise of one's ability may be absent, nor need one be aware of this absence. Russell and Evans to the contrary, it is not uncommon to be mistaken about the object of one's thought on particular occasions. That is, even though you do have an ability to identify the object of your thought, hence do know what you are thinking of, you can still make mistakes about the object of your thought. Similarly, having the ability to walk will not prevent you from sometimes tripping. If not soon corrected, however, mistaking the identity of an object of thought produces equivocation in thought, hence the beginning, at least, of change in the object of thought.

In Chapter 14, I will examine "Russell's principle" in another light, asking whether there are other kinds of mental representation, the identities of whose intentional objects remain unknown to the thinker. This will turn out to be the same as the question whether there are non-conceptual mental representations.

§13.2 ISOLATING THE PROBLEM

To inquire whether it is possible to make a judgment or think about something without knowing what one is thinking of we first need to understand what it would *be* to know what one is thinking of. Externalism concerning mental content clearly implies that we cannot "know what we are thinking about" in the strictest Russellian way. In Russell's view, what can be "thought about," in the strictest sense is only what is within or directly before the conscious mind. On a representationalist view on the other hand, what is within the mind when one thinks of an object is a representation of the object, not the object itself. Or if the object should happen to be "in" the mind, for example, if it is itself a mental representation, still it is not by being in the mind that it becomes an object of thought. Thinking of one's thoughts cannot be supposed to be thinking of or knowing in some completely different sense than thinking about the empirical world. *What thinking of something consists in cannot be supposed to change with the object of thought.* If one thinks about one's representations, this must be by means of other representations. Representations do not represent themselves. Similarly, on a representationalist view, what the mind is "aware of" when it successfully represents an object is the object represented, not the vehicle in the mind that represents the object. But if that is so, against Russell, Julius Caesar may indeed be "before our minds" in the only sense that *anything* can be "before our minds." What is in our minds and what is before our minds must be sharply distinguished. We must not confuse the vehicle of thought with its content (Chapter 8).

Nor can we interpret Russell's dictum to mean, say, that I cannot make a judgment about Alice unless I also judge *that* my judgment is about Alice. Knowing *that* I am thinking of Alice is surely posterior rather than prior to thinking of Alice. I cannot know that I am thinking of Alice unless I first think of Alice, any more than I can know that I am hungry unless I am first hungry. Nor is knowing *that* I am thinking of Alice necessitated by my thinking of Alice. Knowing *that* requires judging *that*, and judging that I am thinking of Alice requires the capacity to think about thoughts. But this is a capacity there is no reason to suppose every thinker must have. There is evidence, for example, that children don't have this capacity until well after they acquire fluent speech.

Again, consider what it would *be* to know *that* I was thinking of Alice. Barring Russell's view of thought as direct confrontation of mind with object, this knowing could not involve directly comparing my thought with Alice. Rather, I would have to think of my thinking and I would have to think of Alice and perhaps also of the relation that made the one a thought *of* the other. In any event, I would surely have to think of Alice. But if thinking of Alice involves knowing that I am thinking of Alice, and this requires thinking of Alice again, we have a regress. It is not regressive (though I believe it is surely false) to claim that it is necessary to have the capacity or the disposition, whenever my thought turns to Alice, to think that I am thinking about Alice. But it is not possible that *actualizing* this capacity should be *constitutive* of having thoughts about Alice.

§13.3 EVANS ON KNOWING WHAT ONE IS THINKING OF

Gareth Evans was an externalist and he believed, nonetheless, that there was a way of explaining "what Russell's Principle means" that makes it come out not only sensible but true (Evans 1982). A central move in Evans' analysis was interpreting "knowing what one is judging about," at crucial junctures, not as a kind of knowing *that* (as we have so far been interpreting it) but as a kind of knowing *how*. As Evans understood it, knowing what one is thinking of is having some sort of "ability" or – he conflated all these – "capacity" or "disposition" or "knowing how."

Evans held that knowing what one is judging about is "a capacity to distinguish the object of [one's] judgment from all other things" (1982, p. 89). Using our example, thinking of Alice, he would have claimed, involves the capacity to distinguish Alice from all other things. Having this capacity, Evans said, is what makes the difference between being capable only of judging, say, that *a* person has such and such attributes and being capable of judging that *Alice* has them (pp. 127–8).

Evans was clear that this ability to discriminate Alice could not be merely the ability to call to mind an idea that was, in some manner inaccessible to the thinker, *externally* (e.g., causally) hooked to Alice and Alice only. Rather, Evans thought, its being hooked to Alice must, at least in part, "reside in facts about what the [thinking] subject can or cannot do at that time" (p. 116), facts determining that the thinker has a "concept" or, in the case of objects as distinguished from properties, an "adequate Idea" of the target of his thought. A concept or Idea, for Evans, is a general ability that (1) "makes it possible for a subject to think of an object in a series of indefinitely many thoughts, [(2)] in each of which he will be thinking of it in the same way" (p. 104).

Consider (2) first. A concept or Idea, for Evans, corresponds to a single (neo)-Fregean mode of presentation of its referent. But recall also that for Evans, there are such things as "dynamic modes of presentation" (Section 11.4). The ability to keep track of an object currently perceived, along (as we will see) with one's ability to locate the egocentric space within which one perceives it within one's representation of objective or public space, constitutes one sort of concept of that object.

Now consider (1). (1) says that to have an Idea of Alice, I must be able to think of Alice not only, say, in the context of the thought that she is slim, but also in the context of the thought that she is trim, that she is walking, that she is city mayor, and so forth for all attributes any arbitrary person might have, given only that I possess the relevant predicate concepts. More precisely, I must understand what it would be for *Alice*, as distinguished from all others, to have any arbitrary one of these various attributes. Evans calls this constraint on concepts "the generality constraint" (1982, Section 4.3). Evans' "generality constraint" is not just the familiar contemporary view that thought must be compositional. The verificationist background from which Evans' thought emerged lends it quite another flavor and use. It implies, rather, a general capacity to understand what it would be to reiterate the thought *Alice* in other *evidenced* or *grounded* judgments about her. The generality constraint, as Evans understands it, is an epistemological constraint. It concerns one's capacities to come to know things of certain very general *kinds*.

"[I]n order for a subject to be credited with the thought that *p*, he must know what it is for it to be the case that *p*" (p. 105), a kind of knowing that it "is hard to give any substance to . . . when this is not to be equated with an ability to determine whether or not [*p*] is true" (1982, p. 106). But Evans wishes to avoid the antirealist conclusion that empirical truth can only be verificationist truth. He wants to be a realist about truth. He attempts to accomplish this, as I understand it, in part by analyzing capacities to understand whole propositions as composed of more generally applicable component capacities to recognize objects, properties, and so forth, corresponding to the concepts these propositions involve. He applies the principle of compositionality in order, for example, to avoid problems about whether verification of propositions about inaccessible things such as those in the past is possible. He supports his realism, second, by understanding the capacities of which concepts are composed to concern interactions with the external world, and by recognizing that whether or not such capacities have been exercised properly cannot always be guaranteed by the character of a thinker's subjective experience. Concepts are not described in a verificationist way, by their relations only to sensory evidence.

Evans begins his analysis by unpacking "know what it is for it to be the case that" (say) it is *Alice* who has this or that property, by referring to possession of a "fundamental Idea" of Alice. The fundamental Idea of Alice is based, first, on grasp of the fundamental "ground of difference" for entities of her defining category, presumably, in this case, the category *person*. "For there is no thought about objects of a certain kind which does not presuppose the idea of *one* object of that kind, and the idea of one object of that kind must employ a general conception of the ways in which objects of that kind are differentiated from one another and from all other things" (p. 108). In the case of persons, for example, the fundamental ground of difference will be being in its own unique place at each given time. A "fundamental Idea" of Alice will require a grasp of her as being at some particular place at some particular time. And in the case of individual objects, a fundamental Idea must consist, also, in grasp of the criteria of identity for that kind of object over time. For Alice, presumably, this must involve at least that the place-times she occupies are contiguous.

Evans now unpacks what it is to "know what it is to be the case that" Alice has properties *not* attributed to her under her "fundamental

Idea, δ'. This requires that one understand "what it is for it to be the case that . . . $\lceil \delta = a \rceil$" for various other kinds of ideas, a, of Alice, such as definite descriptions and "demonstrative thoughts" (thoughts of Alice via current perceptions of her). Thus the problem is reduced, in part, to the question what it is to "know what it is for it to be the case that" various identity equations hold. For example, one concept that I have of Alice may be my ability to recognize her on sight ("recognition based identification," Evans 1982, Chapter 8). That is, I will know that the object of certain "demonstrative" thoughts, "that woman," equal the object of my fundamental Idea, δ, of Alice. Similarly, where P is a demonstratively indicated position in egocentric space and p a position in public space, "[that] in which knowledge of what it is for identity propositions of the form $\lceil P = p \rceil$ to be true consists" is "the capacity to discover . . . where in the world one is" (p. 162), that is, "[the] ability to locate [one's] egocentric space in the framework of a cognitive map" (p. 163).

That I have the ability to think of Alice thus implies that I would know how to reidentify her, either directly, or as mediated by a series of intermediate identity judgments, for purposes of applying each substantive predicate I grasp as possibly true of a person. That is, I take it, for each of these substantive judgments, I would know to make it were occasions to arise on which the relevant linking propositions were evidenced to me in the right way. And for each such possible substantive judgment there must exist ways by which I could grasp the relevant linking propositions. Ignoring worries about whether there are such things as identity judgments (Chapter 12), and tentatively identifying Evans' "capacities" and "abilities" with abilities as we have defined them (Chapter 4), this would surely entail my having a concept of Alice exactly in the sense I have described in previous chapters. That is, it would entail (1) my having a capacity to reidentify Alice, roughly in the sense of "reidentify" I have explicated, and (2) my understanding, for certain predicates, that they could apply to her. But the converse entailment does not hold. I have required very much less than Evans for having a substance concept.

§13.4 DIFFERING WITH EVANS ON KNOWING WHAT ONE IS THINKING OF

It is central to my thesis that the ontological ground of a substance, the principle that accounts for the invariance of certain of its properties

182

over encounters, need not be grasped in order to have a concept of it. Similarly, no criteria of identity or difference need be grasped for members of its class. The tiny infant (or the dog) who identifies Mama by smell so as to learn how to respond in her presence surely has no idea of an objective four-dimensional frame through which Mama-the-space-time-worm crawls on her way. Neither is the infant's (or the dog's) ability to identify Mama dependent on there being, necessarily, no one else in the world who smells exactly like Mama. The infant knows in practice when Mama is present again, which is all she needs for collecting knowledge about Mama. There is no need to know how to distinguish Mama from all other things in principle so long as she manages, for the most part, to do so in practice.

Evans holds that all concepts of objects of the same kind, all "modes of presentation" of these objects, are linked together in the following way. I must know for each such mode what it would be for it to present the same object as that presented by a certain fundamental idea of this kind of object, hence I must know for each such mode what it would be for it to present the same object as each other mode. No concept or set of concepts of the same thing form an island, isolated in principle from other concepts of the same thing. For this reason, Evans holds, watching an object on TV does not, simply as such, afford me a concept of that object, for it does not afford my knowing how to locate the space it is in within my conception of objective space. Merely by seeing the object on TV, I cannot, in principle, identify it with any fundamental idea that I could have of that kind of object. Only if I were *also* to think of the object seen by a description such as "the object of such and such kind that is causing this TV image" could I understand what would be involved in reidentifying it, hence know what it was I was thinking of. Similarly, Strawson spoke of "story-relative identifications" that one might make, (co)identifying various references to the same person in a true story that one hears. But unless one knows independently who this person is *outside* the story, Strawson held, such "identifications" do not really identify any particular person (Strawson 1959, p. 18). Evans agrees (p. 151). I do not agree.

What seems to be *yearned* for in the notion of knowing which object my thought is about is a sort of confrontation of thought, on the one side, with the object bare, on the other, taking place, per impossible, within thought itself. (Of course Russell's view was that exactly this sort of confrontation *is* possible – the object bare is, roughly speaking, *part* of the thought.) Barring that, the next best thing, apparently, is having the *essence* or *nature* of the object's particular identity before the mind, that which makes it different from all other things. And how does one get an individual nature before one's mind? Suppose, for example, that the nature involves being a member of a certain kind or category and being at a certain place at a certain time. What is it for me to think of this particular kind and this particular place and this particular time, as differentiated from all other kinds, places and times? Do these things have individual natures too? Must I have fundamental ideas of each of them too?

I diagnose Evans' position as follows. Interpreting the aboutness of a thought as needing to involve grasp of a "fundamental idea" of its object is merely a hankering left over from the Fregean/internalist/verificationist position that something *internal to me* must somehow determine a distinct object for my thought. The thought must somehow be hooked onto its object *in my mind*. Similarly, Evans' constantly reiterated phrase that we must somehow "know what it is for it to be the case that" *p* in order to understand the proposition *p* strikes me as a transparent rehearsal of the sort of verificationist/internalist suggestion he should be anxious to avoid. This phrase strongly suggests that something like my ability to imagine *p* being directly evidenced is what *constitutes* my meaning something in thinking that *p*.

The closest thing that actually makes some sense, I suggest, to the yearned-for ideal of comparison of a thought with its object bare within thought itself, is a confrontation of one *thought* of an object with another *thought* concerning that same object, this taking place within thought itself, and constituting a recognition *of* the sameness of the object (as described in Chapter 10). Putting this picturesquely, if you imagine the various thoughts that you have about, say, Noam Chomsky, as a sort of story that you tell yourself using various thought tokens that concern him, then knowing who you are thinking of in this story corresponds to your ability to make what Strawson called "story-relative identifications" of the person *in your story*. There is no way that you can cut through the stories that you tell yourself about Noam Chomsky in order to tack them *inside your mind* directly onto Noam, or onto his individual nature, in order to know in any more direct way than that who you are thinking of. Knowing what I am thinking of is being capable of coidentifying (Section 10.2) various of my thoughts with other thoughts of the same. It is being able to distinguish thinking of a thing again from thinking of a different thing.

Now I have argued that abilities are not the same as any kind of dispositions, nor does having an ability entail that one is necessarily able, in one's actual circumstances, to exercise that ability (Chapter 4). Similarly, knowing what one is thinking of obviously cannot be a simple disposition always, under every possible condition, correctly to identify incoming natural information concerning a thing.[2, 3] No one has that kind of ability with regard to the identity of anything. If that were required it would follow, for example, that the ancients did not know what they were thinking of when they thought of Hesperus and when they thought of Phosphorus, since they did not grasp that these were the same heavenly body. And it would follow that if I could ever, even momentarily, mistake someone else for my spouse, then I do not know who I am thinking of when I think of him. Rather, to have an ability to identify the object of my thought, I need only to have a disposition to do so correctly under certain definite kinds of historically determined conditions, namely those under which this ability, or the various more general components of which it is composed, were successful in the past, hence were acquired (Section 4.6). It only needs to be true that incoming natural information about this object, arriving in *certain kinds of packages*, piped through *certain definite kinds of information channels*, will be marked with identity markers as being about the same.

Nor does Evans require that one *actually* identify every source of incoming information. He requires only that no concept or set of concepts of the same thing form an island, wholly isolated in principle from other concepts of the same thing. One must possess conceptual abilities that could in principle bridge the gap between. This is because each

---

2 Evans himself is very unclear about what abilities or capacities are, and especially, on how they can be fallible. For example, in discussing recognition-based concepts, he tells us "It is essential for him to have an adequate Idea of a particular object that there be one, and only one, object which he is disposed to pick out in this way" (p. 271). In other places he makes passing reference to the necessity of information systems, perceptual systems, and so forth, operating properly. An information system can "malfunction" (p. 128). But there is no attempt to give a general characterization of conditions under which the disposition to pick out the object corresponding to a recognitional capacity must be realized.

3 "Natural information" in this passage is "informationC," defined in Appendix B.

nonfundamental Idea must be tied firmly by some capacity to the fundamental idea of its object, hence each idea of an object to every other idea of the same object. If we, in contrast to Evans, dispense with fundamental ideas of objects, will this leave us with the possibility of unbridgeable gaps between coreferential conceptual islands?

The question needs to be posed more carefully. I have argued (Chapters 10–12) that there cannot be modes of presentation of objects that are ways of thinking of them and that are also individuated according to ways of identifying them. Ways of identifying objects are not ways of thinking of them but ways of being guided by experience in marking identity for incoming information. They are ways of knowing how correctly to bind various packets of incoming information together. Moreover, it is not possible to individuate ways of identifying in a way needed for the traditional uses of the notion of modes of presentation (Section 11.5). We might make sense of the question about conceptual islands, however, by reference to naive Strawson-model modes of presentation (Section 11.2). Must I have an ability, if granted enabling conditions, to coidentify any two naive Strawson modes that present the same object, and an ability to separate any that present different objects (thus eliminating redundancy and equivocation in thought)?

One problem is that having an ability and having the ability easily to acquire or develop an ability are not sharply distinguishable. If I have the ability instantly and unhesitatingly to compound numerous more general abilities to yield, on demand, a specific complex ability then, we might suppose, I already have the more complex ability. If I would have to practice before I could do a thing then, reasonably, I don't already have the ability. But what if I would have to think for a while in order to figure out how to put more general abilities of mine together to obtain a certain complex result, such as in figuring out how to hang curtains over these bulky indoor shutters? I might need, for example, to do some calculations. How long will I be allowed to think and still be said to know how already? Suppose that instead of just figuring it out, I will need to acquire some information. I will need, for example, to make some measurements. Do I know how to hang these curtains already?

What kinds of information may I still need to acquire while knowing how already? I know how to get from home to school by following the Gurleyville road, but as I follow it, I have to take in the information how far each next curve is by sight. I know how to get to Boston by following I-84 East and then I-90 East, but I do so by following the I–84E and I–90E signposts, which inform me where to make various turns along the way. Suppose, instead, that I manage to get there just by following all the signs that say "Boston"? Or suppose that I know how to get there, not just by reading signposts, but in part by consulting a map. Similarly, suppose that I know how to make a cake by following a recipe. And I know which cookbook to open to find the recipe. Or suppose that I know how by knowing exactly who to ask for directions, for example, I know that Grandma knows? Can I know how to get to Boston merely by knowing how, in general, to ask for directions, assuming circumstances will afford someone to ask who happens to know? Can I know how to do something if applying my ability would require just the right information-bearing circumstances to come along serendipitously?

Evans returns several times to an example of a man who retains the memory of a steel ball he once saw, but retains no information as to when or where he saw it, nor concerning any other characteristic that would distinguish it from an identical ball he also once saw but forgot. Evans claims that this man has no Idea of the remembered ball. This is because "our subject's supposed idea of that ball is completely independent not only from any possible [distinguishing] experience, but also from everything else in his conceptual repertoire. There is no question of his recognizing the ball; and there is nothing else he can do which will show that his thought is really about one of the two balls (about *that* ball), rather than about the other" (1982, p. 115). Evans takes it, that is, that this man is debarred in principle from ever making another grounded judgment about that ball – from ever reasonably coidentifying his supposed thought of it with any other thought of it. According to Evans' original story, however, the man fails to remember the second ball he saw because of a blow on the head. Now imagine Evans' story as truly describing the realization of a perverse philosopher's thought experiment. The philosopher purposefully showed the man one ball, then hit him on the head, then showed him the other. Years later the philosopher returns, pulls the actually remembered ball out of his pocket, and explains the whole episode to his victim, who then correctly coidentifies the ball of his memory with the ball he sees. So he was not debarred in principle from ever making another grounded judgment about that ball after all. True, Evans does stipulate that the man does not think of his remembered ball *as* the one that caused his memory. But if he already has the capacity to *come* to think of it that way on momentary reflection, this stipulation seems quite beside the point.

187

With examples such as these in mind, how should we answer the question, for example, whether the ancients did or did not know how to coidentify Hesperus with Phosphorus? Presumably in principle something could have lead them to this, even without additional conceptual training. Perhaps the ancients already knew how to separate weight from mass but hadn't happened yet on the experience that would enable them actually to do it? I don't think that principled answers to questions of this sort are possible. In practice, undoubtedly many coreferential islands do remain separate in various people's thoughts, and some naive Strawson modes do remain equivocal.

§13.6 THE ABILITY TO REIDENTIFY, OR BEING ABLE TO REIDENTIFY?

Earlier I mentioned Strawson's notion of "story-relative identification." Strawson explains this notion with an example. A speaker is telling a factual story, which begins "A man and a boy were standing by a fountain . . . The man had a drink." The hearer identifies the references of the two tokens of "man" as being to the same man, but does not identify this man with anyone outside the story. Strawson says of this kind of identification that it is "identification within [the] story; but not identification within history," hence that it is not "full identification" (1959, p. 18). Yet given that the story is factual, the hearer surely knows means of further tracking. He can, for example, ask the speaker who the man was. Thus identification of people in stories is not necessarily isolated from "history." But perhaps the speaker himself does not know who the story is really about, or the hearer does not ask and later forgets who told him the story. On the other hand, perhaps these links can be reestablished. The hearer knows a way to find out who told him the story, and a way to find out who told the story to the hearer, hence who the man was. But now suppose this method is chancy. He will be lucky if it works, but he can try. Does he still "have an ability" to identify the man in the story with someone outside the story?

Notice that there are cases that Strawson would consider to involve "full identifications" that are more tenuously connected than many stories to any practical capacity actually to mark sameness in grounded judgments. Consider my thought, *the person who wove this part*, as I inspect a particularly intricate tiny section of a mediaeval wall hanging of unknown origin. This thought contains a perfectly clear definite description based (as Strawson prefers identifying descriptions to be) on an unambiguous demonstrative. But undoubtedly there is no way at all of my ever marking sameness between the thought of this wonderful weaver and any thoughts in new grounded judgments. Certainly having knowledge of the ontological structures in the world that relate that weaver to me, say, understanding the "criteria of identity" for pieces of tapestry and for persons over time, is insufficient when it comes to the practical business of actually tracking information about this weaver.

Having an ability to reidentify something is obviously a pretty vague sort of affair. Earlier (Section 4.2) I drew a distinction between knowing how to do a thing and actually being able to do it. Actually being able generally requires the presence of supporting conditions that merely knowing how does not. Actually being able to do A might be defined, for example, as having a disposition, right now, to do A if I try. Or a disposition, right now, if I try, to proceed to get into a position to do A if I try . . . and so forth. Clearly the edges are not sharp here either. But the distinction between knowing how and actually being able may cast some light on how we should understand what *knowing what one is judging about* entails. Perhaps we should draw a similarly vague distinction between having a concept of an object and being able to reidentify it in practice. Then we would note that there are degrees of knowing how to reidentify. I may command myriad ways or only a few. Also there are degrees of being able to identify in practice. I may get thousands of opportunities I can utilize or none. But however we divide things up, it is clear that knowing what I am thinking of is always a matter of degree. No one is in principle infallible at reidentifying anything, even should they happen always to succeed in practice. Nor, unlike the case of many more ordinary abilities, need they always know, either immediately or at all, whether they have succeeded.

Not only are substance concepts always imperfect abilities, the means used for many of them may be in our command only temporarily. Sometimes this is because our memories are short. For example, although I can usually remember C sharp for five minutes so as to reidentify it when I hear it again, I always forget it overnight – I don't have "absolute pitch." Luckily my concept of C sharp has other conceptual means. I know how to reidentify it by going to the piano, or the flute, or by asking my friend Brian who has completely infallible pitch. Because I know C sharp's name, I also know how to mark sameness for the thought of C sharp in new grounded judgments as I hear or read about C sharp. I may read what its frequency is, or about the difficulty of playing this or that instrument in its key.

New faces can be, for me, a bit like C sharp. I can identify them over the next hour, but not always over the next week. If I have forgotten both the new face and the name, I may have to act very fast to pick up the scent. Descriptions are sometimes useful, but their usefulness may be short lived. I may need to call on the memories of others quite soon, before *they* forget who fits the description, before they forget, say, who all was present on the occasion. Sometimes there may be no way to pick up the scent, and I will never "know who that was" that I met, never "know who it is I am remembering." But as a limiting case, of course, I do know who I'm remembering. I *would* know how to pick up the scent *were* I to come across certain kinds of information. I have relevant abilities. It's just that I haven't had, and perhaps won't get, a chance to apply them.

§13.7 MISTAKING WHAT I'M THINKING OF

To lack the ability always to identify correctly – to be disposed some-times to error – is part of the human condition. Merely to be disposed to error, however, is not yet to have made an error. And it is only in so far as one actually makes errors in identification that one's thoughts be-come equivocal.

One result of mistaken sameness markings may be invalid inference. For example, suppose that I see that something in the tree is a squirrel and then I see that "it" takes off and flies. I may conclude that some squirrels can fly. But the inference will be invalid if I unknowingly had lost track of the squirrel and some other "it" did the flying. Since invalid inferences can lead from true premises to false conclusions, misidentifi-cations can of course give rise to false beliefs. More interesting however, is when misidentifications give rise to confused or *equivocal* thoughts.

A person who has very basic misinformation about a thing may be said to be "confused" about it, but that sort of confusion is not equivo-cation. "Do you see that woman?" Jane says, pointing to Ann, and then she tells you a whole kettle of lies about Ann, all of which you believe. Perhaps you never learn anything else much about Ann, but once in a while you do see her again on the street, and then you review in your mind all those dreadful lies. You are woefully confused about Ann, but your thought of her is not equivocal. For it is definitely about *Ann* that you are confused, and not about something ambiguous. Perhaps you even believe a lot of wrong individuating descriptions of Ann, but that is not equivocation either. As long as you don't actually *use* any of these descriptions in such a way as to result in actual misidentifications of Ann, you will not yet have an equivocal thought.

Suppose, on the other hand, that you mistake Carol whom you see on the street for the city mayor. Having heard that the mayor was in Washington just this morning, you conclude that she must have taken a plane home. That WHO must have taken a plane home? – Carol, or the mayor? That is what I mean by an equivocal thought. It isn't a thought *of* the one woman any more or less than it is of the other, but hovers between.

On a descriptionist theory (Section 3.5), an equivocal thought might, I suppose, be one that was governed equally by two or more definite descriptions that were not coreferential. Or on a conceptionist theory (Section 3.5), an equivocal thought or concept might correspond to a disposition to recognize incompatible things as part of the same extension. I'm not sure that either of these suggestions is entirely coherent, but the point I would make is that where the conception is taken to determine the extension of a concept, equivocation, should it exist, would be found in mere *dispositions* of the concept user. My claim, on the contrary, is that equivocation is found only where actual information, derived from distinct sources, is marked as being about the same. One *always* has *dispositions* to misidentify things, given sufficiently awkward conditions.

Suppose that I think John is the president of the local chapter of the AAUP, but he's not. Bill is instead. Do I have an equivocal concept, or just a false belief about John? That depends on whether or not I have gathered *information* about the president of the local chapter of the AAUP and applied it to John. Nor need this mean that I have applied information derived from Bill to John. More likely, I have gathered general information about the presidency of the AAUP. I know what the president's duties, privileges, and some of his probable locations are (e.g., at the meeting in Mannly Hall on Friday). The president (timeless) of the local chapter of the AAUP is a rough sort of substance. It is something I can learn about and the information will remain valid over time. If I have falsely identified John with the current presidency, I have probably mixed information about two things together. I have probably made wrong mediate inferences, inferring, for example, that John will be in Mannly Hall on Friday. On the other hand, if I merely take John to be the tallest man in the room and he's not, granted I have no information about the tallest man in the room, as such, there is not as yet, and likely there won't be, any hint of equivocation in my idea of John. False information is not, as such, equivocation.

To have two things or more confused in one's mind is surely a common condition. For example, much of the history of science might be told in these terms. What is astonishing is not that it happens, but that in dealing with common objects, properties, and kinds it doesn't happen more often. What is astonishing is how good we usually are at keeping track of those ordinary things in our world that (unlike which glass is which in the cupboard – Section 5.5) matter to us – at not mixing them all up together. What is astonishing is how good our concepts tend to be, despite the fact that they must operate, as must our other abilities, on principles resting not just on the character of our minds, but on the structure of the world outside.

14

How Extensions of New Substance Concepts are Fixed: How Substance Concepts Acquire Intentionality

§14.1 WHAT DETERMINES THE EXTENSIONS OF NEW SUBSTANCE CONCEPTS?

In the first section of this chapter, I will use the results of the last chapter to explain more exactly how the extension of a substance concept is fixed. I will be concerned, especially, with how the extensions of new substance concepts, acquired directly on first meeting with their referents, are fixed. The rest of the chapter will be devoted to fitting the theory of substance concepts defended here into the more general theory of intentional representation developed in Millikan (1984, 1993a).

Evans concluded, about the man with the memory of the ball he was unable to identify, that the man did not have the capacity to think of *that* ball at all, but only to think of *a* ball (Section 13.4). But, I have argued, the question whether he could think of that individual ball doesn't turn on whether he was actually able to reidentify it. It doesn't turn on whether his *situation* was right for reidentifying it. It depends, rather, on whether his thought was produced by his cognitive systems in such a way as to have, as its first assigned function, that it be coidentified, specifically, with thoughts of *that particular* ball. And to that question the answer would seem to be *yes*.

As Evans describes the case, when the man was looking at the ball he understood it to be an individual ball, indeed, one that happened to be steel and shiny. It is not in question, then, whether he had the general ability to think of individual balls. Presumably at that time he applied a relevant sort of primary-substance (individual-object) template to the ball and was conceptually ready to track it for purposes of collecting

193

certain sorts of information about it. He had various skills in place for tracking individual physical objects, and some understanding of what might be learned about this particular physical object. The *cognitive* representation produced by seeing the ball – the *thought* it produced – was thus designed to be taken up by an interpreting system having, among other functions, the function of conceptually tracking and reidentifying this particular ball. Had the system tracked and reidentified this particular ball, it would have been working entirely in accordance with principles it was *already* designed (selected for, trained, or tuned) to instantiate.[1] Thus the man's idea of the ball was a fully intentional cognitive representation of it. The fact that he also saw, but then forgot, a similar ball at another time does not change that matter. Nor is the matter changed by the fact that in this case he couldn't perceptually *discriminate* that ball from the other (Section 14.1). Nor is it changed by the fact that no one happened to show up later to explain to him which ball it was (Section 13.4). Similarly, if I spot a new kind of lizard in the grass, one that is completely unfamiliar to me, and propose to find out what I can about its species, granted that the general abilities I have already acquired with regard to tracking lizardlike species are adequate, my concept of this species may already be completely determinate in extension.

Also, any new substance concept that I acquire just by remembering the name of that substance and understanding in what general category it falls (Chapter 6), may immediately have a perfectly determinate extension. I have an ability to recognize this same name when I encounter it again. Suppose then that the name has a determinate referent in the public language. This requires that others in the language community, past or present, have or have had an ability to recognize this referent, and have sometimes or do sometimes broadcast information about it by using this name. I then have the (fallible) ability to identify this *as* being information about the same. My concept has the same referent as the public term, and by holding the steadying hand of language, I have the ability to learn how to extend my conception of this referent to include nonlinguistic means of identifying it. Thus, Burge (1979, 1982) is right that what I mean by a term may depend directly on what others in my language community mean by it, indeed, that what I am *thinking* of can depend on what others mean.

1 In the terminology of Millikan (1984), it would have been performing an "adapted proper function." For details on the derivation of adapted proper functions, see also Millikan (in press b).

194

Contrast these cases with one where an apparent cognitive representation has no referent at all. In one place Evans remarks that "[a]n informational state may be of *nothing*: this will be the case if there was no object which served as input to the information system when the information was produced" (1982, p. 128).[2] Similarly, it certainly is possible that the cognitive systems should sometimes be triggered to produce apparently intentional representations, apparent concepts, by sources entirely foreign to any proper use of them. It is possible to seem to perceive and to seem cognitively to represent objects that are not objects at all. That is, there is no way that the cognitive systems could proceed to reidentify an intentional object in this case that would constitute these systems proceeding in accordance with principles they were designed to instantiate.

As it first begins to develop, then, a substance concept may have a completely determinate extension, or it may be determinate that it has no extension at all. Between these two possibilities are others in which the germ of a substance concept might develop normally from here in any of several ways. These are the cases in which a reference has yet to be "focused" (Perner 1998) thus hovering between possible extensions (Section 6.3).

Also, as has been a central theme of this book, if the content of any substance concept proceeds actually to be *misidentified*, and the mistake is not corrected, so that information about two things is bound together as though they were one, although the representation is not empty, it is at least to a degree equivocal. Correctly identifying a substance in thought has the logical form of contributing to the solution of a coordination problem or, say, of directing one light ray toward a focus with others. Identifying correctly is like focusing the eyes. When both eyes are open but not focused on the same thing, neither eye sees anything clearly, but when both are focused on the same thing, then both see, both see the same, and both see clearly.

§14.2 INTENTIONAL REPRESENTATION

According to Russell's principle, thinking of something is always grounded in some sort of "acquaintance" in the Russellian sense implying a kind of knowledge of what that thing is. There is no such thing as an object of thought the identity of which is unknown to the

2   On Evans' use of the term "information," see Appendix A.

thinker. It cannot be that I first think of something and subsequently grasp (or fail to grasp) what it is I am thinking of. This claim is correct, I have argued, for conceptual thought, so long as we understand knowing what one is thinking of as a fallible ability, compatible with the possibility that one can make mistakes about the object of one's thought (Section 13.5 and Section 13.6). What I am thinking of conceptually is not determined prior to my *ability* to reidentify, though it *is* determined prior to my actual *acts* of identifying, which may not properly express that ability.

Russell's principle is mistaken, however, if "thought" is understood to cover all forms of mental representation. It is mistaken if taken to be required of intentionality more generally. *Conceptual* representation is marked off by requiring a matching capacity to reidentify its content, but not all intentionality involves concepts. Perception, for example, may have content that the perceiver has no need or ability to reidentify. A full treatment of these more general claims about intentionality is offered in Millikan (1984, 1993a). Here, I will abbreviate only some aspects of that work, enough to show how the claims about substance concepts fit into the overall picture of intentional representation sketched in those earlier essays.

Natural information, as this notion has usually been understood, is contained in an output signal pattern that covaries with the pattern of input from some source of information, through some physical medium or "channel," according to physical law. I call this sort of information "informationL" ("L" for "law").[3] This is not the sense of "natural information" used in most of this book, that sense being explained in Appendix B, but it is likely to be familiar to the reader, so I will use it as a starting point in explaining the general notion of intentional representation.

InformationL is ubiquitous, both in animate and inanimate nature. It has, merely as such, nothing to do with intentionality, nor is it, just as such, of any use to an organism. There are certain conditions, however, under which an output signal containing informationL about a configuration at its source is also an intentional representation of that configuration. To make this the case, the signal carrying informationL has to carry this information "intentionally" in the following sense. It must carry it in accordance with the natural purpose or function of some

---

3 This is roughly the way in which Dretske, Fodor, and Gibson use the term "information." For discussion, see Appendix B

transmitting or relaying mechanism, a mechanism that has been selected or trained for exactly that job.

If a mechanism has been selected or trained for the job of producing or relaying a certain kind of informationL, that will be because some cooperating or coordinate mechanism, perhaps another phase of the same mechanisms, has a use for this informationL. But informationL, arriving from the environment, relayed through an animal's sensory organs to its brain, arriving in a certain code or vehicle, cannot be of use to the animal unless the animal is designed or has learned to be *guided* by this sort of vehicle in ways appropriate to the configuration at the information's source. That is, informationL is of no use to an organism unless it can be "interpreted" through the arousal of inner or outer activity of the organism that is appropriate to the state of affairs the information concerns. In sum, informationL that is embodied in an *intentional* representation is produced or channeled in accordance with the proper functioning of some designed mechanism, where a further proper function of that mechanism is to cooperate with a corresponding "interpreting" mechanism to guide that interpreter in accomplishing some (ultimately practical) function or functions beyond, under the circumstances represented.

Now let me generalize this idea. Only some mechanisms designed to produce intentional representations are designed to do so by producing or transmitting natural informationL. This may well be how direct perception of the spatial layout of the immediate environment is normally accomplished for purposes of direct action guidance. Gibson was probably right about that. But this is not, for the most part, how cognition is accomplished. In its more general form, intentional representation requires only that there be a mechanism designed to produce items bearing a certain *correspondence* to the distal environment, correspondence in accordance with some definite rules ("semantic rules"), which items ("intentional representations") are to be used to guide another system (the "interpreter") in the performance of certain of its functions.

Now an enormously important feature of designed mechanisms is that they do not always accomplish the functions for which they were designed. Many mechanisms designed either by natural selection or by learning manage to perform their assigned tasks only occasionally. Only occasionally does the slap of a beaver tail on the water actually perform its proper function of saving the beaver's relatives from a danger. In part, this is because its timing only occasionally corresponds to the timing of any real danger. Mechanisms designed to produce intentional representations that correspond by a rule to the distal environment can have these functions yet frequently fail. Compatibly, mechanisms designed to produce intentional representations may be designed to do so, not by the use of channels of natural informationL, where output form corresponds to input form in accordance with natural law, but by the use of quite unreliable statistical methods (see Appendix B). The output of the system may correspond to the distal environment just often enough to be more useful than if the organism had no such system in place at all.

What makes intentional representations "represent" their intentional objects is thus quite different from what makes photographs "represent" their subjects. Intentional representations represent what they would need to correspond to for their interpreting mechanisms to use them productively in accordance with design. If they fail to correspond in this way but the interpreting mechanisms are guided by them in the normal way, the result will be unproductive. It is unproductive for beavers to waste energy and time diving under when there is no danger present. It is unproductive for a worker bee to fly off in the direction a bee dance says unless there is nectar in that direction. But that the intentional representation needs to correspond to the world by a certain rule in order to be productive does not imply that there exists any method by which it can be produced that would guarantee this correspondence. It does not imply, for example, that there must be some method by which its object could always be discriminated from all other objects in accordance with natural law. To represent something it is not necessary that one be able to tell it from all other things.[4]

The "correspondence" that a system producing intentional representations is designed to establish between these representations and their representeds can be thought of as an abstract isomorphism, in this way. Transformations (in the abstract mathematical sense) of the representations correspond to transformations of what is represented, such that different representations map different representeds in a systematic or "productive" way. Intentional representations have, as such, not ordinary extensions but *truth conditions*.[5] They are not analogous to names or open sentences. Rather, intentional representations always make claims.[6]

---

4   For discussion, see Appendix B.
5   More accurately, they have satisfaction conditions. I have omitted discussion here of representations that are imperative rather than indicative. See Millikan (1984, Chapter 6).
6   Indicative ones do. See note 5 above.

If they did not make claims, they could not be such as to guide activity appropriately given the existence of their extensions. About *danger*, for example, there is nothing to be done, nor is there anything to be done about *here* or about *now*. But about *there is danger here now* there may well be something to be done. Similarly, about *nectar fifty yards southeast of here* there is nothing to be done, unless one reads this as an assertion that *there is* nectar fifty yards southeast of here.

§14.3 CONCEPTUAL AND NONCONCEPTUAL INTENTIONAL REPRESENTATIONS

As I have just described it, the intentionality of an intentional representation need not involve concepts of any of the things referred to in its truth conditions. Neither the beaver nor its relatives need a concept of danger – a way of collecting information that regards just danger, *as such*, over time – in order to produce appropriate beaver slaps or to respond to them appropriately by diving under. Similarly, an animal's perception of the spatial layout of its immediate environment for purposes of moving about in it, avoiding obstacles, getting through passages, climbing up things or over things and so forth, need not involve any concepts. Being guided by perception of a tree so as to avoid it as you run by does not require a concept of it, not even merely as an obstacle. You need not be collecting information about it, nor about trees or obstacles generally, for future use, nor need you be making any inferences concerning these objects based on previous experience. You might be doing so, of course, but you need not. Certainly, say, a deer need not. There can be mental representation, then, without a grasp of the identity of what is represented, hence without knowing *what* is represented. To suppose otherwise, I suggest, is to relapse into a "passive picture theory of *conception*" (compare Section 8.1). Knowing what one is mentally representing requires the ability to track it conceptually, to mark its identity with sameness markers, preparatory to using the information it bears in mediate inference or an analogue (Chapter 13). There is no reason to suppose this sort of marking is required for all uses of perception.[7]

On the other hand, very simple acts of identifying are involved in many nonconceptual tasks. In Section 10.2, I pointed out that any

---

7 In Millikan (1984), I called intentional representations that did their jobs without their semantic values having to be identified "intentional icons," reserving the term "representations" for those whose values did need to be identified for them to perform properly.

coordinations among sensory modalities, such as eye–hand coordination, and even the perception of depth using binocular vision, involve simple acts of coidentifying. Similarly, the ability to learn over time how to handle or behave in the presence of an individual, or a stuff, or a kind, requires the ability to reidentify that substance over a variety of encounters with it. Clearly the ability to grasp the identity of what is represented is crucial for routine uses of a great number of representations that are simpler than what one would naturally call "thoughts" or "judgments." When the direction of a sound alerts me to the direction in which a bird can be seen, I have (re)identified a location. I then know (minimally – see Sections 4.3, and 13.4) what direction the bird is in. When the look of a rope combines with its feel so that these jointly guide my activity of tying a knot, I (re)identify various parts of the rope. I know (minimally) what parts of the rope I am seeing and feeling. On the other hand, knowing what rope I am feeling as I coordinate its sight and its feel is not knowing whether it is the rope Sally was hunting for or the rope I used yesterday for tying the canoe. Similarly, seeing how far off the dart board is for purposes of learning, over a period of time, how to hit the bull's-eye at that distance is not seeing how many *feet* off it is. And I can see how far the dart board is for throwing darts and also know how far off the eye chart is in feet without knowing whether these are the same or different distances. Knowing what my inner representations are representing can be a relatively simple affair, involving minimal identifications, certainly not yet involving full-fledged cognition. This suggests that the distinction between perception and cognition is not a sharp one. There are gray areas between.

Perhaps something reminiscent of Evans' "generality constraint" (Section 13.3) marks off the level of true cognition in the sense of "thought" and "judgment" from more primitive and fundamental levels of mental representation and identification, in the following way. Perceptual representations that guide immediate action need to be rich in specific kinds of information, showing the organism's exact relations to a number of aspects of its current environment directly as they unfold during action. These representations may need to have variable structure of a kind that conforms closely to the variable structure of the organism–environment relations that need to be instantly taken into account. And because they need to be constructed quickly and reliably, they may be constructed by modular systems that are relatively cognitively impenetrable (compare Fodor 1989).[8] The first job of the more disinterested, more general-purpose, cognitive representations, on the other hand, is easy participation in mediate inference. This job makes different demands, there being no way to specify in advance in what specific kinds of inferences such a representation may need to be used. The information captured in cognitive representations is collected for whatever, if anything, it may happen to prove useful for. While the representations of perception need to be cast in highly structured multidimensional media suitable to the immediate purposes to which they are dedicated, cognitive representations should be cast in a simpler uniform medium that makes them easy to compare and combine.

Whether or not information can interact in inference depends not on its content but on its vehicle. Putting it graphically, if the first premise of an inference is represented with a mental Venn diagram and the second with a mental sentence, it is hard to see what inference rules could apply to yield a conclusion. Similarly, one might suppose, if the information coming in through the various senses were not translated into something like a common medium for the purposes of theoretical and practical inference, it could not interact in a flexible way. Evans' generality constraint requires that any subject of judgment might be thought with any relevant predicate. The requirement here would be twofold. First, every proposition should be represented such that it could be combined with any other having an overlapping content, so as to make suitable mediate inferences possible. Second, each should be represented such that new identity markers could be inserted wherever needed, thus facilitating expansion of one's grasp of identities in the cognitive domain.

§14.4 THE INTENTIONALITY OF MENTAL TERMS FOR SUBSTANCES

Intentional representations are produced by systems designed to align them with the world according to the semantic rules to which their interpreting devices are adapted or adjusted. The intentional content of an inner sign, what it is about, rests directly on how it is designed to be used by the organism that harbors it. We have seen that it isn't always necessary that these interpreting devices should identify the semantic

---

8 Fodor thinks inference must be involved in this construction, however, whereas I do not.

values of an intentional representation in order to use it. Many intentional representations do their jobs properly without their contents being identified. But the very first function of any discursive or, as I shall say, *cognitive* representation is to be ready to participate in inferences. Thus the intentional content of the cognitive attitudes must rest directly on this primary function. A cognitive representation is dependent for its very intentionality on its interpreting mechanisms' ability to identify its intentional objects, to know what it represents (Chapter 13). This is the truth, I believe, in Evans' claim that where there is no concept of an object there can be no thinking of it. And it is the truth in the claim made by many philosophers of this century that thinking of a thing necessarily involves dispositions to make inferences concerning it, that intentionality is inseparable from rationality. The intentionality of cognition (but of cognition only) *does* happen to be inseparable from rationality.

Substance concepts used for cognition are designed for use in mediate inference. Inference moves, paradigmatically, from one cognitive attitude to another. Thus the functions of these substance concepts always require them to appear as elements in complete intentional representations having satisfaction conditions. A word, Frege said, has meaning only in the context of a sentence. Similarly, a discursive concept has a function only in the context of a complete cognitive attitude. That it has an intentional content, that it means anything, is entirely dependent on its capacity to participate in the creation of a variety of complete cognitive attitudes, that is, a variety of intentional representations, as these were described in Section 14.1.

15

Cognitive Luck: Substance Concepts in an Evolutionary Frame[1]

Steven Pinker (1994b) chides the educated layman for imagining Darwin's theory to go something like Figure 1 (the vertical lines are "begats").

Pinker says, "evolution did not make a ladder; it made a bush" (p. 343), and he gives us the diagrams shown in Figures 2 and 3 instead, showing how it went, in increasing detail, down to us. "Paleontologists like to say that to a first approximation, all species are extinct (ninety-nine percent is the usual estimate). The organisms we see around us are distant cousins, not great grandparents; they are a few scattered twig-tips of an enormous tree whose branches and trunk are no longer with us" (pp. 343–4). The historical life bush consists mainly in dead ends.

Moreover, when we look more closely at the life bush, examining in detail the various lineages that form the littlest twigs (the species), we see the same pattern over again. The vast majority of individual animals and plants forming these various lineages didn't make it. The twigs are largely made of fuzz – of myriad little lives that broke off before reproduction. An indication of a species' mortality rate is how many more offspring than one per parent are conceived on average. Consider, then, spiders, fish, and rabbits. And recall that Octavius was a common Roman name. To a first approximation, all individual animals die before reproducing.

Species went extinct, typically, because of changing environments, including the comings and goings of other living species. The study of

1   This chapter is a revised version of "Cognitive Luck: Externalism in an Evolutionary Frame" from *Mindscapes: Philosophy, Science, and the Mind*, Martin Carrier and Peter K. Machamer, Eds., © 1997. Used by permission of the University of Pittsburgh Press.

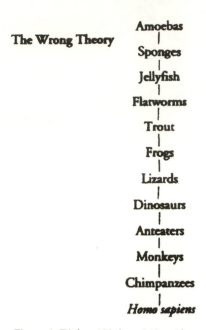

Figure 1 (Pinker 1994b, p. 343, with permission)

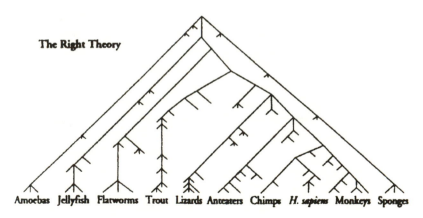

Figure 2 (Pinker 1994b, p. 344, with permission)

these changes and resulting extinctions is, of course, a purely historical study, a study of the disposition of historical bits of matter, positioned at particular points in space and time, running afoul of other historical bits of matter, positioned in accidental juxtaposition. The places where the streamlets of life managed to flow on, through little chinks in the bar-

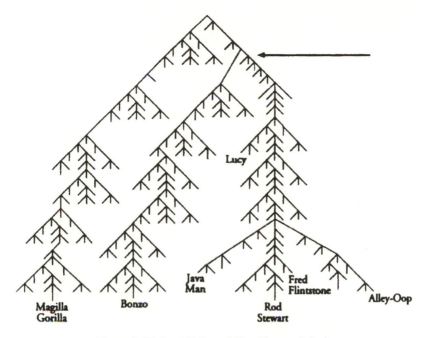

Figure 3 (Pinker 1994b, p. 345, with permission)

riers thrown up by geological history and other competing life forms, were also accidental in the very strongest sense. There are no empirical laws of evolution. There are only applicable and interesting mathematical models of certain aspects of evolution, ways of calculating the necessary outcomes of certain assumptions, as when demonstrating that WERE Johnny to continue to earn 5 percent a year on his $10,000 investment for fifteen years, and WERE he not to spend any of it, he WOULD accumulate $20,000. Models of this kind are not empirical laws. The results of the evolutionary process we still have with us today are the outcome of sheer cosmic luck, no more and no less.

There are, however, two great and simple principles that, conjoined, account for the fact, despite vastly changing historical circumstances, that there still exists life, indeed, vastly abundant life. Call these principles "multiplication" and "division." "Multiplication" says that the more progeny each member of a group bears, the more chance there is that some of these progeny will be lucky enough to happen upon accidental chinks in the environmental barriers through which they may slip to the next generation. If enough baby sea turtles are born, a few will accidentally avoid being eaten on the journey from their birth nests to the sea. "Division" says that if enough variety of life is produced, then there is a good chance that some of the environments that chance by will be suited to someone or other. "Division" is effected both by the vast number of species and by polymorphism within species. The history of life is like a lottery that was bound to be won by some, because so many bought tickets and there were so many different kinds of drawings.

Turning to life within a single species, it is easy wrongly to suppose that there is another principle that keeps lineages going. Natural selection, we suppose, has acted to preserve only the "fittest" characteristics for any given species, so that these are had pretty much by all members of the species. The result, we suppose, is that each normal little animal is nearly ideally designed for its own particular niche. Then why do so many species need to have so many babies? Why the thick long fuzz on all the lineage lines if all the animals are so "fit"? The reason is that, like everything else having to do with the propagation of life, fitness is a matter of statistics. Higher fitness lends only a higher *probability* of survival and reproduction. A die loaded with sixes on two sides doesn't help if you throw one of the other four sides, and that is what you are most likely to do.

The tossing, here, is done by the enormous variety among individual environments. The kitten with an immune system resistant to feline distemper is run over by a car. The kitten who exhibits sensible behavior on the roadway gets exposed to distemper. The kitten with both strengths gets into rat poison at a neighbor's. There is no way to be "fit" for all contingencies. Where environmental barriers are diverse and shifting, introducing numerous and diverse kittens raises the chances that a few will manage to pass through, but it doesn't raise the chance for *each* kitten. Assuming probabilities pertinent to relevant environmental factors remain constant over time, one could confidently predict that a species will continue to survive. But to predict how the individual lineages within the species will go so as to make this happen would require a detailed knowledge of every cranny in the environment at every time. Predicting that someone will win is easy enough, predicting *who* will win is impossible. For the system that propagates a lineage is not contained in the individual bodies of the organisms making up the lineage. It rests also upon statistically reliable yet accidental episodes of environmental cooperation. Individual lineages do not advance lawfully.

Instead of laws for lineage advance, there are mechanisms. Given a propitious environment by the luck of the draw, there are various mechanisms by which selected individual organisms composing a particular species have historically projected themselves forward in time. The working of these mechanisms is explained, not by laws of the particular species, but by laws formulated in more basic sciences. Physical structures with which the organism is equipped, coupled with just the right propitious supporting physical structures in the environment, project the lineage in accordance with physical laws. There is, for example, a mechanism by which newly hatched green turtles reach the sea when they do. But of course there is no law that they reach the sea – not even a *ceteris paribus* law, any more than there is a *ceteris paribus* law that little boys grow up to be president. Similarly, there is a mechanism whereby sand is sometimes prevented from entering our eyes (the eye-blink reflex) but there is no law that sand is kept out of our eyes.

Suppose now that we magnify the little lines that are individual organisms moving moment by moment through their individual life cycles. Over here under the lens is a barnacle. It waves its little fan foot through the water once, twice, ten times, a hundred and ten times, and the hundred and eleventh time it picks up a microscopic lunch. Over here is Tabby, after a squirrel. Whoops, missed! Now she is after a bird. Missed again! An hour of stalking with no profit. Never mind, here she comes now to *cry* for her dinner, where environmental circumstances are more likely, for her, to bear fruit. Over there, now, is Grackling the goose, doing a mating dance for his chosen. She spurns him today, but perhaps she will not tomorrow. Or he will find another instead, either this season or next. Over here is Rover, kicking up sand as he runs. Despite his healthy eye-blink reflex, one sand grain goes into his eye. The eye waters profusely, but does not wash out the sand. Rover rubs the eye with his paw and eventually manages to clear it. Similarly, looking to less visible behaviors, there are membranes to keep harmful bacteria from entering Rover's body. And there is also a whole series of mechanisms designed to destroy those bacteria that still manage to get through. Often one or another of these various filters works but it can also happen that none do.

In this manner, at every point where an organism interacts with its environment as needed to spin out its lifeline, we find innumerable failures. Counterbalancing these, we again find Multiplication and Division. We find numerous trials, many of which fail for each success. We find numerous redundant mechanisms, designed to perform the same basic tasks. The result is that the lifeline occasionally proceeds, small step by small step, right through to the next generation. But there are no laws that govern this process. There are only numerous and diverse mechanisms operating in a stochastic environment hoping for a possible drawing. There are lots of fuzzies everywhere along each individual lifeline, lots and lots of deadend trials.

Up to now without comment I have been treating biological species not as classes but as big, scattered, historical entities, enduring for longer or shorter periods through time. What species an individual organism belongs to depends not on its timeless properties but on its historical relations to other individuals. Dogs must be born of other dogs, not just be like other dogs; sibling species count as two or more for the same reason that identical twins count as two, not one. Earlier (Section 2.3) I mentioned that both Ghiselin and Hull have argued that species are actually *individuals*, a position that appears reasonable, certainly for the case of familiar sexually reproducing animals. Hull concluded that because species are really historical individuals, "their names function in no scientific laws" (1978), for example, "[t]here is no such thing as human nature." Crossing this current, I claimed, however, that the members of the various biological species, as well as members of various other biological types, form real substance kinds, over which many well founded generalizations, though not strict laws, can be run entirely legitimately. Inductions from one member of a species to the next often hold up for very good reason. Were this not so, there could be no science of biology. Nor could there be any science of psychology. But we must be careful not to analogize the subject matter of the life sciences and other historical sciences too closely to that of the eternal sciences.

Biological species form historical substance kinds in part because of historical connections among their members. Roughly, the members have been copied from one another, and natural selection, operating on a variety of levels has enforced a high degree of copying fidelity. Adult members of a species are alike also in part because they have developed in what is relevantly the same historical environment. And they continue to be alike – indeed, may continue to survive – only insofar as they continue to inhabit what is, in relevant respects, the same environment. They live on land, or in the sea, or alone, or in groups, or in language communities, and so forth.

Now it is always possible to study the properties that are common to most individuals of a given species at a given stage of life, apart from their normal environment. You can study these properties just as you might study the properties of any chunk of inorganic matter lying on the lab table. In this case, any dispositions that characterize the kind, or that would characterize the kind in any physically possible environment, are as legitimate to study as any other. These dispositions may show up, for example, when the species members are in the wild, or in cages, or in spaceships, or in laboratory apparatuses, or under the microscope, or after injection with chemicals, or under 5 atmospheres pressure, or subjected to 5,000 volts current. For what these objects are disposed to be like and to do in one environment is as much a part of their objective nature as in any other. Their nature as such objects makes no reference to an environment. The environment will have been instrumental in the past of these objects, molding them into a roughly uniform substance kind, but truths can be discovered about their relations to many possible environments, not just their historical environment.

Clearly there is another way to study a species scientifically, however. It can be studied with an eye to the properties that allowed it to survive through time as a Hullian historical individual. This sort of study is intrinsically ecological, deeply interested in the environment. It focuses on the contrast between the individual lifelines, and individual episodes within these lives, that have pushed on in contrast to those that have failed. It studies the various *mechanisms* by which the life bush has thrust forth new shoots in those episodes in which the environment happened to be cooperative. It studies the mechanisms that helped to bias the species' chances in favor of winning the vast lottery of life. It is interested in the environment, not just as some sort of average container for members of a species, but in just those respects that have historically been *propitious* for that particular kind of organism engaging in these or those particular productive activities. This sort of study is a study of organisms as *life* forms, rather than merely as collections of like physical objects.

Now no one will deny, of course, that the study of normal human psychology should be a study of the human mind as it operates, in some sense, "in its normal environment." Just as we study fish in the water, pigs on land, and birds in the air, we study human cognizers surrounded by air containing oxygen, at about one atmosphere pressure, with a supporting surface underneath, within a certain range of temperatures, whose heads are not in strong electric fields, or being banged on too hard, or chewed on too eagerly by tigers. It is against this sort of stable background that the normal human cognizer is studied as a natural kind. Thus we study human cognizers not just as a current kind of interesting physical object, but after having taken a peek at historical human life lines, as opposed to human life ends, and after examining the environmental contexts of these differences. A question that needs examining, however, is what it means exactly to claim that the sort of environment just described is "the normal one" in which human cognition takes place.

First, it will help to ward off a possible confusion in the wake of the discouraging words uttered above about survival chances for most species. Haven't I claimed that in the environment that is statistically normal for a species, the environment in which animals of that species typically find themselves, the animal dies? It dies before maturing or reproducing. Then doesn't it follow that we must study the individual not in the normal environment but in an especially lucky one? But of course it is only over their whole lives that the statistics on individuals are so terrible. Hour by hour, supporting rather than threatening environments may be statistically normal. So there may after all be some relatively fixed and stable set of conditions, for many species, relative to which the lifeline mechanisms of its members can be studied, deaths before reproduction being viewed as caused by temporary disruptions of these conditions. Similarly, although nobody doubts that human cognition requires a supporting environment, perhaps it requires, on the whole, merely the same mundane set of stable supporting conditions that sustains the human body from hour to hour. Against this steady background environment, the human, including the cognitive systems, might be studied purely as a natural kind. That, I believe, is the image most have of the study of human cognition.

But there is something important left out of this picture. What is left out is the fuzz on the *individual* lifelines. Remember Tabby in search of her dinner, Grackling in search of a mate, and Rover with sand in his eye. In general, the behaviors of animals effect loops through the environment that feed back into their lifelines only under quite special conditions, conditions that are not statistically average at all. Moreover the various mechanisms controlling different kinds of behaviors each require different supporting conditions. Each behavior has its own special needs. Tabby's hunting behavior requires a proximate mouse or bird that is not too wary and fleet; Grackling's dancing behavior requires a proximate female who is willing, and so forth. The job of the cognitive systems is to collect information about the specifics of the environment on which such behaviors will be based. The question arises, then, whether the cognitive systems also have fuzz on them – whether they, too, require special supporting conditions that vary with the tasks to be performed.

A contemporary tradition in epistemology has it that whether a thinker has knowledge as opposed to true belief is determined by a partly serendipitous relation between thinker and environment. Contrary to Plato's claims, there is cognitive luck involved in knowing. More fundamental, cognitive luck is required for success in thinking OF things, for success in entertaining coherent propositions. Environmental luck is required for the cognitive systems to maintain a coherent inner representational system. This means that cognitive psychology must be the study of happy interactions with the environment, an essentially ecological study. This follows from the externalist view of mental semantics I have been presenting in this book.

Assume that the central job of the cognitive systems is to collect information over time, to amplify this information through inference, and to bring it to bear in determining action. Note that amplificatory inference always depends on a middle term (Section 10.2). In order to make valid amplificatory inferences, then, the cognitive systems must be able to tell when various separate bits of information that have been collected over time concern the same thing and when they concern different things. Similarly, whenever information that has been collected is brought to bear upon action. From this we have concluded that a crucially important task that must continually be performed by the cognitive systems is managing to recognize when new information coming in concerns the very same thing again, something one already knows something about. Without this, none of the information taken in can be used. Without this the representational system would become wholly corrupted. Its representations would cease to have any clear meanings, becoming hopelessly referentially equivocal or, at the limit, referentially empty. The capacity correctly to recognize sources of incoming information[2] is a requirement for having any coherent thought at all.

This then is the question to be pressed. Does this capacity rest merely on the same mundane set of stable supporting conditions that sustains the human body from hour to hour, or does it have its own special environmental needs, differing perhaps from one cognitive task to another?

That our powers of recognition can fail is obvious enough. Take places or spouses, colors, minerals, tunes, species, buildings, diseases – whatever it is, you can misidentify it. It is possible to construct conditions – external conditions – under which someone completely familiar with it may still fail to recognize it. Are such failures the fault of the cognitive systems, or is it epistemic bad luck that sometimes puts these systems beyond their powers?

2   – informationC. See Appendix B.

We should keep clearly in focus what the cognitive systems are for. Their mission is not, for example, the acquisition of justified certainty. They are not at fault or malfunctioning when they take risks, when they rely on environmental stability. As modern skeptics are well aware, no one lives by justified certainty. Justified certainty is not what is needed to advance the lifeline. Instead, once again we find at work the principles of multiplication and division. Having many different fallible methods of recognizing the same person, the same mineral, the same species, the same disease, some methods that can be used under some conditions, others under other conditions, employing these methods redundantly whenever possible, employing each whenever an opportunity for it happens to arise – this is the strategy that gets us by. Much of the time it gets us by. But every one of these diverse methods requires its own unique sort of environmental support.

Consider a stereoscope that produces an illusory three-dimensional image by causing the visual systems to misidentify. It causes them to take visual contents derived from two different objects as though derived from the same source, thus creating the illusion of a three-dimensional scene (Section 10.3). The illusory image is not formed due to a malfunction within the (internal) visual system. The visual system is not broken or reacting in a way it should not when forming such an image. Instead, the environment is abnormal – not abnormal in some general feature constantly needed to sustain human life, but in a very specific feature, needed to sustain correct binocular vision.

Sometimes we recognize people by their faces, sometimes by their stature and walk, sometimes by their voices, sometimes by their names. But an uncooperative environment can produces two people who look (at least for the moment, or at least from here) just too much alike, or who sound (in this context) just too much alike, or who have exactly the same name. No matter how carefully our recognizing abilities are tuned, and no matter how clever the various mechanisms by which they work, providence will sometimes put up misleading signs. Coherent thinking rests, not on some one steady set of normal environmental conditions, but on a vast variety of special circumstances, each required for proper exercise of a different recognition skill.

Like the species lines, and the individual lifelines, and the little lines representing behaviors, the cognitive lines, too, often get broken off by the environment. Just as the ability to live on and to multiply requires environmental support, the ability to maintain coherent thoughts – to have clear ideas – requires environmental support.

Appendix A

Contrast with Evans on Information Based Thoughts

The theory I have presented of substance concepts and the thoughts governed by them is similar in a number of respects to Evans' theory of "information based thoughts" in *The Varieties of Reference* (1982). Evans' information based thoughts were thoughts containing information derived from perception or testimony, where the thinker also had "an adequate concept" of the information's source. Evans is not altogether clear, however, on what "information" is supposed to be. Initially (p. 122*n*), he refers us to J. J. Gibson (1968), but his subsequent discussion, which makes reference to informational states that "fail to fit" their own objects, "decaying" information (p. 128*n*), "garbled" information (p. 129), informational states that are "of *nothing*" (p. 128) and so forth, is glaringly inconsistent with Gibson's conception of information.

The clearest images Evans presents us are information contained, on the one hand, in a photograph, and on the other, it seems, in a *percept* (not, as Gibson would have had it, in energy impinging on sensory surfaces). But "[a]n informational state may be of *nothing*: this will be the case if there was no object which served as input to the information system when the information was produced" (p. 128). On the other hand, "two informational states embody the same information provided they result from the same informational event . . . even if they do not have the same content: the one may represent the same information as the other, but *garbled* in various ways" (pp. 128–9). Thus it seems that an "informational state" need not contain any information at all, and that when it does "embody" or "represent" information this need not coincide with its "content." What then makes it into an "informational state"? What determines its "content"? And what determines what the informational state "represents"?

213

Of a photograph, Evans says,

A certain mechanism produces things which have a certain informational *content*. ... The mechanism is a mechanism of information storage, because the properties that figure in the content of its output are (to a degree determined by the accuracy of the mechanism) the properties possessed by the objects which are the input to it. And we can say that the product of such a mechanism is *of* the objects that were the input to the mechanism when the product was produced. Correspondingly, the output is *of* those objects with which we have to compare it to judge the accuracy of the mechanism at the time the output was produced. ...

Now this structure can be discerned whenever we have a system capable of reliably producing states with a content which includes a certain predicative component, or not, according to the state of some object. (The structure is of course discernable even if, on some particular occasion, the system malfunctions.) (Evans 1982, pp. 124–5)

From this I take it that Evans' "information" results from operation of a system that "reliably" produces certain output properties as a function of certain input properties even though it may sometimes be inaccurate or malfunction, and that its "content" is determined by reference to the properties that the input either has, or would have had if that same output had been produced when the mechanism was functioning properly. The information is *about* the object or objects directly causing the input, granted these objects are of the same sort that produce input to the device when functioning properly. Otherwise we have an "informational state" that is not "about" anything hence carries no "information." The properties of the inputting object(s) about which the informational state embodies information are those properties of the object that the mechanism would have been guided by in producing its output had it been functioning properly. Evans calls these properties, granted there was some input object of the right sort, "the information represented." Thus it happens that an informational state that misrepresents "represents the same information" as one that represents correctly.

Clearly we must be very careful here not to equivocate on the notion "what is represented." Perhaps we usually think of "what is represented" as the intentional content of a representation. But for Evans, the intentional content is called "content" and "what is represented" is *what was supposed to have been the intentional content*, that is, what would have been the intentional content had the mechanism operated properly. "What is represented" is whatever properties are at the source that produces the informational state, granted the source is of the right general kind.

This notion of information is blatantly non-Gibsonian, and (more familiar to philosophers, perhaps) blatantly non-Dretskean (Dretske 1980). It is not the kind of "information" that was a "common commodity" in the world long before organisms came along to use it. Rather, this notion loudly demands prior analysis of the normative notions, "accuracy," "malfunction," and even, I suggest, "reliable" – notions that can find no footing prior to the interests of organisms.

Leave aside, for the moment, questions about what kind of normativity might be involved with this kind of "information." I have proposed an interpretation of Evans' analysis of the intentional content corresponding to the "predicative component" of an information bearing state. This content is given by reference to what the properties at the source causing the informational state would have to be if the informational system were giving this output when functioning properly. It is not given by the actual properties of the input. Similarly, Evans is very insistent that the fact that a certain *object* causes the input to the informational system does not constitute its being an *intentional* object (subject) of the information bearing output. To adopt that position would be to adopt the "photograph" model of what a thought is of, against which Evans argues at length. Rather, it seems, for the information bearing state to have an *intentional* subject – for it to be a *thought of* something – a "fundamental idea" of its object must be supplied/applied. I have advocated abandonment of the theory of fundamental ideas, however (Section 13.4). And we can, I believe, easily reconstruct an account of the intentional object (subject) of thought along Evans' lines without reference to fundamental ideas.

Evans remarks on "what is perhaps the central feature of our system of gathering information from individuals: namely the fact that we group pieces of information together, as being from the same object – that we collect information into bundles" (p. 126). This collecting together, Evans calls "*re*identification" of the subject of information. Evans' thesis is that only when thinkers "have the capacity" to *re*identify the objects of their thought, are they actually thinking of anything. Capacities, for him, seem to be something like reliable dispositions. (Actually, it is very unclear what they are, so we must guess.) Thus, it appears, just as one thinks of a property when one's cognitive systems are "capable of reliably producing states with a content which includes a certain predicative component, or not, according to the state of some object" (p. 125), similarly, one thinks of an object only when one's cognitive systems are capable of reliably producing informational states about that object that get bundled together, the object thus being *re*identified.

To get from Evans' position, thus interpreted, to the one I advocate, a number of adjustments are required. First, we must replace Evans' idea of what the system regularly does, with what it has the *ability* to do, that is, in part, what it is the, or a, proper function of the system to do, given its evolutionary history and its learning history (Section 4.6). That is the way I would unpack the normativity implicit in Evans' references to "accuracy" and "malfunction."

Second, we must replace Evans' notion "*re*identify" with the notion "coidentify" (Section 10.2) or, when the intentional significance of this act is our focus, with the notion "reidentify." Reidentifying something is not just thinking of it again, nor is it making an identity judgment. It is marking an informational state with a sameness marker, in preparation for its use as a middle term in inference, or an analogue of inference (Section 10.2).

Third, we must take the notion "information" apart, carefully separating natural information from intentional information, that is, from the content of an intentional representation such as an inner representation. The form of natural information that is important here is the general form that I call "natural informationC," as contrasted with Gibson's and Dretske's notions of natural information (see Appendix B). Intentional information is what is represented by an intentional representation when the representation is true, and true in accord with a normal explanation for proper functioning of the representation producing devices that formed it. Now we can put the matter this way. One thinks of an object (represents it conceptually) only when one's cognitive systems have the ability (Chapter 4) to translate natural informationC about the object into intentional information about it such that the mental representations carrying this information are correctly marked with sameness markers as suitable for coidentification (Section 10.2).

Appendix B

What Has Natural Information to Do with Intentional Representation?[1]

"According to informational semantics, if it's necessary that a creature can't distinguish Xs from Ys, it follows that the creature can't have a concept that applies to Xs but not Ys."

(Jerry Fodor, *The Elm and the Expert*, p. 32)

There is, indeed, a form of informational semantics that has this verificationist implication. The original definition of information given in Dretske's *Knowledge and the Flow of Information* (1981, hereafter KFI), when employed as a base for a theory of intentional representation or "content," has this implication. I will argue that, in fact, most of what an animal needs to know about its environment is not available as natural information of this kind. It is true, I believe, that there is one fundamental kind of perception that depends on this kind of natural information, but more sophisticated forms of inner representation do not. It is unclear, however, exactly what "natural information" is supposed to mean, certainly in Fodor, and even in Dretske's writing. In many places, Dretske seems to employ a softer notion than the one he originally defines. I will propose a softer view of natural information that is, I believe, at least hinted at by Dretske, and show that it does not have verificationist consequences. According to this soft informational semantics, a creature can perfectly well have a representation of Xs without being able to discriminate Xs from Ys.

I believe there is some ambivalence in Dretske's writing about natural information, especially noticeable when comparing KFI to *Explaining Behavior* (1991, hereafter EB), but if we ignore some of Dretske's

1 This chapter is drawn from a paper that was originally presented at the Conference of the Royal Institute of Philosophy on Naturalism, Evolution and Mind in July 1999.

examples, the explicit statement of the theory in KFI is univocal. This theory is also strongly suggested in Fodor's work on mental content (1990, 1994, 1998) and seems to be consonant with J. J. Gibson's use of "information" as well.

According to Dretske,

A signal *r* carries the information that *s* is F = The conditional probability of *s*'s being F, given *r* (and *k*), is 1 (but, given *k* alone, less than 1). (KFI, p. 65)

Dretske's "*k*" stands for knowledge already had about *s*. Knowledge that p is belief that is caused by information that p. It follows that a signal carries the information that *s* is *F* when either it alone, or it taken together with some other signal that has also been transmitted to the receiver, returns a probability of 1 that *s* is *F*. Thus, I suggest, we can drop the parenthetical "and *k*" in the formulation and just say that a signal carries the information that *s* is *F* if it is an operative part of some more complete signal, where the conditional probability that *s* is *F*, given the complete signal, is 1 but would not be 1 without the part. Thus we eliminate reference to knowing.

What is meant by saying, in this context, that the occurrence of one thing, "the signal," yields a probability of 1 that another thing, "*s* being *F*," is the case? In a footnote, Dretske explains:

In saying that the conditional probability (given *r*) of *s*'s being F is 1, I mean to be saying that there is a nomic (lawful) regularity between these event types, a regularity which *nomically precludes* *r*'s occurrence when *s* is not F. There are interpretations of probability (the frequency interpretation) in which an event can fail to occur when it has a probability of 1 . . . but this is *not* the way I mean to be using probability in this definition. A conditional probability of 1 between *r* and *s* is a way of describing a lawful (exceptionless) dependence between events of this sort. . . . (KFI, p. 245)

and in the text he tells us:

Even if the properties F and G are perfectly correlated . . . this does not mean that there is information in *s*'s being F about *s*'s being G. . . . For the correlation . . . may be the sheerest coincidence, a correlation whose persistence is not assured by any law of nature or principle of logic. . . . All Fs can be Gs without the probability of *s*'s being G, given that it is F, being 1. (pp. 73–4)

218

The probability that *s* is *F* given *r* must follow, it appears here, *given merely logic and natural law*. That is, the necessity must be strict natural necessity.[2]

The next question concerns the reference classes intended when referring to "the probability that *s* is F, given *r*." *r* was said to be a signal and *s* being *F* would seem to be a state of affairs, but if there are causal laws necessitating the one given the other, these laws must be general. There must be certain general aspects under which we are considering *r*, and the fact that *s* is *F*, by which they are connected in a lawful way. They cannot be connected in a lawful way merely as an individual occurrence and an individual fact. It must be a certain type of signal that determines, with a probability of 1, a certain type of fact. And this will yield two reference classes for the probability, the class of "signals" of a certain type and the class of facts of a certain type, such that the probability that a signal of that type is connected with a fact of that type is 1. What reference classes are intended, then, when it is said that a certain *r* carries the information that a certain *s* is *F*? When Dretske says that the pointer on my gas gauge being at the ½ mark carries the information that my gas tank is half full, in which two reference classes are these two conditions being considered, so as to make that so?

Clearly the reference classes cannot be (1) all pointers on gas gauges that point to the one half mark and (2) all gas tanks that are in the same cars as those gauges. For some gas gauges are broken or disconnected or badly calibrated, and even if none were, it would not be a matter of natural law that they couldn't be broken or disconnected or badly calibrated. Rather, as Dretske emphasizes in KFI, a reference must be made here to the presence of certain "channel conditions." In this case, channel conditions consist in a fairly intricate collection of surrounding conditions including various connecting parts the presence of which is needed before natural laws will guarantee that the gas gauge will read half full only if the gas tank is half full. One kind of thing carries information about another in accordance with strict natural necessity only given specified channel conditions. The two reference classes concerned contain only members connected by these channel conditions.

We can contrast this to the notion of a *ceteris paribus* law. According to the classical view, a *ceteris paribus* law is one that is true in accordance

---

2 The necessity may go in either temporal direction. For example, an effect might carry information about another effect of the same cause.

with natural necessity given certain surrounding conditions, where exactly what these conditions are is not specified, indeed, may or may not be known. Usually the idea is, however, that whatever these conditions, they are for the most part realized in the contexts in which the law is used. The *ceteris paribus law*, then, makes reference to both kinds of probability that Dretske mentioned above. First, given the surrounding conditions to which it implicitly refers, it holds true with a probability of 1 in accordance with strict natural necessity. Second, the surrounding conditions to which it implicitly refers are themselves assumed to hold true with high statistical frequency.

But on the above reading of Dretske's definition of information, the second sort of probability is not involved. The frequency with which the channel conditions hold, relative to which a certain kind of signal bears information about a certain kind of fact, is not part of the definition of information. Suppose, for example, that many gas gauges are badly calibrated (indeed, they are) so that the gas tanks connected to them are half full when the pointer is on the one quarter mark, others when the pointer is on the three quarters mark, and so forth. In each case, when the gas tank is half full, no matter what it reads, the pointer carries the information that it is half full, relative to its own particular channel conditions. How often each of these various kinds of channel conditions holds is quite irrelevant. To be sure, Dretske often talks as if the relevant reference class in which *this* reading on *this* gas gauge should be put is restricted to those times when this very same gas gauge does or, counterfactually, would have given this same reading. Still, the assumption has to be that we are talking only about times when this very same gas gauge is found surrounded by the very same relevant channel conditions. Or suppose the reference class consists only of this particular reading on this particular occasion, the idea being just that if the tank had not been half full the pointer would not have pointed to this number. This way of thinking of the matter is in every way equivalent. The point is that the counterfactuals have to be run on the assumption that the relevant channel conditions still hold, and nothing has been said about how often conditions of this sort do hold in the world.

This is the only way I can see to interpret Dretske's definition and remarks on information quoted above. On the other hand, this way of interpreting Dretske's definition of information does seem to be inconsistent with certain things he says about "natural meaning," "natural signs," and "indication" in EB, despite the fact that he explicitly associates all three of these with signals that bear "information" in the sense of KFI (EB, p. 58). Dretske tells us, for example, that although otherwise such tracks would indicate quale, "[i]f pheasants, also in the woods, leave the very same kind of tracks, then the tracks, though made by a quail, do not indicate that it was a quale that made them" (p. 56). Here, not natural law but statistical frequencies at the source end of the information channel appear to be determining whether the tracks carry natural information. And Dretske tells us that "[t]he red spots all over Tommy's face mean [natural meaning] that he has the measles, not simply because he *has* the measles, but because people without the measles don't have spots of that kind" (p. 56). Contrast Fodor, who seems to use the term "information" more in the way we interpreted it above following the explicit definition in KFI. He says, "If the tokens of a symbol have two kinds of etiologies, it follows that there are two kinds of information that tokens of that symbol carry. (If some 'cow' tokens are caused by cows and some 'cow' tokens aren't, then it follows that some 'cow' tokens carry information about cows and some 'cow' tokens don't)" (1990, p. 90). Fodor also often speaks of "covariation" between represented and representation, which is plausible only if one imagines a reference to some one definite though unspecified channel of influence, making the signal depend nomically on whether *s* is F and vice versa. Fodor's usage fits not only Dretske's original definition but also a cautious physician's offering: "Those spots may mean Tommy has the measles, but they could also mean scarlet fever. I think we had better take a culture." Dretske's modified claim, that if some people with spots like that don't have the measles then those spots don't mean measles, apparently refers instead to statistical frequencies at the source.

Alternatively, perhaps it refers to the frequency of certain channel conditions. It might well be, for example, that given certain channel conditions, only measles virus would cause spots like that, but that given other channel conditions, only strep bacteria would. Just as, given certain channel conditions, only a half full tank of gas would cause that reading, but given other channel conditions, only a quarter full tank would. Then by Dretske's original definition, Tommy's spots might mean measles even if on another child they would mean scarlet fever. But if Dretske's modification here involves assigning certain channel conditions themselves a probability of one, such a probability would also seem to be merely a statistical frequency.

Indeed, both Dretske's KFI and his EB waver at points between the two kinds of probability in discussing information. Dretske tells us, both in KFI and in EB, that if his doorbell rings, that carries the information that someone is at the door. But in EB we are told:

"It is partly the fact, presumably not itself a physical law, that animals do not regularly depress doorbells . . . that makes a ringing doorbell *mean* that some *person* is at the door. . . . As things *now* stand, we can say that the bell would not be ringing if someone were not at the door. It therefore indicates or means that someone is at the door. But this subjunctively expressed dependency, though not a coincidence, is not grounded in natural law either. . . . Normally, though, these things don't happen. . . . And this is no lucky coincidence, no freaky piece of good fortune. . . . There must actually be some condition, lawful or otherwise, that explains the persistence of the correlation . . . [for the doorbell to indicate a person]."

But, of course, if the condition that explains the correlation is not lawful but "otherwise," then it is grounded in mere facts about the state conditions characterizing the world at certain times and places – either conditions at the source or existent channel conditions. It has the status merely of a local statistical frequency – based lawfully, perhaps, hence explainably, upon prior local statistical frequencies, but that does not change its essential nature as merely a statistical frequency.

The vacillation here seems to be twofold. First, it concerns whether or not mere statistical frequencies at the source, rather than strict natural law, should be allowed to determine signals as bearing "natural information." Second, it concerns whether we should count a signal that is not univocal except as harnessed to a particular information channel. But, of course, most of the interesting examples of signals carrying "information," defined Dretske's original way, are of a sort that either do not always carry the same kind of information (because channel conditions vary) or if they do, that is a matter of convenient empirical fact, not natural necessity. The fact that a signal carries "information," defined Dretske's original way, has no bearing whatever upon whether, by the mere fact that the signal has arrived, one can tell anything about *what* information, if any, it carries.[3]

I propose to stay for a while with Dretske's original definition of natural information. To my knowledge, no other well-defined notion of natural information is currently available. Allowing merely statistical

---

3 Dretske worries about something close to this in KFI, pp. 111–23, but he does so in the confusing context of worrying about what "knowledge" is, and thus he never confronts the basic problem. – Or so I would argue, but my main project here is not Dretske exegesis.

considerations on board poses an intractable problem concerning the reference classes within which the frequency of 1 should be required to hold. Do spots like that mean measles if small pox, though now extinct, used to, and may in the future, cause spots like that? If the Skinner-trained pigeons in your neighborhood start pressing doorbells, how close may my neighborhood be to yours for my ringing doorbell still to carry the information that a person is at my door? More important, mixing frequencies with natural necessities muddies the issues involved in trying to understand phenomena connected with intentional representation. These issues can be seen much more clearly if we separate issues of natural law from issues that concern mere frequencies. For clarity, I will call natural information purified of all mere frequencies, natural information as originally defined by Dretske, "informationL" (for "law").

InformationL is an entirely objective commodity and it is ubiquitous. Often its channels are complex, and such as seldom if ever to be duplicated. Channels that are often duplicated tend to be fairly simple channels, such as reflections in calm water. Channels carrying reflections in choppy water, though not much more complex, are seldom repeated. The more numerous and irregular the intervening media between source and signal are, the less likely repetition becomes.

InformationL is everywhere, but the problem, of course, is to interpret it. For no signal that makes up only part of the world can carry the informationL that its own channel conditions hold. And that means that it cannot carry the information that it carries informationL, nor what code this information is in. This opens the question why an organism could possibly care whether or not it ever encounters any of this ubiquitous but uncommunicative informationL. What good will it do an animal to have informationL?

The problem is twofold. First, a signal carrying informationL is, as it were, in code. It is of no use to an organism unless the organism can "read" the code. Second, the informationL that reaches an organism is not all in the same code.

Consider first the easy problem, that of reading the code. Suppose that the information all arrives in the same code. Then for a signal to be of use to a creature – to be "read" by it – it would only be necessary that the creature should be guided by the signal in a way that diverts it from activities less likely to benefit it to ones more likely to benefit it, this likelihood being contingent on the fact conveyed by the signal. For example, if the fact conveyed is the relative location of water, given that

223

the creature is thirsty, all that is needed is that the signal should cause the creature to turn toward the location indicated. The beneficial activity need not, of course, be overt. It might be an inner state change. The basic idea here is well known, I believe, and has been given numerous expressions, for example, by Dretske and myself.

The "same code" problem is the harder one, and is itself two-sided. First, we have not yet offered a reason to suppose that informationL about the same thing always or ever reaches an organism in the same code or packaging. Second, we have offered no reason to suppose that the same packaging always or ever carries the same informationL, indeed, any informationL. Why suppose, for any signal that the organism receives, that all signals of that kind reaching the organism, carry the same informationL. But for the organism to be able to use the informationL it receives, the same kind of informational content needs to affect the organism in the same kind of way, and different kinds of informational content need to affect it in different ways. Information about the same must, as it were, look the same to the organism, and information about different things must look different to the organism. (This may put us in mind of Fodor's "formality constraint" [1980].)

A central tenant of contemporary ecological psychology of the sort introduced by J. J. Gibson is that there is far more consistency in the natural information received by an organism than was formerly supposed. The claim is, first, that if you look for the right aspect of the signals that arrive by way of the ambient energy surrounding an organism, you find that a surprising number of superficially or apparently different channels of informationL can be described as really being the same channel once you have located the right high order invariances in the signals. And it is these invariances, these univocal codes,[4] that the evolving animal has become sensitive to, so as to "pick up" the relevant information and use it.

Second, the Gibsonian claim is that the very same relevant channel conditions are present under environmental conditions that the animal frequently or nearly always finds itself in, or that it knows how to maneuver itself into. In the animal's normal environment, the relevant channel conditions are always the same, or always possible for the ani-

---

4 Gibsonians protest that the natural information used by organisms is not in the form of a "code." Their point, however, is merely that it is constituted by changing energy structures that do not require translation into some other medium in order to be used by the organism.

mal actively to intercept, so that relevant features of the source lawfully produce informationL about themselves in the same code. There are "ecological laws" such that the signals covary with the relevant environmental features.

Third, the Gibsonian claim is that informationL of this sort that is relevant to the animal's needs is much more complete than had previously been supposed. Information about exactly those environmental conditions to which the animal needs to adjust is frequently presented in an unequivocal way. "The stimulus is not impoverished."

These three claims are not generally separated in the tradition of Gibsonian psychology, but they are independent. Gibsonian "information" is not only informationL, but also lawfully carries complete information needed for guidance with respect to important aspects of the environment, and is frequently present in the environment, coming in always through the very same information channels, that is, exemplifying the very same *ceteris paribus* laws, arriving in a single code. All the animal has to do is to tap into these rich sources of information (for example, by developing eyes with lenses) and funnel them directly into guidance of appropriate behavior.

Mechanisms by which various perceptual constancies are achieved, such as recognition of same color, same shape, same size, same voice, and so forth, through a wide spectrum of mediating conditions, insofar as these constancies are sometimes detected over wide ranges of input in accordance with univocal principles, illustrate the use of Gibsonian information. Then it is a very complex signal indeed, one in which the significant invariances are (from the physicist's point of view) highly derived, that yields informationL through a complicated but still univocal channel in a single code. The job of tapping into such informationL channels and using the information to guide useful action is, as a biological engineering feat, extremely challenging. Yet natural selection has managed to solve many of these problems.

Surely there does exist in our world at least a certain amount of Gibsonian information, or at least very close to that, which serves as the bedrock foundation making sentient life possible at all. This foundation guides the most basic immediate responses to the environment of all animals, and also supports all information-gathering activities and faculties that make use of less tractable, less user-friendly, forms of information that are also naturally found in the environment. But there is also that useful information in the environment that is not fully Gibsonian.

InformationL becomes less Gibsonian, for example, as it becomes less ubiquitous. Darkness and dense fog, for example, impede transmission of normal visual information. InformationL becomes less Gibsonian as it arrives in more alternative packagings, in alternative codes. For example, we use a number of alternative visual cues for depth. More interesting are cases in which the same signal form varies in the information it carries. Consider light and sound when reflected off smooth surfaces. Like a gas gauge that carries informationL but reads "¼" when it is half full, reflections carry perfectly good informationL but informationL that needs to be read differently than usual. A puddle in the woods is not a hole in the ground with upside down trees hanging inside. Animals, after brief exposure, generally treat reflections simply as irrelevant noise in the data, holes in the normal flow of information. But a kitten's first experience with a mirror can be very amusing to watch, a dog will bark at its own echo, sometimes for hours, and a Canada goose once spent a whole afternoon doing a mating dance to his reflection in the basement window of our building on the Connecticut campus. We humans, on the other hand, are able to tap many such sources of informationL and to read them correctly. We can comb our hair in the mirror, we understand that Clinton is not inside the TV set nor our friends inside the telephone. We build gadgets to collect thousands of different kinds of informationL – various indicators, meters, gauges, scopes, audios, videos, and so forth – and we learn to read them correctly.

When a variety of channels of informationL about the same are intermittently available to an organism, the animal must understand when each is open, distinguishing informationL both from mere noise and from informationL arriving in similar vehicles but differently coded. Nor should we take for granted that an animal can integrate the sources of informationL that it uses. There is a story circulating (though probably apocryphal[5]) that certain venomous snakes strike mice by sight, trace the path of the dying mouse by smell, and find its head (so as to swallow it first) by feel, and that none of these jobs can be done using any other sensory modality. The lesson is, anyway, logically sound. InformationL about the same that comes in a variety of codes requires "translation" if it is to be used in a versatile way.

Suppose then that informationL about the same things arriving through a variety of media is translated by mechanisms in the organism

---

5 The original source seems to be the zoologist Sverre Solander, who gives no references and, despite requests, has offered no data yet to my knowledge.

into a common code.[6] Insofar as this result is achieved, whatever appears in that code is correlated always in the same way with the same source or kind of source in the environment, even when the channels that control this effect are variable. In this way, a great deal of informationL that is not fully Gibsonian as it originally reaches the organism may be translated into the practical equivalent of Gibsonian informationL inside the organism. As I will now argue, however, relatively few things that an animal needs to know can be communicated in this direct way.

InformationL depends on a channel between the information source and the signal producing a correspondence between the two in accordance with natural necessity. But unfortunately, relatively few things that an animal needs to know about can figure as sources for this kind of information. The mouse, for example, needs to know when there is a hawk overhead, but there are no natural laws that apply to hawks overhead and hawks only. The existence of hawks is not a matter of law, nor, for any given channel, is the nonexistence of things other than hawks that might cause the same effects as a hawk on the output of that channel a matter of natural necessity. Similarly, if there are channel conditions under which cows cause mental "cow" tokens as a matter of natural law, surely there can be none under which mental "cow" tokens are caused by cows. They might instead be caused by something that looked like a cow, or sounded like a cow, or smelled like a cow, or all three, but that wasn't a cow. It is the *properties* of objects like hawks and cows that enter into natural laws, not the hawks and cows themselves, and it is never a matter of natural law that only hawks or cows have these properties.

There is, of course, an old-fashioned way out of this difficulty. You can argue that it is a matter of nominal definition that cows and only cows have certain properties, and then argue that information concerning the copresence in one and the same object of all these defining properties could indeed be transmitted through an information channel. Then there might be natural informationL about the presence of a cow. As a preliminary, however, first notice that you can't take this route for information concerning individuals. Even quite primitive animals are often able to recognize and keep track of various of their conspecifics individually, to learn things about them, and so forth. But there are no

6   By "translated into a common code," I mean only that sameness or overlapping in content is marked.

laws that concern any individuals as such. No signal can carry the in-formationL that it is *Tommy* who has the measles. Second, although a classical position that some still occupy gives natural kinds such as gold and water definitions in terms of necessary and sufficient characteristics, it is no longer plausible that biological kinds, such as cow, can be de-fined that way. A large proportion of the kinds that we name in every-day speech are "historical kinds," kinds that are not defined by their possession of certain properties at all, but instead through "historical" connections – connections in the spatial/temporal/causal order – that their members have to one another (Millikan 1999, Chapter 2 above). Exactly as with individuals, these kinds cannot be subjects of informa-tionL. They fall under no laws, not even ceteris paribus laws, and they support no counterfactuals.

Thus we are returned to the problem addressed earlier when Dretske observed that it is not a matter of natural necessity that your ringing doorbell "indicates" there is some person at the door. In what sense of "natural information" then, exactly, does the doorbell carry natural in-formation? Is there a way to define a softer notion of "natural informa-tion" to do the work required here?

To answer this we must have firmly in mind what work it is that is required. What do we need a theory of natural information for? In this context, we require it to support a theory of "intentional" representa-tion, in the sense introduced by Brentano. This is the kind of represen-tation that displays Brentano's mark of the mental. Intentional represen-tations can represent nonexistent things, for example, nonexistent facts. They can be misrepresentations. All agree, of course, that natural infor-mation is not itself intentional, that it cannot misrepresent or be false. "Informational semantics," as Fodor calls it, is an attempt to show how, despite this difference, intentional representation still rests at base on natural information.

How to move from a theory of natural information to a theory of intentional representation is, however, a problem. That is what Fodor's theory of "asymmetrical dependency" is designed to do (1990, Chapter 4). And that is what Dretske's addition of teleology is designed to do – his claim that it is only a function, not always realized, of intentional representations to carry natural information (1981, 1991). Fodor's asym-metrical dependency theory seems, quite explicitly, to rest on informa-tionL, but I won't argue that case here. Rather, I will try to show how teleology can be combined with a theory of soft natural information to produce the variety in forms of intentional representation that animals require. But there has been some confusion about the relation of teleological accounts of intentionality to informational semantics. So let me first remark on that relation.

Naturalized teleological theories of the content of representations are attempts to explain Brentano's mark of intentionality: How can representations be false or represent nonexistent things? But teleological theories are only overlays, minor additions, veneers superimposed, on prior underlying theories of representation, and there can be considerable variety among these underlying theories. When looking at any teleological theory, the first thing to ask is on what kind of more basic theory of representation it rests.

Suppose, for example, that you think of mental representations as items defined in a classical functionalist way, in accordance with patterns of causal/inferential dispositions. And suppose that you have a theory that tells what dispositional relations one of these representations must have to others, and the collection as a whole to the world, for it to be a representation, say, of its raining. Then the teleological theorist, call her Tilly, will come along and point out that surely some of the causal roles of actual representations in actual people's heads correspond to bad inferences. What you must say, says Tilly, is that what the representation represents is determined by what its causal role *would* be if the head *were* operating correctly, that is, in the way it was designed, by evolution or learning, to operate. Similarly, suppose that you think of mental representations as items that "stand in for" the things they represent, running isomorphic to them, with differences in the representations producing differences in the behaviors guided by them, thus making the behaviors appropriate to the presence of the things represented. Then Tilly will come along and point out that some representations are false, that is, not isomorphic to things in the world as required to guide behavior appropriately. What you must say, says Tilly, is that the representations represent what would be in the world, running isomorphic to them, if the cognitive systems were operating correctly. That is, what a teleological theory of content does is to take some more basic theory of content, point out that the application of that theory to actual creatures requires idealizing them in certain ways, and then offer the teleological principle to explain which idealization is the right one to use in interpreting intentional contents, namely, the one that fits how the cognitive systems were designed or selected for operating. You give your naturalistic analysis of what a true or correct representation is like, and Tilly merely adds that systems designed to produce true representations don't always work as designed, claiming that correctness in perception and cognition is defined by reference to design rather than actual disposition.

Accordingly, the teleologist who is an information semanticist begins with the idea that representations are signals carrying "natural information" and then adds teleology to account for error. My claim is that adding teleology to informationL will not yield the rich variety of intentional representation that either we or the animals employ, but that there is a softer kind of natural information that does underlie all intentional representation. This softer kind, however, offers no help whatever to the verificationist.

Let us return, for a few moments, to the animal whose perceptual/cognitive systems are capable of translating informationL about the same things arriving through a variety of media into a common code. Whatever appears in that code is correlated always in the same way with the same source or kind of source of informationL in the environment. But, Tilly reminds us, it is not plausible that errors will never occur. If this arrangement has been built by natural selection, however, it will at least be a *function* of these mechanisms, which tap into and converge these channels of informationL, to produce signals that carry informationL in a univocal code. Their function is to transmit signals that are controlled by certain external sources of information so that these sources then control the behavior of the organism in ways that are adaptive. Surely this is the sort of thing that Dretske had in mind in saying that the function of a representation is to indicate (1986, 1991). Or, being very careful, what has really been described here is not the function of the representations themselves, but the function of certain mechanisms that produce representations. The first job of such a mechanism is to complete a specific type of channel of information flow, or to bring to focus in a single code a number of such channels, so as to produce an informationL-bearing signal in a specific code. This is the way to add teleology to the idea that intentional representation is, at root, natural informationL. False intentional representations result when such a mechanism fails to perform this job properly.

I say that I think this is what Dretske has in mind. Dretske has sometimes wavered, however, on whether it can be a function of information gathering systems to gather information about affairs that are distal to the organism. I will explain.

230

The job of bringing information arriving through different channels, perhaps through complex media, in different codes, to a focus is obviously difficult and very risky. Tilly is surely right that systems responsible for accomplishing this feat inevitably will sometimes fail. Recall the Canada goose in love with itself, and the dog trying to communicate with its echo. When this sort of thing happens, however, it is not usually because there is anything wrong with the organism. Without doubt, perhaps definitionally, almost none of the mistakes in informationL gathering that are made by healthy animals are due to malfunction of the animals' informationL-focusing systems. Mistakes are due to an uncooperative environment, which fails to supply those informationL channels that the animal has been designed or tuned to recognize and employ. Gibson to one side, concerning some informationL that an animal needs to gather, the environment may be rife with decoy channels, nor is there anything the animal can do about that, perhaps, without evolving completely different perceptual systems. Both Dretske (1986) and Neander (1995) have concluded from this, however, that the information-gathering systems of animals may not actually have the function of gathering information about *distal* affairs at all. The argument is that when representations of distal affairs are apparently mistaken, since typically this is not because the animal's information systems are failing to function properly, it must be that these systems do not have as their function to gather this kind of information. Neander then seriously claims that all representation must be only of proximal stimuli. The effect, of course, will be a very strong form of verificationism indeed. The organism can only represent what it can verify conclusively, granted it's not sick or damaged.

But the idea that nothing can have a purpose or function that it requires help from anything else to achieve is mistaken. Consider the can opener on the wall in my kitchen. It is not now opening cans. It is not now performing its function. It would need my help in order to do that. Certainly it doesn't follow that it is malfunctioning, or that opening cans is not its function.[7] In the case of information-gathering systems, exactly as with can openers or, say, with the famous walking

7 If, however, you do insist, as Neander does, that in the *ordinary* sense of "function" things really can't have distal functions, then I refer you to the definition of "proper function" stipulated in Millikan (1984), in accordance with which most of the many proper functions that most biological items have are distal, and I suggest that the notion of function we need to use to gain insight here is "proper function" as there defined.

mechanisms in cockroaches, a cooperative environment plays a lead role in helping them serve their functions. (Nor, of course, does it follow that it is the environment's function to help cockroaches walk or to help us focus information.)

Let us now look more closely at the result of adding teleology to natural informationL to produce intentional representation. The first job of a system that uses informationL to produce representations is to complete a specific type of natural-informationL channel so as to project that informationL into some standard code. But systems of this kind also have jobs beyond. The codes into which they translate informationL must be ones that the behavioral systems of the animal are able to use. The problem, posed first during evolutionary development, then to the developing individual animal, is to coordinate these two kinds of systems. Suppose, however, that the representation-producing systems and the behavioral systems fail to cooperate on some task. Suppose that a signal carrying informationL about one state of affairs is used by the behavioral systems in a way appropriate instead to some contrary state of affairs. For example, the informationL that the height to be stepped up is, say, eight inches, is coded in a representation that guides the legs to step up only seven inches. Which has erred, the perceptual side of the system or the motor side of the system? Is the representation wrong, or is its use wrong? Has the message been written wrong, or has it been read wrong? What does the *intentional* representation say, eight inches or seven inches?

Notice that the signal, as carrying informationL, definitely says eight inches. Compare the informationL carried by a miscalibrated gas gauge. The miscalibrated gauge carries informationL telling the *actual* level of the gas in the tank. If we interpret it wrongly, that does not make it carry the informationL we wrongly take it to carry. What it itself naturally means just is whatever it *actually* carries informationL about, even though in a difficult or uninterpretable code. In the same way, the coded informationL about the height of the step cannot be wrong. The attributes *right* and *wrong*, *true* and *false*, don't apply to the code considered as a natural sign.

Recall that a signal carries informationL, not as considered within the reference class of all items in the world having the same physical form, but only as a member of the class of signals linked to sources through the same kind of information channel, that is, in accordance with the same natural necessities implemented through the same mediating conditions. As an *intentional* representation, however, the representation of the height of the step is a member of a different reference class altogether. It is a member of the class of all representations like it in form,[8] produced by the same representation-producing systems, for use by the same representation-using systems. In this class there may also be representations identical to it but that carry natural informationL in a different code, and representations that carry no natural informationL at all. In which code, then, is its *intentional* content expressed?

Exactly here is the place to apply teleology, as I see it, to the analysis. We suppose that the system that codes and uses the information about the step is a system where the coding and using parts of the system have coevolved, either phylogenetically and/or ontogenetically. During evolution of the species and/or during learning or tuning, they have been selected or adjusted for their capacities to cooperate with one another. The operative features of both halves of the system have been selected for and/or tuned as they have because these features and settings have sometimes succeeded in guiding behavior appropriate to the informationL encoded. If this is so, inevitably it is true that these coordinations were achieved by settling on some single and quite definite code. Only if there was constancy or stability in the code employed by the representation maker and user could coordinations have been achieved systematically. It is this code then that the representation producer was designed to write in, and it is this code that the representation user was designed to read. And it is this code that determines the *intentional* content of the message about the height of the step. In any particular case of error, whether it is the representation producers or the representation users that have erred depends on whether or not the natural informationL appears in this code.

My proposal is now that we should *generalize* this result. Intentional representations and their producers are defined, are made to be such, by the fact that it is their job to supply messages that correspond to the world *by a given code*. That is the essence. But notice that *that* formulation makes no reference to informationL. If that is the essence of the matter, then the *mechanisms* by which the producers manage to produce messages that correspond by the given code drops out as irrelevant to their nature as intentional representation producers. If there exist systems with the function of supplying messages that correspond to the world by a given code but that manage to achieve this result, when successful,

8   More accurately, the class of all representations that the systems designed to use it are designed to identify as having the same content.

233

without tapping into any channels of natural informationL, they too will be producers of intentional representations. They will be producers of intentional representations that are not defined with reference to natural informationL. I will now argue that such systems do exist, indeed, that the bulk of our mental representations necessarily are of this type. Rather than informationL, they tap into channels of softer natural information. How should we define this "softer" form of natural information?

Dretske wishes to eliminate *de facto* perfect correlations that are "lucky coincidences" or "freaky piece[s] of good fortune" as possible supports for any notion of natural information. But does anything stand in the middle between, on the one hand, statistical frequencies resulting from lucky coincidence and, on the other, the necessity of natural law? The answer Dretske gave to this question, though inadequate, I believe, is still a very interesting one. He said, "[t]here must actually be some condition, lawful or otherwise, that explains the *persistence* of the correlation" [emphasis mine]. About this I remarked earlier that the fact that a local statistic is based lawfully upon prior local statistics, hence that a correlation is explainable, does not alter its nature as a mere statistical frequency. If the frequency of black balls in the urn today is 1, and if nothing disturbs the urn, then by natural necessity it follows that the frequency of balls in the urn tomorrow is 1. That does not change the probability of being black if a ball in the urn into a probability of some kind other than mere statistical frequency. It does not help being-a-ball-in-the-urn to carry the informationL being-black.

But it does do something else. It explains how, by sampling the urn today and adjusting my expectations of color accordingly, this adjustment in expectation can turn out to be adequate to my experience tomorrow, *not by accident but for good reason.* Many statistical frequencies *persist* over time in accordance with natural necessity, and many produce correlate statistical frequencies among causally related things, in accordance with natural necessity. If measles are producing spots like that in this community today, then measles will probably be producing spots like that in this community tomorrow. Measles, after all, are contagious. And if a nose like that is correlated with the presence of Johnny today it will probably be correlated with the presence of Johnny tomorrow. Johnny's nose, after all, tends to sustain both its shape and its attachment to Johnny. There are no laws that concern individuals as such, but there are many kinds of local correlations that do. Notice, however, that whether the persistence of a correlation may be explained in this sort of way does not depend on its being a perfect correlation. Conditional probabilities of 1 have nothing to do with the matter.

This yields a way that an organism may come to possess systems that produce representations that correspond to the world by a given code *often enough* to have been selected for doing that job, but that do this job without tapping into any natural informationL. Systems of this sort run on bare statistical frequencies of association – on correlations – but on correlations that persist not by accident but for good reason. Probably these correlations typically obtain between properties of the not-too-distant environment that *do* supply informationL to the organism, and more distal properties, kinds, situations, individuals, and so forth, of interest to the organism but that *don't* supply it with informationL. The intentional contents of representations of this sort are determined not by any natural informationL that it is their function to carry, but merely by the codes in which their producers were selected to write, so as to cooperate with the systems designed to read them.

It follows that a representation producer, basing its activities on past local statistical frequencies, may indeed be representing Xs, and yet be unable perfectly to distinguish Xs from Ys. It may have no disposition under any conditions infallibly to distinguish Xs from Ys. *To perform properly*, its representations of Xs – its code tokens of a certain type – must correspond to Xs, but this does not entail that there exist any information channels at all, actual or possible, through which it could infallibly discriminate Xs from Ys. That having grown up with gray squirrels around, I am thinking of gray squirrels has nothing to do with whether I can discriminate gray squirrels from Australian tree possums, even if someone introduces tree possums into my neighborhood. Similarly, the determinacy of content of my representation of cows is not threatened by the possibility of a new species arising that I couldn't distinguish from cows, or by the possibility of Martians arriving with herds of facsimile cows. The alternative that I should sometimes actually be at the other end of an informationL channel from cows is not even coherent.

Consider, in this light, Pietroski's tale about the kimus and the snorfs (1992). The snorfs are attracted by the red morning glow over their local mountain so that they climb up it each day. Thus they conveniently avoid their chief predators, the snorfs, who don't take to mountain terrain. Pietroski claims that since no current kimu would recognize a snorf if it ran into it head on, it is implausible that the perception of red means snorf-free terrain to the kimus. A mere correlation between the direction of the red glow and the direction of the snorfs is not enough to support intentional representation. Now first, we should note that the injection of phenomenology here is perversely distracting. The question is not whether a red qualia, should there exist such things, could mean *no snorfs this direction* rather than *red*. Bats perceive shapes by ear and, goodness knows, maybe squares sound to them like diminished seventh chords do to us. Pietroski's question should be whether *any* inner representation that merely directs the kimu toward the sunlight could represent for it the snorf-free direction. Nor should the idea be that the kimu reads or interprets the inner representation as meaning "the snorf-free direction" the way you or I would interpret a sign of snorfs. To interpret a sign of snorfs, you or I must have a prior way of thinking of snorfs, and that, by hypothesis, the kimus do not have. The question, put fairly, is whether something *caused* by red light could *constitute* an inner representation of the snorf-free direction for the kimus. Also, we should be clear that the kimus' sensitivity to and attraction by the red light is not supposed to be accidental, but is a result of natural selection operating in the usual way. Kimu ancestors that were not attracted to red light were eaten by the snorfs.

Put this way, the situation is parallel to that of certain tortoises, who are attracted to green things, because green correlates with edible vegetation. They will move on the desert toward any green seen on their horizon. Nor do the nutritious properties of the vegetation produce the green light. These properties are merely correlated with green light. Can the green mean "chow over there" to the tortoise? Obviously not in so many words. But your percept of an apple doesn't mean "there's an apple over there" in so many words either. If the green doesn't mean chow over there to the tortoise, then what on earth *could* mean chow over there to anyone? Is it really plausible that there could be a genuine informationL channel open to any of us, for you or for me, that would communicate the informationL that there was chow on the table? Does human chow, as such, figure in any causal laws? If not, then in what sense are we "able to discriminate" when it is chow time? Unless, that is, we rely on mere statistical correlations.

Besides natural informationL, then, we should recognize another equally important kind of support for intentional representation, resting on what may also be called "natural signs" carrying – to keep the terminology parallel – "informationC" (for "correlation"). Natural signs bearing informationC are, as such, instances of types that are correlated with what they sign, there being a reason, grounded in natural necessity, why this correlation extends through a period of time or from one part of a locale to another. One thing carries information about another if it is possible to learn from the one something about the other not as a matter of accident but for a good reason. But no vehicle of information is transparent, of course. How to read the information through its vehicle has to be discovered, and it has to be possible to learn this in an explainable way, a way that works for a reason. The vehicle carries genuine information only if there is an ontological *ground* supporting induction that leads from prior experience to a grasp of the information carried in new instances. There must be a connection between the various instances exhibiting the correlation, a reason for the continuation of the correlation. Correlations that yield true belief only by accident do not carry genuine information.

Natural signs carrying informationC are correlated with what they represent because each sign instance is connected with what it represents in a way that recurs for a reason. Typically, however, the correlations are not perfect, and informationC, like informationL, cannot be false by definition. A token indistinguishable from a natural sign but that is not connected in the usual way with its usual represented is not a natural sign. The correlations that support informationC may be weak or strong. For example, a particular instance of a small shadow moving across the ground is a natural sign carrying informationC that a flying predator is overhead if it is actually caused by a flying predator, but the correlation that supports this natural signing, though it persists for good reason, may not be particularly strong.

If we allow ourselves to use the term "natural information" to cover informationC as well as informationL, then, we must keep firmly in mind that this sort of natural information has nothing to do with probabilities of one. Nor does the presence of this kind of information directly require the truth of any counterfactuals. If a shadow is a natural sign of a predator it does not follow that if a predator weren't there a shadow wouldn't be there, hence that such shadows can be used to discriminate predators from nonpredators. Nor does it follow that if a shadow weren't there a predator wouldn't be there – not on a cloudy day. Thus it is that a creature can perfectly well have a representation of Xs without being able to discriminate Xs from Ys.

References

Atran, S. 1989. Basic conceptual domains. *Mind & Language* 4, nos. 1 and 2, 7–16.

Barsalou, L. W. 1987. The instability of graded structure: Implications for the nature of concepts. In Neisser 1987, 101–40.

Bartlett, F. C. 1932. *Remembering*. London: Cambridge University Press.

Billman, D. 1992. Modeling category learning and use. In Burns 1992, 413–48.

Block, N. 1986. Advertisement for a semantics for psychology. *Midwest Studies in Philosophy*, 10, 615–78.

Blum, P. 1998. Different structures for concepts of individuals, stuffs and real kinds: One Mama, more milk and many mice. *Behavioral and Brain Sciences* 21.1, 66–7.

Boyd, R. 1991. Realism, anti-foundationalism and the enthusiasm for natural kinds. *Philosophical Studies* 61, 127–48.

Boyer, P. 1998. If 'tracking' is category-specific a 'common structure' may be redundant. *Behavioral and Brain Sciences* 21.1, 67–8.

Bridgeman, B. 1982. Multiplexing in single cells of the alert monkey's visual cortex during brightness discrimination. *Neuropsychologia* 20, 33–42.

Burge, T. 1979. Individualism and the mental. In P. French, T. Uehling, and H. Wettstein (eds.), *Studies in Metaphysics: Midwest Studies in Philosophy* IV, 73–121. Minneapolis: University of Minnesota.

Burge, T. 1982. Other bodies. In A. Woodfield (ed.), *Thought and Object*, 97–120. Oxford: Clarendon.

Burge, T. 1986. Individualism and psychology. *Philosophical Review* 95, 3–45.

Burns, B. (ed.) 1992. *Percepts, Concepts, and Categories: The Representation and Processing of Information*. Amsterdam and New York: North-Holland.

Byrnes, J. P. and Gelman, S. A. 1991. Perspectives on thought and language: Traditional and contemporary views. In Gelman and Byrnes 1991, 3–27.

Calvert, G. A., Bullmore, E. T., Brammer, M. J., Campbell, R., Williams, S. C., McGuire, P. K., Woodruff, P. W., Iverson, S. D., and Davis, A. S. 1997. Activation of auditory cortex during silent lipreading. *Science* 276, 593–96.

Campbell, J. 1987/88. Is sense transparent? *Aristotelian Society Proceedings*, New Series. Vol. LXXXVIII, 273–92.

Cangelosi, A. and Parisi, D. 1998. Concepts in artifical organisms. *Behavioral and Brain Sciences* 21.1, 68–9.

Carey, S. 1985. *Conceptual Change in Children*. Cambridge, MA: MIT Press.

Carey, S. and Gelman, R., eds. 1993. *The Epigenesis of Mind: Essays on Biology and Cognition*. Hillsdale, NJ: Erlbaum.

Carroll, L. 1894. What the tortoise said to Achilles. *Mind*. Reprinted in I.M. Copi and J. A. Gould, *Readings on Logic*. New York: Macmillan, 1964.

Choi, S. and Gopnik, A. 1993. Nouns are not always learned before verbs: An early verb spurt in Korean. In *The Proceedings of the Twenty-fifth Annual Child Language Forum*, 96–105. Stanford: Center for the Study of Language and Information.

Chomsky, N. 1995. Language and nature. *Mind* 104, 1–61.

Clark, E. V. 1991. Acquisitional principles in lexical development. In Gelman and Byrnes 1991, 31–71.

Crane, T. 1989. The waterfall illusion. *Analysis* 483, 142–7.

Dennett, D. C. 1995. *Darwin's Dangerous Idea*. New York: Simon & Schuster.

Dennett, D. C. and Kinsbourne, M. 1992. Time and the observer: The where and when of consciousness in the brain. *The Behacioral and Brain Sciences* 15, 183–247.

Dodwell, P., Humphrey, K., and Muir, D. 1987. Shape and pattern perception. In Salapatek, P. and Cohen, L. (eds.), *Handbook of Infant Perception Vol. 2: From Perception to Cognition*, 1–77. Orlando, FL: Harcourt Brace Jovanovich.

Dretske, F. 1980. *Knowledge and the Flow of Information*. Cambridge, MA: Bradford Books/MIT Press.

Dretske, F. 1986. Misrepresentation. In Radu Bogdan (ed.), *Belief: Form, Content, and Function*. New York: Oxford, 17–36.

Dretske, F. 1991. *Explaining Behavior*. Cambridge, MA: MIT Press.

Dromi, E. 1987. *Early Lexical Development*. Cambridge: Cambridge University Press.

Dummett, M. 1973. *Frege: Philosophy of Language*. New York: Harper & Row.

Eldredge, N. and Gould, S. J. 1972. Punctuated equilibria: An alternative to phyletic gradualism. In T. J. M. Schopf (ed.), *Models in Paleobiology*, 82–155. San Francisco: Freeman, Cooper and Company. Quoted in Hull 1978.

Engel, A. K. 1993. Temporal coding in the visual system; implications for the formation of representational states in neuronal networks. Presented at the conference on Naturalistic Approaches to Representation and Meaning, Zentrum für interdisziplinäre Forshung, Universität Bielefeld, December 1–3.

Evans, G. 1980. Things without the mind. In Zak van Stratten (ed.), *Philosophical Subjects: Essays Presented to P. F. Strawson*, 76–116. Oxford: Clarendon Press. Reprinted in Evans 1985b.

Evans, G. 1981. Understanding demonstratives. In H. Parrett and J. Bouveresse (eds.), *Meaning and Understanding*. Berlin and New York: deGruyter. Reprinted in Evans 1985b.

Evans, G. 1982. *The Varieties of Reference*. Oxford: Clarendon Press.

Evans, G. 1985a. Molyneux's question. In Evans 1985b, 364–99.

Evans, G. 1985b. *Collected Papers*. Oxford: Clarendon Press.

Fodor, J. A. 1972. Some reflections on L.S. Vygotsky's *Thought and Language*. *Cognition* 1, 83–95.

240

Fodor, J. A. 1980. Methodological solipsism as a research strategy in cognitive psychology. *Behavioral and Brain Sciences* 3, 63–73.

Fodor, J. A. 1989. Why should the mind be modular? In A. George (ed.), *Reflections on Chomsky*. Basil Blackwell. Reprinted in Fodor, 1990, 207–30.

Fodor, J. A. 1990. *A Theory of Content*. Cambridge, MA: MIT Press.

Fodor, J. A. 1994. *The Elm and the Expert*. Cambridge, MA: MIT Press.

Fodor, J.A. 1998. *Concepts: Where Cognitive Science Went Wrong*. Oxford: Oxford University Press.

Fodor, J. A. 1999. There are no recognitional concepts; not even RED. In E. Villanueva (ed.), *Concepts: Philosophical Issues* Vol. 9, 1–14. Atascadero, CA: Ridgeview Publishing.

Fumerton, R. 1989. Russelling causal theories. In C. W. Savage and C. A. Anderson (eds.), *Rereading Russell: Essays in Bertrand Russell's Metaphysics and Epistemology, Minnesota Studies in the Philosophy of Science*, vol. 12, 108–18. Minneapolis: University of Minnesota Press.

Gallistel, C., Brown, A., Carey, S., Gelman, R., and Keil, F. 1993. Lessons from animal learning for the study of cognitive development. In Carey and Gelman 1993, 3–36.

Gelman, S. A. and Byrnes, J. P., eds. 1991. *Perspectives on Language and Thought*. Cambridge: Cambridge University Press.

Gelman, S. A. and Coley, J. D. 1991. Language and categorization: The acquisition of natural kind terms. In Gelman and Byrnes 1991, 146–96.

Gendler, T. S. 1998. Why language is not a 'direct medium'. *Behavioral and Brain Sciences* 21.1, 71–2.

Gentner, D. 1982. Why nouns are learned before verbs; linguistic relativity versus natural partitioning. In S. Kuczaj (ed.), *Language, Thought and Culture: Language Development* vol. 2, 301–334. London: Erlbaum.

Ghiselin, M. 1974. A radical solution to the species problem. *Systematic Zoology* 23, 536–44.

Ghiselin, M. 1981. Categories, life and thinking. *Behavioral and Brain Sciences* 4, 269–83.

Gibbons, John. 1996. Externalism and knowledge of content, *The Philosophical Review* 105, no. 3, 287–310.

Gibson, J. J. 1968. *The Senses Considered as Perceptual Systems*. London: George Allen and Unwin.

Gilbert, D. 1993. The assent of man: Mental representation and the control of belief. In D. M. Wegner and J. W. Pennebaker (eds.), *Handbook of Mental Control*. Englewood Cliffs, NJ: Prentice-Hall.

Gleitman, L. R. 1990. The structural sources of verb meanings. *Language Acquisition* I, 1–55.

Goodman, N. 1966. *The Structure of Appearance*, Second Edition. Indianapolis: Bobbs-Merrill.

Gopnik, A. and Meltzoff, A. 1993. Words and thoughts in infancy: The specificity hypothesis and the development of categorization and naming. In C. Rovee-Collier and L. Lipsitt (eds.), *Advances in Infancy Research* 8, 217–49. Norwood, NJ: Ablex.

Gopnik, A. and Meltzoff, A. 1996. *Words, Thoughts and Theories*. Cambridge, MA: MIT Press.

Grice, H. P. 1957. Meaning. *The Philosophical Review* LXVI, no. 3, 377–88.

Grimshaw, J. 1994. Lexical reconciliation. In Lila Gleitman and Barbara Landau, *The Acquisition of the Lexicon*, 411–30. Cambridge, MA: MIT Press.

Hacking, I. A. 1991a. On Boyd. *Philosophical Studies* 61, 149–54.

Hacking, I. A. 1991b. A tradition of natural kinds. *Philosophical Studies* 61, 109–26.

Hempel, Carl G. 1950. Empiricist criteria of cognitive significance: Problems and changes. Reprinted in *Aspects of Scientific Explanation and Other Essays in the Philosophy of Science*. New York: The Free Press, Macmillan Co., 1965, 101–22.

Hempel, Carl G. 1966. *Philosophy of Natural Science*. Englewood Cliffs, NJ: Prentice-Hall.

Hull, D. L. 1978. A matter of individuality. *Philosophy of Science* 45, 335–60. Reprinted in Sober 1994, 193–216.

Ingram, D. 1989. *First Language Acquisition: Method, Description and Explanation*. Cambridge: Cambridge University Press.

Jarrett, G. 1999. Conspiracy theories of consciousness. *Philosophical Studies* 96.1, 45–58.

Johnson, M. H., Dziuawiec, S., Ellis, H. D., and Morton, J. 1991. Newborns' preferential tracking of face-like stimuli and its subsequent decline. *Cognition* 40, 1–21.

Johnson-Laird, P. N. 1983. *Mental Models*. Cambridge, MA: Harvard University Press.

Kaplan, D. 1990. Words. *Proceedings of the Aristotelian Society*, Supplementary Vol. 1990, 93–119.

Katz, J. 1972. *Semantic Theory*. New York: Harper & Row.

Katz, J. and Fodor, J. A. 1963. The structure of a semantic theory. *Language* 39, 170–210.

Keil, F. C. 1979. *Semantic and Conceptual Development: An Ontological Perspective*. Cambridge, MA: Harvard University Press.

Keil, F. C. 1983. Semantic inferences and the acquisition of word meaning. In T. B. Seiler and W. Wannemacher (eds.), *Concept Development and the Development of Word Meaning*. Berlin: Springer-Verlag.

Keil, F. C. 1987. Conceptual development and category structure. In Neisser 1987, 175–200.

Keil, F. C. 1989. *Concept, Kinds and Cognitive Development*. Cambridge, MA: MIT Press.

Keil, F. C. 1991. Theories, concepts, and the acquisition of word meaning. In Gelman and Byrnes 1991, 197–221.

Komatsu, L. K. 1998. Mapping Millikan's conceptual work onto (empirical) work by psychologists. *Behavioral and Brain Sciences* 21.1, 76–7.

Komatsu, L. K. 1992. Recent views of conceptual structure. *Psychological Bulletin* 112.3, 500–26.

Kripke, S. 1972. *Naming and Necessity*. Cambridge, MA: Harvard University Press.

Lakoff, G. 1987. *Women, Fire, and Dangerous Things. What Categories Reveal About the Mind*. Chicago: Chicago University Press.

Liberman, A. M. and Mattingly, I. G. 1985. The motor theory of speech perception revised. *Cognition* 21, 1–36.

Liberman, A. M. and Mattingly, I. G. 1989. A specialization for speech perception. *Science* 243, 489–94.

Liberman, I. Y., Shankweiler, D., Fisher, F. W., and Carter, B. 1974. Explicit syllable and phoneme segmentation in the young child. *Journal of Experimental Psychology* 18, 201–12.

Lorenz, K. 1962. Kant's doctrine of the a priori in the light of contemporary biology. *General Systems* VII, 23–35. Reprinted in H. C. Plotkin, ed., *Learning, Development and Culture*. New York: John Wiley & Sons, 121–42.

Lundberg, I., Frost, J., and Petersen, O. P. 1988. Effects of an intensive program for stimulating phonological awareness in preschool children. *Reading Research Quarterly* 23, 263–84.

MacFarlane, A. 1977. *The Psychology of Childbirth*. Cambridge, MA: Harvard University Press.

MacLennan, B. J. 1998. Finding order in our world: The primacy of the concrete in neural representations and the role of invariance in substance identifications. *Behavioral and Brain Sciences* 21.1, 78–9.

Mandler, J. M. 1997. Development of categorization: Perceptual and conceptual catogories. In G. Brenner, A. Slater, and G. Butterworth (eds.), *Infant Development: Recent Advances*. Hillsdale, NJ: Erlbaum.

Mandler, J. M. 1998. Whatever happened to meaning? *Behavioral and Brain Sciences* 21.1, 79–80.

Markman, E. 1989. *Categorization and Naming in Children*. Cambridge, MA: MIT Press.

Markman, E. 1991. The whole-object, taxonomic and mutual exclusivity assumptions as initial constraints on word meaning. In Gelman and Byrnes 1991, 72–106.

Marler, P. 1993. The instinct to learn. In Carey and Gelman 1993, 37–66.

Marr, D. 1982. *Vision*. San Francisco: W. H. Freeman and Co.

Mattingly, I. G. and Studdart-Kennedy, M., eds. 1991. *Modularity and the Motor Theory of Speech Perception*. Hillsdale, NJ: Erlbaum.

Mayr, E. 1981. Biological classification: Toward a synthesis of opposing methodologies. *Science*, 510–16. Reprinted in E. Sober, ed., *Conceptual Issues in Evoloutionary Biology*, second edition. Cambridge, MA: MIT Press 1994, 277–94.

Medin, D. L. 1989. Concepts and conceptual structure. *American Psychologist* 44.12, 1469–81.

Medin, D. L. and Ortony, A. 1989. Psychological essentialism. In S. Vosniadou and A. Ortony (eds.), *Similarity and Analogical Reasoning*, 179–95. New York: Cambridge University Press.

Medin, D. L. and Schaffer, M. M. 1978. Context theory of classification learning. *Psychological Review* 85, 207–38.

Medin, D. L. and Smith, E. E. 1981. Strategies and classification learning. *Journal of Experimental Psychology: Human Learning and Memory* 7, 241–53.

Medin, D. L. and Smith, E. E. 1984. Concepts and concept formation. *Annual Review of Psychology* 35, 113–38.

Millikan, R. G. 1984. *Language, Thought and Other Biological Categories*. Cambridge, MA: MIT Press.

Millikan, R. G. 1991. Perceptual content and Fregean myth. *Mind* 100.4, 439–59.

Millikan, R. G. 1993a. *White Queen Psychology and Other Essays for Alice*. Cambridge, MA: MIT Press.

Millikan, R. G. 1993b. On mentalese orthography. In Bo Dahlbom (ed.), *Dennett and His Critics*, 97–123. Oxford: Blackwell.

Millikan, R. G. 1993c. Knowing what I'm thinking of. *Proceedings of the Aristotelian Society*, Supplementary Volume 67, 109–24.

Millikan, R. G. 1993d. White Queen psychology. In Millikan 1993a.

Millikan, R. G. 1994. On unclear and indistinct ideas. In James Tomberlin (ed.), *Philosophical Perspectives* vol. VIII, 75–100. Atascadero, CA: Ridgeview Publishing.

Millikan, R. G. 1996. On swampkinds. *Mind and Language* 11.1, 103–17.

Millikan, R. G. 1997a. Cognitive luck: Externalism in an evolutionary frame. In P. Machamer and M. Carrier (eds.), *Philosophy and the Sciences of Mind, Pittsburgh-Konstanz Series in the Philosophy and History of Science*, 207–19. Pittsburgh, PA: Pittsburgh University Press and Konstanz: Universitätsverlag Konstanz.

Millikan, R. G. 1997b. Images of identity. *Mind* 106, no. 423, 499–519.

Millikan, R. G. 1998a. A common structure for concepts of individuals, stuffs, and basic kinds: More mama, more milk and more mouse. *Behavioral and Brain Sciences* 22.1, 55–65. Reprinted in E. Margolis and S. Laurence, eds., *Concepts: Core Readings*, 525–47. Cambridge, MA: MIT Press, 1999.

Millikan, R. G. 1998b. With enemies like these I don't need friends: Author's response. *Behavioral and Brain Sciences* 22.1, 89–100.

Millikan, R. G. 1998c. How we make our ideas clear. *Proceedings and Addresses of the American Philosophical Association*, November 1998, 65–79.

Millikan, R. G. 1999. Historical kinds and the special sciences. *Philosophical Studies* 95.1–2, 45–65.

Millikan, R. G. (in press a). The myth of mental indexicals. In Andrew Brook and Richard DeVidi (eds.), *Self-Reference and Self-Awareness, Advances in Consciousness Research* Vol. 11. Amsterdam/Philadelphia: John Benjamins.

Millikan, R. G. (in press b). Biofunctions: Two paradigms. In R. Cummins, A. Ariew, and M. Perlman (eds.), *Functions in Philosophy of Biology and Philosophy of Psychology*. Oxford: Oxford University Press.

Millikan, R. G. (in press c). In defense of public language. In L. Antony and N. Hornstein (eds.), *Chomsky and His Critics*. Oxford: Blackwell.

Millikan, R. G. (manuscript). Some Different Ways to Think.

Minsky, M. 1975. A framework for representing knowledge. In P. H. Winston (ed.), *The Psychology of Computer Vision*, 211–77. New York: McGraw-Hill.

Morais, J., Cary, L., Alegria, J., and Bertelson, P. 1979. Does awareness of speech as a sequence of phones arise spontaneously? *Cognition* 7, 323–31.

Murphy, G. L and Medin, D. L. 1985. The role of theories in conceptual coherence. *Psychological Review* 92, 289–316.

Neander, K. 1995. Misrepresenting and malfunctioning. *Philosophical Studies* 79, 109–41.

Neisser, U. 1975. *Cognition and Reality*. San Francisco: W. H. Freeman.

Neisser, U. (ed.) 1987. *Concepts and Conceptual Development*. Cambridge: Cambridge University Press.

Nelson, C. and Horowitz, F. 1987. Visual motion perception in infancy: A review and synthesis. In Salapatek and Cohen 1987, 123–53.

Nelson, K. 1991. The matter of time: Interdependencies between language and thought in development. In Gelman and Byrnes 1991, 278–318.

Peacocke, C. 1983. *Sense and Content*. Oxford: Clarendon Press.

Peacocke, C. 1986. Analogue content. *Aristotelian Society Proceedings*, Supplementary Vol. LX.1–17.

Peacocke, C. 1987. Depiction. *The Philosophical Review*, XCVI, 383–411.

Peacocke, C. 1989a. Perceptual content. In J. Almog, J. Perry, and H. Wettstein (eds.), *Themes from Kaplan*, 297–329. Oxford: Oxford University Press.

Peacocke, C. 1989b. *Transcendental Arguments in the Theory of Content: An Inaugural Lecture Delivered before the University of Oxford on 16 May 1989*. Oxford: Clarendon Press.

Perner, J. 1998. Room for concept development? *Behavioral and Brain Sciences* 21.1, 82–3.

Piaget, J. 1926. *The Language and Thought of the Child*. New York: Harcourt Brace.

Pietroski, P. M. 1992. Intentionality and teleological error. *The Pacific Philosophical Quarterly* 73, 267–82.

Pinker, S. 1994a. How could a child use verb syntax to learn verb semantics? In Lila Gleitman and Barbara Landau (eds.), *The Acquisition of the Lexicon*, 377–410. Cambridge, MA: MIT Press.

Pinker, S. 1994b. *The Language Instinct*. New York: William Morrow and Co.

Pribram, K. H. 1991. *Brain and Perception: Holonomy and Structure in Figural Processing*. Hillsdale, NJ: Erlbaum.

Pribram, K. H., Speielli, D. N., and Kamback, M. C. 1967. Electrocortical correlates of stimulus response and reinforcement. *Science* 157, 94–6.

Putnam, H. 1975. The meaning of 'meaning'. In Keith Gunderson (ed.), *Language, Mind and Knowledge, Minnesota Studies in the Philosophy of Science* vol. 7. Minneapolis: University of Minnesota Press.

Quine, W. V. 1953. Two dogmas of empiricism. In *From a Logical Point of View*, 20–46. Cambridge, MA: Harvard University Press. [Pagination as reprinted in A. P. Martinich (ed.), *The Philosophy of Language*, 3rd ed. Oxford: Oxford University Press, 1996.]

Quine, W. V. 1956. Quantifiers and propositional attitudes. *The Journal of Philosophy* 53, 177–87.

Quine, W. V. 1960. *Word and Object*. Cambridge, MA: MIT Press.

Rifkin, A. 1985. Evidence for a basic-level in event taxonomies. *Memory and Cognition* 13, 538–56.

Rosch, E. 1973. Natural categories. *Cognitive Psychology* 4, 328–50.

Rosch, E. 1975. Universals and cultural specifics in human categorization. In R. Brislin, S. Bochner, and W. Honner (eds.), *Cross Cultural Perspectives on Learning*, 177–206. New York: Halsted.

Rosch, E. and Mervis, C. B. 1975. Family resemblances: Studies in the internal structure of categories. *Cognitive Psychology* 7, 573–605.

Rumelhardt, D. E. 1980. Schemata: The building blocks of cognition. In R. J. Spiro, B. C. Bruce, and W. F. Brewer (eds.), *Theoretical Issues in Reading Comprehension*, 33–58. Hillsdale, NJ: Erlbaum.

Russell, B. 1912. *The Problems of Philosophy*. New York: H. Holt Inc.

Russell, B. 1948. *Human Knowledge, Its Scope and Limits*. London: Allen and Unwin.

Salapatek, P. and Abelson, R. P. 1987. *Handbook of Infant Perception*. Orlando, FL: Academic Press.

Schank, R. C. and Abelson, R. P. 1977. *Scripts, Plans, Goals and Understanding*. Hillsdale, NJ: Erlbaum.

Selfridge, O. (unpublished). *Tracking and Trailing.*

Sellars, W. 1956. Empiricism and the philosophy of mind. In K. Gunderson (ed.), *Minnesota Studies in the Philosophy of Science*, vol. I, 253–329. Minneapolis: University of Minnesota Press. Reprinted in Sellars 1963.

Sellars, W. 1963. *Science, Perception and Reality*. London: Routledge and Kegan Paul. Reprinted, Atascadero, CA: Ridgeview 1991.

Sellars, W. 1975. The structure of knowledge; Lecture II: Minds. In Hector-Neri Castaneda (ed.), *Action, Knowledge and Reality: Critical Studies in Honor of Wilfrid Sellars*, 318–31. Indianapolis: Bobbs-Merrill. Reprinted in D. M. Rosenthal (ed.), *The Nature of Mind*. Oxford: Oxford University Press 1991, 372–9.

Sellars, W. 1982. Sensa or sensings: Reflections on the ontology of perception. *Philosophical Studies* 41, 83–111.

Shepard, R. 1976. Perceptual illusion of rotation of three-dimensional objects. *Science* 191, 952–4.

Shepard, R. 1983. Path-guided apparent motion. *Science* 220, 632–4.

Singer, W. 1995. Time as coding space in neocortical processing: A hypothesis. In M. S. Gazzaniga (ed.), *The Cognitive Neurosciences*. Cambridge, MA: MIT Press.

Smith, C., Carey, S. and Wiser, M. 1985. On differentiation: A case study of the development of the concepts of size, weight, and density. *Cognition* 21, 177–237.

Smith, Edward E. and Medin, Douglas L. 1981. *Categories and Concepts*. Cambridge, MA: Harvard University Press.

Sober, E. (ed.) 1994. *Conceptual Issues in Evolutionary Biology*. Cambridge, MA: MIT Press.

Spelke, E. 1989. The origins of physical knowledge. In L. Weiskrantz (ed.), *Thought Without Language*, 168–84. Oxford: Oxford University Press.

Spelke, E. 1993. Physical knowledge in infancy: Reflections of Piaget's theory. In Carey and Gelman 1993, 133–70.

Strawson, P. F. 1959. *Individuals*. London: Methuen and Co.

Strawson, P. F. 1974. *Subject and Predicate in Logic and Grammar*. London: Methuen and Co.

Ward, T. B. and Becker, A. H. 1992. Intentional and incidental learning. In B. Burns 1992, 451–91.

Waxman, S. R. 1991. Semantic and conceptual organization in preschoolers. In Gelman and Byrnes 1991, 107–45.

Wettstein, H. 1988. Cognitive significance without cognitive content. *Mind* 97, 1–28.

Winograd, T. 1975. Frame representations and the declarative-procedural controversy. In D. G. Bobrow and A. Collins (eds.), *Representation and Understanding: Studies in Cognitive Science*, 185–210. New York: Academic Press.

Wittgenstein, L. 1953. *Philosophical Investigations*. Oxford: Blackwell.

Xu, F. and Carey, S. 1996. Infant metaphysics: The case of numerical identity. *Cognitive Psychology* 30, 111–53.

Names Index

Index

capacities (*cont.*)
  to recognize, 185, 211
  to reidentify, 76, 108, 182, 196, 215
  to think about thoughts, 179
  to track, 75, 80
categories, 26, 29, 43, 44, 46
  early, 8
  of language, 45
  of substances, 32
  ontological, 73
categorization, 34, 36, 44
causal theory of reference, 49
channel conditions, 219ff, 227
Christmas lights model, 136, 138, 160
circumstances
  for success, 56, 101, 212
  historical, 205
  likely, 53, 55, 58
  of identification, 10
  represented, 197
  unfavorable, 53, 145
  varying, 55, 101, 108
classes, 37, 39
classification, 25, 35, 37, 39, 41, 45, 81
  function of, 34
  of concepts, 174
  principles of, 31
  structure of, 71
  systems of, 31, 35, 36, 38
classifiers, 34, 36, 39, 42, 48, 83
code, 197, 223ff
  token, 235
  type, 235
cognition, 114, 146
  central problem of, 5, 172
  environment for, 210
  intentionality of, 202
  teleology in, 230
  theory of, 1, 2
  vs. perception, 200
cognitive role, 87
coidentification, 144, 167, 172, 176,
    184, 187, 193, 200
communication, 35, 36, 37, 79, 148
commutativity, 163
complements, 106
completeness

demand for, 114, 119, 122, 125
  importation of, 119, 122
  in formal systems, 166
conceptionism, 42, 43, 47, 49, 191
conceptions, 11, 12, 39ff, 56, 60, 64, 67,
    73, 77, 91, 93, 155, 173, 174, 194
  adult, 93, 94
  aspects of, 151, 174, 175, 176
  separate from substance concepts,
    145, 173
concepts
  adequate, 104, 213
  analytical, 39, 40, 71, 72, 79
  and classification, 34, 37
  apparent, 195
  application of, 87
  as necessary for cognition, 202
  as properties, 43
  discursive, 202
  early, 71, 87
  empirical, 96, 98, 100, 103, 105, 108
  epistemology of, 96, 101, 102
  equivocation of, 13, 68, 91, 103, 191
  Evans' sense, 134, 180, 183
  examples of, 1
  extension of, 11, 42, 49, 194
  Fodor's sense, 217
  formation of, 30, 49, 83, 99, 104
  grounding of, 105
  holism of, 102
  honing, 106
  in inductions, 4
  individuation of, 74
  learning of, 44
  linguistic, 93
  nontheoretical, 101
  of classes, 39
  of individuals, 10
  of properties, 42, 66, 69, 78, 79, 81,
    106
  of the mental, 97
  predicate, 16, 41
  prelinguistic, 76
  psychological theories of, 43
  redundancy of, 13, 103
  relative to theories, 47
  same, 11, 12, 92, 171, 173

laws, 24, 99, 219, 228, 234, 236
  ceteris paribus, 146, 207, 219, 225, 228
  ecological, 225
  natural, 15, 227
learning, 33, 50, 57, 63, 164, 197, 229, 233
  early, 69
  perceptual, 117, 139
  trial and error, 65
logic, 30, 72, 106
logical form, 112, 171, 195

meaning, 45, 47, 48, 91ff, 100, 115, 177, 202
  natural, 220
means, 10, 11, 39, 59, 60, 91, 145, 151, 155, 156, 173, 174, 189, 194
medium, 14, 84, 89, 90, 196, 201, 224
memory, 35, 37, 80, 153, 168, 187
mental equals sign, 137, 147, 161, 169
mental sentence, 159
mental word, 2, 137, 167
minitheory, 101
mistakes, 65, 66, 68, 124, 125, 146, 178, 231
mode of presentation, 110, 116, 128, 130, 133, 147ff, 167ff, 180, 183, 186
  equivocal, 149
Molyneux's question, 115, 120, 128, 134, 143
Müller-Lyer arrows, 105, 121, 122, 128
multiplication, 205, 212

naming explosion, 69
natural kinds, 1, 15, 16, 17, 18, 48, 228
natural necessity, 18, 27, 33, 219, 220, 222, 227, 228, 234, 236
natural selection, 51, 61, 63, 64, 67, 146, 197, 208, 225, 230, 236
negation, 106, 163
nominal kinds, 15
nominalism, 44
normal conditions, 53, 56, 62, 66, 67, 102, 103, 146, 212, 224
Normal conditions, 62

normal explanation, 216
normal function, 67
normal structure, 65

observations, 16, 28, 31, 82
ontological ground of induction, 2, 16, 17, 18, 20, 23, 24, 39, 41, 46, 47, 48, 70, 71, 81, 182, 237
  historical, 20
opacity, 175
operational definitions, 39

passive picture theory, 112, 113, 115, 123, 124, 130ff, 160, 166, 199
perception, 85, 87, 109ff, 124, 127, 139, 199, 217
  direct, 85, 197
  of speech, 87
  theories of, 110
  through language, 88, 89
phonemes, 87, 88
Phosphorus, 93, 185, 188
possible worlds, 12, 22, 24, 35, 49
predicates
  projectable, 25
predicative component, 214, 215, 216
probability, 57, 222
  conditional, 218
productivity, 88, 198
projectories, 154, 155, 156
proper functions, 63, 65, 197, 216
  adapted, 63, 194
  derived, 63
properties, 21, 23, 27, 35, 36, 38, 45, 46, 71, 80, 104, 107, 111ff, 123, 129, 215, 218, 227
  conditional, 22
  not definitional of real kinds, 16
  projectable, 15, 25
prototypes, 43, 44, 45
psychological kinds, 46

qualia, 97, 126, 127, 129, 236

real kinds, 3, 5, 15, 16, 17, 18, 23ff, 45, 69, 70, 74
realism, 44, 45, 46, 181

256